The Crocodile Tears

A Manifesto for Palestinian Rights

Hamdoon A. Khan

Contents

Introduction

In the labyrinth of human history, where echoes of ancient civilizations resonate through the ages, there exists a patch of land that has borne witness to the rise and fall of empires—the storied Philistia and Canaan. Beyond its archaeological treasures and cultural tapestry lies a contemporary saga, a diary of discord that reverberates through the hearts of Palestinians and Israelis. As we step into the corridors of time, let us unravel the intricate threads of history that weave through the Israeli-Palestinian war, seeking clarity in a narrative often obscured by the fog of contention.

In this exploration, we embark not merely on a journey of remembrance but on a quest for truth: a truth that transcends the boundaries of political rhetoric and national narratives. It beckons us to peer beyond the veil of decades and centuries, to understand the genesis of a conflagration that has entrenched itself in the very soil of Philistia and Canaan.

Amongst the echoes of historical grievances and contested claims, this book aims to be a torchbearer of illumination, shining light on the innocence of a people and the shadows that obscure their narratives. In this pursuit, join me not as passive observers but as seekers of understanding, for it is only through the unraveling of historical complexities that we can hope to forge a path towards a just resolution.

The narrative unfolds not amongst the present turmoil but within the ancient whispers of Philistia and Canaan, where the origins of the Israeli-Palestinian war delve into the profound intertwining of two peoples' destinies. The cradle of antiquity unveils Philistia and Canaan, a land steeped in rich history, where the sands bear witness to the footprints of civilizations long faded into the annals of time. Resting along the eastern Mediterranean coast, this region became a crossroads of cultures, a convergence for empires that left enduring imprints on its landscape. From the mysterious Philistines to the influences of the Hellenistic era, Philistia's history is a palimpsest of conquests and cultural exchanges.

The tale begins with the Philistines, a people shrouded in mystery, their origins traced to the Aegean world. As seafarers and traders, they navigated the ancient waters, eventually settling in the coastal plains of Philistia and Canaan around the 12th century BCE. The echoes of their presence can still be found in the archaeological remnants that dot the landscape—cities, pottery, and artifacts that speak of a flourishing civilization. Over the centuries, Philistia and Canaan witnessed the rise and fall of empires—Persians, Greeks, Romans—all leaving their imprint on this coveted land. The lure of its strategic location, a bridge between continents, drew the gaze of ambitious powers seeking dominion over trade routes and cultural crossroads.

As we peer into the annals of Philistia and Canaan's history, we encounter not only the clash of swords but also the melding of diverse cultures. The Hellenistic period brought forth cities adorned with Greek architecture, testaments to the fusion of Eastern and Western influences. This intricate interplay of cultures set the stage for the complex mosaic that is modern Philistia and Canaan.

In our exploration of the intricate terrain that is the Israeli-Palestinian war, the layers of civilizations that have trodden upon this land contribute to the multifaceted identity of its current inhabitants. In this historical context, the roots of the Israeli-Palestinian strife reach deep into the soil, entwined with the narratives of a land that has borne witness to the ebb and flow of centuries.

As we stand on the precipice of modern history, the roots of the Israeli-Palestinian war extend back through the turbulent aftermath of World War II. The ink on the pages of global geopolitics was still wet when the stage was set for a complex drama that would unfold in the heart of Philistia. The post-World War II era witnessed a confluence of political, ideological, and territorial forces that would shape the destinies of both Palestinians and Israelis. In the wake of the Holocaust, a profound sense of collective guilt and responsibility gripped the international community. The horrors suffered by the Jewish people during the war ignited a fervent determination to establish a homeland—a sanctuary free from alleged persecution.

The United Nations, ostensibly endeavoring to address this humanitarian crisis, proposed a partition plan in 1947. This plan aimed to divide the land of Palestine into separate Jewish and Arab states, with Jerusalem as an international city. However, this solution sowed the seeds of discord, rather than harmony. The lucid bias in the approach of the UN inadvertently contributed to the seeds of discontent. The Arab population's resistance was immediate, rooted in a sense of displacement and injustice caused by an external authority carving up their ancestral land. The ensuing conflict marked the genesis of a battle that would become entrenched, defining the identity and aspirations of both Palestinians and Israelis.

In the chapters that follow, we will dissect the intricacies of this war, examining the geopolitical forces that came into show and the resistance that burgeoned among the Palestinian population. The narratives of dispossession, displacement, and a quest for self-determination unfolded against a backdrop of competing nationalisms, striving for recognition and justice.

The United Nations' partition plan proved insufficient to quell the flames of discord. Instead, it laid the groundwork for a protracted combat, the echoes of which resonate through the decades. As we navigate the historical contours of the Israeli-Palestinian war, we must unravel the complexities that have shaped the narratives of innocence and guilt, justice and injustice, weaving together a fabric that reveals the human stories beneath the political rhetoric.

In the corridors of historical inquiry, this book unfurls its pages with a purpose that transcends the mere recounting of events. It seeks to be a scrupulous investigation, a journey through the layers of time and the complexities that underpin the Israeli-Palestinian war. As the quill scratches the parchment, the purpose of this endeavor emerges with clarity and conviction.

The primary aim of this book is to foster a nuanced understanding among readers-a comprehension that goes beyond the binary of right and wrong. It is an invitation to ponder the shades of gray that often escape the stark black-and-white frames presented by political discourse. By dissecting the intricacies of history, politics, and human experience, this book endeavors to be a catalyst for informed dialogue and thoughtful reflection.

As the author, my aspiration is not to wield the pen as a weapon of accusation but as a tool for reconciliation through truth. By conducting thorough research and maintaining an unwavering commitment to impartiality, I endeavor to offer a comprehensive perspective that invites readers to navigate the historical labyrinth with an open mind.

In the crucible of the Israeli-Palestinian war, where narratives collide and histories intertwine, the importance of understanding becomes an imperative guiding principle. Beyond the confines of academic inquiry, this understanding serves as a bridge-a connection between the past and present, between divergent perspectives, and, most crucially, between the people entangled in this enduring tussle. At its core, the significance of understanding lies in the potential it holds for fostering empathy and transcending entrenched viewpoints. The complexities of this confrontation demand a nuanced comprehension, one that goes beyond surface-level narratives and delves into the profound historical, cultural, and human dimensions.

Understanding is a tool of enlightenment, enabling readers to discern the intricacies of a narrative often obscured by political rhetoric. It invites us to step into the shoes of those who have borne the brunt of combat, to empathize with the human stories woven into the fabric of this tumultuous history. Moreover, the importance of understanding extends beyond the borders of the region. In an era of global interconnectedness, the Israeli-Palestinian war reverberates far beyond the contested lands. It is a microcosm of broader geopolitical dynamics, and a key to comprehending the interconnectedness of global peace and stability.

For policymakers, academics, and every conscientious global citizen, an informed understanding of this skirmish is paramount. It becomes a foundation upon which informed decisions can be made, interventions crafted, and dialogues initiated. The repercussions of this brawl extend far beyond the immediate region, influencing international relations, shaping perceptions, and challenging the very notions of justice and equity.

Embarking on the journey of writing this book began in mid-2021 alongside my other research endeavors. After investing around twenty-seven months, I had completed eighty percent of the manuscript. However, a significant turning point occurred with the onset of the Al-Aqsa Flood—an orchestrated series of attacks by Hamas, the Palestinian freedom fighters, on the 7th of October this year, 2023. Witnessing the continued support from certain Western countries and the UN for Israeli actions, despite the blatant disregard for their war crimes, compelled me to suspend my other research activities and dedicate myself to expediting the completion of this work.

The term 'Jihad,' repeatedly portrayed in political and media propaganda as a manifestation of extremism and aggression, is fundamentally about standing for justice in all its forms. In this very context, Prophet Muhammad (PBUH) conveyed, "The best fighting (jihad) in the path of Allah is (to speak) a word of justice to an oppressive ruler." Among the spread of fabricated lies about the innocent people of Palestine by media and politicians, my intention is to present the unadulterated truth, supported by historical context and logical arguments within the pages of this book. This endeavor not only challenges the oppressive rulers of the world but also confronts anyone who stands with Israel and supports its terrorist activities within the land of innocent Palestinians, often without an understanding of the historical context and the reality behind this conflict.

In the pages that follow, as we traverse the historical contours of the Israeli-Palestinian saga, let us not merely accumulate knowledge but cultivate understanding-a perspective that transcends bias, embraces complexity, and, in doing so, contributes to the collective wisdom necessary for forging a path towards a just and lasting resolution.

Philistia Through the Ages

Prehistoric Foundations (Before 1200 BCE)

The exploration of early settlements in Philistia unveils a compelling narrative of prehistoric human presence, echoing the footsteps of ancient inhabitants who laid the foundations for the rich tapestry of the region. Archaeological evidence paints a vivid picture of a landscape shaped by the endeavors of those who dwelled in Philistia before the emergence of the Philistine culture.

In excavations conducted across Philistia, remnants of prehistoric settlements have been unearthed, testifying to the enduring connection between ancient communities and the land they inhabited. These archaeological discoveries, ranging from tools to dwelling structures, provide tangible glimpses into the daily lives and activities of the early inhabitants. The artifacts recovered are not mere remnants; they are silent storytellers, revealing the material culture and technological prowess of a people navigating the challenges of their environment.

Among the notable archaeological excavations in Philistia, sites such as Tel Miqne, associated with the ancient city of Ekron, stand as testament to the layered history embedded in the region's soil. The meticulous documentation of findings at these sites offers a chronological narrative, allowing scholars to trace the evolution of settlements over time. The stratigraphy of these excavations becomes a chronological palette, each layer a stroke on the canvas of Philistia's past.

The excavation endeavors in Philistia, particularly those delving into the archaeological discoveries of prehistoric settlements, unfurl a captivating narrative that transcends the boundaries of time. These excavations, akin to carefully peeling back the layers of history, unearth tangible remnants that act as silent witnesses to the lives of early inhabitants, offering a foretaste into the complexities of their existence.

Key archaeological discoveries in the exploration of pre-Philistine cultures lie in the realm of dwellings and structural formations. Sites such as Tel es-Safi, identified with the biblical city of Gath, have revealed the foundations of ancient structures that once stood proudly against the backdrop of the Philistine landscape. The meticulous excavation of these architectural remnants provides a blueprint of the spatial organization and construction techniques employed by the early settlers.

The pottery unearthed in these excavations emerges as a cornerstone in deciphering the material culture and daily rituals of the prehistoric inhabitants. From simple, utilitarian vessels to intricately adorned pieces, the pottery repertoire speaks volumes about the aesthetic sensibilities and functional needs of these ancient communities. The typological analysis of pottery shards allows archaeologists to delineate distinct phases and transitions in ceramic styles, creating a chronological mosaic of cultural evolution.

Beyond the realm of artifacts, the retrieval of human remains in these archaeological digs adds a poignant dimension to the narrative of early Philistia. Skeletal analysis, coupled with forensic techniques, provides insights into demographic aspects, health conditions, and potential societal structures. burial practices, evidenced by grave goods and burial configurations, shed light on the spiritual beliefs and funerary customs of the pre-Philistine cultures.

Furthermore, the exploration of tools and implements within these archaeological sites unveils the technological prowess of early inhabitants. Flint tools, grinding stones, and other implements speak to the resourcefulness and adaptability of these communities. The functional aspects of these tools, identified through use-wear analysis, contribute to the reconstruction of daily activities such as hunting, food processing, and craft production.

The integration of environmental archaeology within these excavations enriches the understanding of the symbiotic relationship between early settlers and their surroundings. Micro botanical analysis of plant remains, along with studies of animal bones, provides a nuanced perspective on subsistence strategies and the exploitation of natural resources. The examination of soil composition and sediment layers further refines our comprehension of the ecological dynamics that influenced settlement patterns.

The exploration of pre-Philistine cultures in Philistia delves beyond the artifacts and structures, extending its gaze to the environmental factors that shaped the contours of early settlements. Geography and climate, as silent orchestrators of the human narrative, intricately woven their influence into the drapery of prehistoric Philistia, guiding the choices of ancient communities in their quest for sustenance and survival.

The geography of Philistia, marked by a diverse topography ranging from coastal plains to inland hills, played a fundamental role in dictating settlement patterns. The coastal plain, with its fertile soils and proximity to the Mediterranean, emerged as a favorable canvas for early inhabitants. Excavations at sites like Tel Gerisa unearthed evidence of agricultural practices, affirming the symbiotic relationship between settlers and the land. The coastal allure, however, did not confine settlement solely to the plains; rather, the hills and inland regions witnessed a nuanced interaction between communities and their environment.

Climate, another determinant of settlement, cast its influence over the choices made by pre-Philistine cultures. The Mediterranean climate, characterized by mild, wet winters and hot, dry summers, sculpted the rhythms of agricultural cycles and resource availability. Archaeobotanical studies, analyzing plant remains from archaeological sites, provide insights into the cultivation practices adopted by ancient communities. Cereal grains, legumes, and other cultivated plants present in these studies unveil the agricultural strategies devised to navigate the climatic nuances of Philistia.

Moreover, the examination of settlement locations in relation to water sources unveils a strategic calculus employed by early inhabitants. Water, a lifeline in the arid landscape, became a determining factor in the establishment of settlements. Springs and water wells discovered in archaeological excavations underscore the significance of these water sources in sustaining communities. The layout of settlements, often clustered around these vital water nodes, reflects a pragmatic response to the challenges posed by the region's climate.

The influence of geography and climate on settlement patterns is further accentuated by the integration of animal husbandry into the economic repertoire of pre-Philistine cultures. Animal bones recovered from archaeological sites serve as a palimpsest, documenting the practices of domestication and exploitation of animal resources. The strategic positioning of settlements in proximity to grazing lands and the careful selection of animal species for husbandry align with the ecological considerations embedded in the decision-making of early inhabitants.

The mosaic of environmental factors shaping settlement patterns in pre-Philistine cultures becomes even more intricate when considering the interplay between geography, climate, and trade routes. The accessibility of Philistia to trade routes, facilitated by its coastal location, influenced economic interactions and cultural exchanges with neighboring regions. The ebb and flow of goods, ideas, and influences across these routes enriched the cultural landscape, leaving indelible imprints on the evolving identity of Philistia.

Philistine Arrival and Iron Age (1200 BCE - 586 BCE)

The origins of the Philistines are a subject of scholarly debate, but it is widely accepted that they were part of the Sea Peoples' migrations that swept across the Eastern Mediterranean. The archaeological evidence suggests a correlation between the collapse of the Mycenaean and Hittite civilizations and the subsequent emergence of the Philistines in the southern coastal regions of Canaan. The emergence of Philistine city-states marked a transformative period in the cultural landscape of ancient Philistia, characterized by distinctive material culture that set the Philistines apart from their predecessors. The examination of Philistine pottery, architecture, and artifacts unveils unique aspects that reflect the dynamic fusion of indigenous and foreign elements, encapsulating the essence of the Philistine identity.

Philistine pottery stands as a hallmark of their material culture, marked by distinctive features that set it apart from the surrounding regions. Notably, the Philistines introduced a style known as Philistine Bichrome pottery, characterized by its distinct two-colored motifs. The application of black and red pigments on a light slip background created intricate designs, often depicting animals, birds, and geometric patterns. This distinctive pottery style not only served functional purposes but also acted as a cultural marker, signifying the emergence of a new identity within the region.

Architectural innovations during this period further attest to the unique character of Philistine city-states. The Philistines introduced a new architectural style characterized by the use of ashlar masonry, a technique involving finely cut and dressed stones. This departure from the prevalent construction methods in the region showcased the Philistines' expertise in adapting and integrating foreign architectural traditions. The city of Ashkelon, with its well-preserved fortifications and monumental structures, stands as a testament to the Philistines' architectural prowess.

Artifacts discovered in Philistine city-states provide additional insights into the material culture of this period. A distinctive class comprises the Philistine pottery figurines, frequently portraying both human and animal shapes. These figurines, with their distinctive features and stylized representations, offer a glimpse into the artistic expressions and cultural symbolism of the Philistines. The deliberate choice of certain motifs, such as warrior figures or animals, may carry deeper cultural significance, reflecting societal values and beliefs.

The integration of foreign elements into Philistine material culture is evident in the presence of Mycenaean and Aegean influences. The adoption of Mycenaean IIIC pottery forms, characterized by stirrup jars and other vessel types, points to connections with the broader eastern Mediterranean world. This intermingling of styles and techniques highlights the Philistines' role as cultural intermediaries, absorbing and reinterpreting external influences to create a unique amalgamation.

The emergence of Philistine city-states was intrinsically linked to the complex interaction of geography, climate, and the migratory patterns of the Philistine people. As we delve into the investigation of Philistine migrations, it becomes evident that these movements were not arbitrary but intricately influenced by the environmental factors inherent to the ancient landscape of Philistia.

Geography, with its diverse topography and ecological features, performed a pivotal task in shaping the migratory routes and settlement patterns of the Philistines. The coastal plain, characterized by its fertile soils and proximity to the Mediterranean, emerged as a beacon for settlement. The allure of arable land and access to maritime resources drew the Philistines towards the coastal regions, setting the stage for the establishment of city-states such as Ashkelon, Ashdod, Ekron, Gath, and Gaza.

The strategic positioning of these city-states was not a mere coincidence but a response to the environmental opportunities and challenges presented by the landscape. Coastal locations facilitated trade, maritime activities, and cultural exchanges with neighboring regions. The interconnectivity between geography and settlement is exemplified by the prominence of Philistine cities as key nodes in the broader network of ancient Mediterranean trade routes.

Climate, as a determining factor in agricultural practices and resource availability, also shaped the migratory patterns of the Philistines. The synergy between geography and climate becomes even more pronounced when examining the specific characteristics of Philistine agriculture. The adoption of innovative agricultural techniques, such as terracotta pipes for irrigation, reveals an adaptive response to the environmental constraints of the region. These technological advancements not only enabled efficient water management but also contributed to the success of Philistine agricultural endeavors.

Furthermore, the investigation of Philistine migrations unveils the dynamic nature of interactions between the indigenous population and incoming groups. The Philistines, believed to have originated from the Aegean and Cyprus regions, brought with them cultural practices, technological know-how, and artistic traditions. The assimilation of these external elements into the local milieu speaks to the cultural adaptability of the Philistine communities and their ability to integrate foreign influences into their evolving identity.

The threads of interaction with neighboring cultures weave a complex narrative, revealing the intricate dynamics that shaped the identity and destiny of these coastal communities. The interactions with neighboring cultures during this transformative period were characterized by a delicate balance of cooperation, cultural exchange, and intermittent conflicts.

The coastal location of the Philistine city-states positioned them as indispensable actors in the broader Mediterranean network, fostering interactions with diverse neighboring cultures. The maritime connectivity facilitated trade, cultural exchanges, and the flow of goods and ideas. The archaeological record attests to the diversity of imported artifacts found in Philistine sites, ranging from pottery to exotic items, indicating the extent of their engagement with neighboring regions.

The noteworthy facets of Philistine interactions with neighbors lies in the realms of trade and commerce. The coastal plain, with its strategic position, became a nexus for maritime trade routes. Philistine cities, such as Ashdod and Ashkelon, engaged in robust trade, importing raw materials, luxury goods, and technological innovations. The evidence of Mycenaean IIIC pottery and other imported items from the Aegean and Cyprus regions underscores the cosmopolitan nature of Philistine city life and the extent of their connections beyond regional borders.

Cultural exchanges with neighboring societies left an indelible mark on the evolving identity of the Philistines. The adoption and adaptation of foreign artistic styles, architectural techniques, and material culture reflect the porous boundaries through which cultural influences flowed. The Philistines, having arrived from the Aegean, infused their own cultural elements into the local milieu while absorbing and reshaping the indigenous traditions, creating a distinctive fusion that characterized Philistine material culture.

However, this narrative of interaction was not devoid of tensions and clashes. The geopolitical landscape of the ancient Near East was rife with power brawls, and the Philistine city-states found themselves entangled in periodic scuffles with their neighbors. The historical records and biblical narratives allude to clashes with neighboring entities, including the Israelites and the Egyptians. These conflicts were not only military but also ideological, reflecting the complex interchange of territorial ambitions, cultural differences, and political rivalries.

The city of Ashkelon, for instance, stood witness to tumultuous periods of destruction and reconstruction, echoing the ebb and flow of geopolitical tensions. The layers of destruction uncovered in archaeological excavations tell a tale of the volatile nature of Philistine interactions with neighboring powers, where the city-states became arenas for the collision of competing interests and aspirations.

Imperial Rule (586 BCE - 330 CE)

The era of Assyrian and Babylonian dominance unfolded as an imperative chapter in the annals of Philistine history, reshaping the landscape of the city-states both politically and culturally. The imposition of imperial rule brought forth a paradigm shift in governance and administration, leaving an enduring impact on the trajectory of Philistine civilizations. This transformative period witnessed intricate changes in the structures of power, as the Assyrians and later the Babylonians asserted their influence over the region. As we delve into the analysis of this imperial rule, we will scrutinize the alterations in political frameworks, the assimilation of cultural identities, and the strategic adaptations made by the Philistines in response to the challenges posed by being part of larger empires.

The Assyrians, renowned for their formidable military prowess and efficient administrative systems, left an indelible mark on the governance of the Philistine city-states. The annals of the Assyrian kings document their campaigns and the incorporation of Philistine territories into the Assyrian Empire. The imposition of Assyrian rule necessitated the establishment of a centralized administrative framework, characterized by the appointment of local governors and the implementation of imperial policies.

A distinctive feature of Assyrian governance was the implementation of imperial officials, referred to as eunuchs, who assumed the role of governors in the conquered territories. Acting as intermediaries between the local administration and the Assyrian central authority, these officials undertook a crucial role. Archaeological evidence, including inscriptions and administrative documents, offers insights into the meticulous record-keeping and bureaucratic structures employed by the Assyrians to ensure efficient control and taxation.

Similarly, the Babylonian dominance that followed further shaped the administrative landscape of the Philistine city-states. The Babylonians, under the rule of Nebuchadnezzar II, exerted control over the region, influencing not only political structures but also societal norms. The Babylonian Chronicles and historical accounts attest to the subjugation of the Philistines and their integration into the Babylonian administrative system.

Under Babylonian rule, changes in governance were intertwined with religious and cultural impositions. The Babylonians sought to assimilate the conquered peoples into their imperial ideology, promoting the worship of Babylonian deities and the adoption of Babylonian cultural practices. This cultural assimilation was often enforced through the appointment of puppet rulers who aligned with Babylonian interests, ensuring a semblance of local governance under imperial control.

Archaeological excavations in Philistine city-states provide tangible evidence of these changes in governance and administration. The discovery of inscriptions, seals, and administrative artifacts offers glimpses into the bureaucratic mechanisms employed by the imperial powers. The meticulous recording of tribute payments, the establishment of imperial garrisons, and the enforcement of imperial decrees underscore the systematic nature of Assyrian and Babylonian rule.

The imprint of Assyrian and Babylonian dominance on the Philistine city-states transcended mere administrative changes, permeating the very essence of local cultures. The cultural transformations that unfolded under imperial rule were marked by a complex relationship of assimilation, resistance, and adaptation, shaping a nuanced narrative of how external powers influenced and molded the identity of the Philistine populace.

The Assyrians, recognized for their imperial strategies of cultural assimilation, aimed to homogenize the conquered territories under their overarching ideology. The archaeological evidence from Philistine sites reveals a confluence of Assyrian and local cultural elements. Artifacts such as seals, pottery, and inscriptions illustrate a fusion of artistic styles, where Assyrian motifs coexist with indigenous designs, reflecting the intricate process of cultural blending.

The propagation of Assyrian cultural influence entailed the endorsement of Assyrian deities and religious practices. Establishing temples dedicated to Assyrian gods in the Philistine city-states served as emblematic focal points of imperial authority. The integration of Assyrian religious iconography into local contexts is discernible in the architectural features and religious artifacts unearthed in archaeological excavations. This syncretism of religious elements emphasized the nuanced negotiation between imperial imposition and local resilience.

Babylonian dominance, following the Assyrian era, brought its own set of cultural transformations to Philistia. The Babylonians, with their penchant for cultural hegemony, sought to imprint their imperial identity on the conquered regions. The archaeological record attests to the introduction of Babylonian architectural styles, artistic motifs, and religious practices. The incorporation of Babylonian deities into the local pantheon and the establishment of Babylonian-style structures reflected a deliberate effort to reshape the cultural landscape.

The adaptation of cuneiform script for administrative and religious purposes further exemplifies the cultural assimilation orchestrated by Babylonian rule. Inscriptions and tablets discovered in Philistine sites bear witness to the utilization of Babylonian writing systems for record-keeping and communication. This linguistic transformation signaled not only a pragmatic adjustment to administrative requirements but also a profound influence on the written expression of local culture.

While cultural assimilation was a dominant theme, the Philistine populace also exhibited elements of resistance and resilience. Local communities navigated the delicate balance between accommodating imperial influences and preserving their distinct identity. The archaeological evidence reveals instances of cultural continuity, where certain aspects of local traditions persisted despite the overarching imperial presence. The persistence of indigenous artistic styles, religious practices, and language attests to the agency of the Philistine communities in shaping their cultural narrative.

Steering the challenges of being part of larger empires, the Philistines during Assyrian and Babylonian dominance displayed a remarkable capacity for adaptation and strategic engagement. As imperial subjects, they confronted the complexities of maintaining a distinct identity while negotiating the demands and pressures exerted by the ruling powers.

The Philistines adopted a diplomatic approach to forge pragmatic alliances with imperial powers. Archaeological evidence substantiates the existence of treaties and agreements between the Philistine city-states and entities like the Assyrians or Babylonians. Unearthed in excavations, these documents outline the terms of engagement, encompassing tribute payments, military alliances, and commitments to imperial agendas. These diplomatic initiatives were a tangible expression of the Philistine leadership's astute political maneuvering, aiming to secure a measure of autonomy within the imperial framework.

Furthermore, the Philistines demonstrated a keen awareness of the importance of cultural accommodation. Embracing aspects of Assyrian and Babylonian culture, the Philistines strategically incorporated imperial motifs into their own artistic expressions. The syncretic blending of local and imperial styles in pottery, architecture, and religious artifacts showcased a nuanced approach to cultural adaptation. This deliberate fusion served not only as a form of homage to the ruling powers but also as a means of navigating the cultural expectations imposed by the empires.

Economic pragmatism took a decisive part in the Philistines' adaptation to foreign powers. The Philistine city-states were strategically positioned as significant trade hubs, connecting various regions within the imperial domains. Archaeological findings, including trade goods, inscriptions, and economic records, underscore the economic interdependence between the Philistines and their imperial overlords. Trade agreements and economic partnerships facilitated a degree of economic autonomy for the Philistines while ensuring their continued relevance within the larger imperial networks.

Military collaboration was another facet of the Philistines' strategic adaptations. Understanding the geopolitical realities, the Philistines occasionally aligned themselves with imperial powers in regional conflicts. The archaeological record hints at military engagements, alliances, and shared military strategies between the Philistines and the imperial forces. These collaborations, while pragmatic, also allowed the Philistines to safeguard their interests and maintain a measure of influence in the ever-shifting political landscape.

The Philistines' adjustment to foreign powers involved a nuanced interplay between strategic compliance and subtle resistance. While they engaged in diplomatic overtures, embraced cultural syncretism, and pursued economic collaborations, there were also instances of retaining elements of their indigenous identity. The archaeological discoveries unveil the delicate balance between assimilation and assertion, providing glimpses into a society adept at navigating the multifaceted challenges of imperial rule.

Hellenistic and Roman Influences
(330 BCE – 330 CE)

The Hellenistic and Roman periods marked a transformative era for Philistine urban developments, witnessing a confluence of architectural innovations, cultural coalescence, and infrastructural advancements. Philistine cities experienced significant growth and underwent changes that mirrored the influences of Hellenistic and Roman civilizations.

During the Hellenistic period, the Philistine cities exhibited a distinctive fusion of Greek architectural styles with local influences. Urban planning saw a shift towards more organized layouts, reflecting the Hellenistic emphasis on grid-based city designs. Archaeological excavations have revealed the remnants of public buildings, agora spaces, and theaters that underscored the civic and cultural aspirations of Philistine urban centers. The introduction of Greek architectural elements, such as colonnades and monumental structures, added a grandeur to the urban landscape.

The urban developments of Philistine cities continued to evolve under Roman rule, with an even greater emphasis on monumental architecture and civic infrastructure. The Romans, known for their engineering prowess, left an indelible mark on Philistine cities through the construction of amphitheaters, aqueducts, and bathhouses. The city of Ashkelon, for instance, boasts a well-preserved Roman theater, exemplifying the integration of Roman entertainment and architectural aesthetics into the urban fabric.

The demographic composition of Philistine cities also witnessed shifts during the Hellenistic and Roman periods. The influx of diverse populations, including Greek and Roman settlers, brought about cultural diversity and contributed to the cosmopolitan character of urban life. This demographic amalgamation is reflected in the material culture, inscriptions, and architectural styles unearthed in archaeological excavations.

The Hellenistic and Roman periods ushered in an era of profound cultural exchange in Philistia, marking a transformative phase where Greek and Roman elements intermingled with the existing fabric of Philistine society. This cultural confluence, characterized by the amalgamation of artistic, religious, and societal influences, had a pivotal impact on shaping the identity of Philistine communities.

Art and architecture served as poignant mediums through which Greek and Roman cultural elements permeated Philistine society. The adoption of classical motifs, architectural styles, and artistic techniques became evident in the construction of public buildings, temples, and private residences. Notable examples include the incorporation of Corinthian columns, mosaic floorings, and frescoes depicting mythological themes. These artistic expressions exhibited a harmonious blend of local traditions with the aesthetic sensibilities imported from Hellenistic and Roman cultures.

Religious practices underwent a transformation during this period, reflecting the syncretism between indigenous beliefs and the introduction of Greek and Roman deities. Temples and religious structures exhibited an eclecticism in their pantheons, with local gods coexisting alongside imported divinities. The worship of Greek and Roman gods, coupled with the preservation of indigenous religious practices, created a unique tapestry of religious expression that defined the spiritual landscape of Philistia.

Theater, a quintessential element of Greek and Roman culture, found resonance in Philistine society, becoming a platform for cultural exchange. Theatrical performances featuring Greek and Roman plays became popular, attracting diverse audiences and fostering a shared cultural experience. The amphitheaters, exemplified by the well-preserved Roman theater in Ashkelon, not only served as entertainment venues but also as spaces for communal gatherings that transcended cultural boundaries.

Language, a fundamental aspect of cultural identity, witnessed a notable shift with the influx of Greek and Latin influences. Bilingual inscriptions and the use of Greek and Latin in official documents reflected the linguistic diversity that emerged during the Hellenistic and Roman periods. This linguistic interchange facilitated communication between different cultural groups and contributed to the cosmopolitan character of Philistine urban centers.

The economic landscape of Philistia also bore the imprints of Greek and Roman influences, particularly in trade practices and commercial interactions. The integration of Roman currency systems, trade routes, and market structures enhanced economic ties with the broader Mediterranean world. Philistine cities became hubs of commerce, attracting merchants and traders from diverse backgrounds, further enriching the cultural tapestry of the region.

The social fabric of Philistine society evolved with the infusion of Greek and Roman social norms. The concept of civic life, modeled after Hellenistic and Roman city-states, influenced the organization of communities and the development of civic institutions. The emergence of local elites with cultural affinities to Greek and Roman traditions contributed to the stratification of Philistine society.

Similarly, during these periods, Philistia rose to prominence, becoming a strategically and economically significant region in the broader context of the Eastern Mediterranean. The geographical location of Philistia, situated at the crossroads of major trade routes and encompassing key coastal cities, had a crucial function in shaping its regional importance during this epoch.

Key port cities like Ashkelon, Ashdod, and Gaza took requisite roles as maritime hubs, fostering trade and communication with Mediterranean and Aegean regions. The accessibility of Philistia from both land and sea routes positioned it as a linchpin for trans-regional exchanges, further solidifying its role as a gateway between the Levant and the broader Eastern Mediterranean.

The coastal cities of Philistia also held military significance, commanding control over maritime trade routes and providing a strategic vantage point for defense. The Roman and Hellenistic powers recognized the geopolitical importance of these cities, leading to their incorporation into broader regional strategies. The well-fortified structures, such as the fortifications in Ashdod and Ashkelon, attested to the strategic value attributed to Philistia by imperial powers.

The production of Philistine pottery, renowned for its distinctive features, became a sought-after commodity in the Mediterranean market. The unique characteristics of Philistine pottery, including the use of specific motifs and styles, reflected both indigenous traditions and influences from the Hellenistic and Roman cultural spheres. This export of pottery not only bolstered Philistia's economic standing but also contributed to the dissemination of its cultural identity across the Mediterranean.

Moreover, the agricultural fertility of the Philistine plain, characterized by fertile soils and favorable climatic conditions, facilitated the cultivation of crops and supported a thriving agrarian economy. The agricultural surplus not only sustained the local population but also became a valuable commodity for trade, further enhancing Philistia's economic importance in the region.

Byzantine Era and Islamic Rule (330 CE - 1200s CE)

The Byzantine and Islamic periods in Philistia marked significant religious transformations, with the spread of Christianity followed by the advent of Islam shaping the spiritual landscape of the region. During the Byzantine era, Christianity gained prominence as the dominant religious force in Philistia. The spread of this faith was facilitated by the establishment of churches and religious institutions, contributing to the Christianization of the local population.

The Byzantine religious developments in Philistia were not only confined to the construction of churches but also encompassed the promotion of Christian doctrines, rituals, and iconography. The emergence of Byzantine Christianity carried out a pivotal duty in influencing the religious practices and beliefs of the Philistine community. The construction of churches, adorned with intricate mosaics and religious symbols, served as physical manifestations of the Byzantine religious presence in Philistia.

As Christianity took root in the region, the Byzantine authorities fulfilled a key responsibility in institutionalizing and consolidating the Christian faith. This period witnessed the establishment of ecclesiastical structures, with bishops assuming leadership roles and overseeing the spiritual affairs of the Christian community. The religious landscape of Philistia became increasingly defined by Christian doctrines, rituals, and the influence of Byzantine religious authorities.

However, the religious dynamics in Philistia underwent a significant transformation with the arrival of Islam during the Islamic period, beginning in the 7th century CE. The spread of Islam in Philistia was not only a religious shift but also a cultural and political transformation. The historical context and events surrounding the arrival of Islam in Philistia were marked by the expansion of Islamic rule across the region.

The adoption of Islamic culture and traditions became integral to the fabric of Philistine society. The spread and adoption of Islamic culture in Philistia encompassed various aspects, including language, arts, and traditions. The Arabic language, as a central component of Islamic identity, became prevalent, influencing communication, literature, and cultural expression in Philistia.

Moreover, the political transformations under Islamic rule profoundly influenced the religious panorama. The governance structures and administrative policies implemented during this period were shaped by Islamic principles. The establishment of mosques and the integration of Islamic governance contributed to the Islamicization of Philistia, creating a new chapter in its religious history.

The blend of different religious and ethnic communities thrived under Islamic rule, contributing to the vibrant religious diversity that characterized Philistia. The dynamics of collaboration and cultural exchange among different religious groups became defining features of the diverse societal framework during this period.

The architectural legacy in Philistia during the Byzantine and Islamic periods, on the other hand, stands as a testament to the rich cultural and religious tapestry woven into the region. This legacy, characterized by distinctive features and stylistic elements, reflects the influence of both Byzantine and Islamic architectural traditions on the cities of Philistia.

During the Byzantine era, the construction of churches became a prominent architectural endeavor, shaping the urban scenery of Philistine cities. Byzantine architecture, known for its grandeur and ornate details, left an indelible mark on the region. The Hagia Sophia in Constantinople served as an architectural archetype, influencing the design and construction of Byzantine churches in Philistia.

The Byzantine era bestowed upon Philistia a lasting architectural legacy, epitomized by the grandeur of basilicas. Characterized by a longitudinal plan, central nave, and aisles, these churches became emblematic of Byzantine religious architecture. The Basilica of St. Hilarion in Gaza, among others, stands as a prime example, highlighting the fusion of Byzantine architectural elements with local adaptations. Intricate mosaic work, domed roofs, and elaborate arches adorned these basilicas, symbolizing the Byzantine commitment to artistic expression within a religious context.

The Byzantine architectural legacy extended beyond churches to include monastic complexes. Monasteries, such as the Monastery of St. Sabas, exemplified Byzantine architectural principles with their compact layouts, centralized courtyards, and interconnected buildings. These monastic structures not only served as centers of worship but also as hubs for scholarly activities and communal living.

As the Islamic period unfolded, a new architectural paradigm emerged, blending Islamic design principles with existing Byzantine structures. The arrival of Islam brought forth a distinctive architectural legacy, characterized by the construction of mosques and other Islamic edifices.

Mosques became focal points of Islamic architectural expression in Philistia. Influenced by Islamic geometric patterns and calligraphy, mosques like the Great Mosque of Gaza exemplified the integration of local building traditions with Islamic aesthetics. The use of pointed arches, domes, and minarets became defining features of Islamic architecture, shaping the skyline of Philistine cities.

Moreover, the adaptation of existing structures demonstrated a pragmatic approach to architecture during the Islamic period. Some Byzantine churches were repurposed into mosques. The Mosque of Omar in Bethlehem, formerly the Church of St. Mary, exemplifies this adaptive reuse, symbolizing the coexistence of different religious traditions within the architectural landscape.

The architectural heritage from the Byzantine and Islamic eras in Philistia acts as a visual testament to the region's cultural metamorphosis. The transition from Byzantine basilicas to Islamic mosques reflects not only shifts in religious dominance but also the seamless integration of diverse architectural styles. This coalescence of Byzantine and Islamic architectural elements created a unique visual language that continues to resonate in the cultural heritage of Philistia.

Philistia, during these periods, served as a dynamic crossroads of cultural and economic exchange, fostering a vibrant tapestry of interactions that left a lasting imprint on the region's identity. The strategic location of Philistia at the intersection of major trade routes and its diverse religious and cultural heritage positioned it as a nexus for cross-cultural encounters, shaping the economic and cultural landscapes of the time.

Trade, a cardinal force in the region, thrived in Philistia during the Byzantine and Islamic periods. The city-states along the coast, such as Gaza and Ashkelon, became bustling centers of commerce, facilitating the exchange of goods, ideas, and artistic influences. The Mediterranean Sea served as a vital conduit for maritime trade, connecting Philistia to distant lands and enabling the flow of commodities like spices, textiles, and precious metals.

The city of Jaffa, with its well-established port, played a crucial purview in maritime trade, serving as a gateway for merchants and travelers. The diverse array of goods that passed through Jaffa's harbor attested to the region's integration into larger trade networks. The bustling markets of Philistine cities became melting pots of cultural exchange, where merchants from various backgrounds engaged in transactions, fostering an environment of diversity and cosmopolitanism.

Moreover, the city-states of Philistia evolved into centers of intellectual exchange, drawing scholars, theologians, and philosophers from diverse cultural realms. The translation movement, where Greek philosophical works were translated into Arabic, flourished in this cosmopolitan environment, contributing to the dissemination of knowledge across linguistic and cultural boundaries. Philistia's role as a cultural crossroads facilitated the exchange of ideas, fostering intellectual growth and creating a rich fabric of thought.

Philistia's significance as a cultural and economic crossroads during the Byzantine and Islamic periods is reflected in the archaeological evidence unearthed in the region. Excavations have revealed a wealth of artifacts, including pottery, coins, and architectural remnants, attesting to the diversity of influences that shaped the material culture of Philistine city-states.

Crusader Period and Ayyubid/ Mamluk Rule (1100s – 1500s)

The era of the Crusaders brought about a significant shift in Philistia's history, as the arrival and establishment of Crusader strongholds reshaped the urban landscape of the region. In the 12th century, European Crusaders descended upon the Holy Land, seeking to reclaim Jerusalem and establish Christian dominion. This crusading fervor led to the establishment of Crusader cities along the coastal plains, profoundly impacting the indigenous Philistine urban centers.

The strategic importance of Philistia's coastal region did not escape the attention of the Crusaders. Cities like Jaffa, Ashkelon, and Caesarea became focal points for Crusader expansion and consolidation. The Crusaders erected formidable fortifications, transforming these coastal cities into bastions of military might and Christian influence. The construction of imposing castles and defensive structures not only altered the skyline but also exerted a palpable influence on the socio-political dynamics of the region.

The impact of Crusader cities on Philistine urban centers was multifaceted. The Crusaders, driven by religious zeal, sought to impose their cultural and architectural imprint on the land. Existing structures were often repurposed or modified to align with Crusader aesthetics and functionality. Churches and cathedrals, adorned with Gothic architecture, emerged alongside existing Islamic and Byzantine remnants, creating a mosaic of religious and cultural influences.

The establishment of Crusader strongholds brought about demographic shifts as well. European settlers, enticed by promises of land and religious pilgrimage, populated the newly founded cities. This influx of Crusader settlers introduced a European demographic element into the historically diverse drapery of Philistine urban life. The coexistence of different cultural, religious, and linguistic groups within these cities created a complex social milieu, characterized by interactions and tensions.

The Crusader impact on trade and commerce was profound. The coastal cities served as vital hubs for maritime trade, connecting Europe to the Levant. The establishment of Crusader-controlled ports facilitated the flow of goods, ideas, and cultural influences between East and West. The fusion of European, Byzantine, and Islamic trade practices contributed to the economic vitality of Philistia during this period.

However, the Crusader presence in Philistia was not without resistance. Indigenous Muslim rulers, particularly the Ayyubids and later the Mamluks, mounted successive campaigns to reclaim these coastal territories. The clash of civilizations and the dynamic relationship between Crusader and Muslim forces shaped the geopolitical landscape, leaving an indelible mark on the history of Philistia.

The transition from Crusader rule to Ayyubid and Mamluk governance marked a vital phase in the history of Philistia, unfolding against the backdrop of the Crusader Period and the subsequent Ayyubid/Mamluk Rule. As the Crusaders established strongholds in the region, their interactions with Muslim rulers became emblematic of the intricate geopolitical dynamics that defined the era.

The decline of Crusader dominance in the late 12th century witnessed the ascendancy of the Ayyubid dynasty, led by the renowned Salah ad-Din (Saladin). Salah ad-Din's capture of Jerusalem in 1187 dealt a significant blow to the Crusaders and initiated a shift in regional power dynamics. The Ayyubids, with a commitment to Sunni Islam, sought to reclaim territories under Crusader control, including those in Philistia.

The interactions between Crusaders and Ayyubid rulers were characterized by a blend of military conflicts, negotiations, and occasional periods of coexistence. Salah ad-Din's chivalrous conduct during the capture of Jerusalem is well-documented, demonstrating a nuanced approach to governance that extended beyond mere conquest. The Ayyubid rulers, by adhering to Islamic principles, displayed harmony in dealing with diverse religious and cultural communities within the territories they reclaimed.

With the decline of the Ayyubid dynasty, the Mamluks rose to prominence in the late 13th century. Their governance, often marked by military prowess and centralized authority, continued the trend of Muslim rulership in Philistia. The Mamluks maintained a vigilant stance against potential Crusader incursions, fortifying existing defenses and securing key strategic points along the coast.

Interactions between Crusaders and Ayyubid/Mamluk rulers were not solely confined to military confrontations. Diplomacy and cultural exchanges had a commitment in shaping the trajectory of the region. Treaties and agreements were formed, delineating spheres of influence and allowing for the coexistence of Crusader and Muslim realms. The fluidity of these interactions reflected the complex geopolitical landscape, where alliances shifted in response to changing circumstances.

Trade and economic considerations further influenced the interactions between Crusaders and Muslim rulers. The coastal cities of Philistia, with their strategic importance for maritime trade, remained focal points of contention. Ayyubid and Mamluk rulers, cognizant of the economic significance of these cities, engaged in diplomatic negotiations and occasional military campaigns to safeguard their interests.

Ottoman Empire (1500s - Early 1900s)

During the Ottoman Period, Philistia underwent significant administrative changes as it became an integral part of the vast Ottoman Empire. The governance structures implemented by the Ottomans reflected the empire's intricate system of administration, characterized by a blend of centralization and local autonomy. At the heart of Ottoman administrative organization was the concept of the millet system. This system recognized various religious communities, or millets, as distinct legal entities with the autonomy to govern their internal affairs. In Philistia, which housed diverse religious communities, this approach allowed for a degree of self-governance among Christians, Muslims, and Jews.

The Ottomans appointed local administrators known as governors or beys to oversee provincial affairs. These officials accomplished a crucial mission in implementing imperial policies, collecting taxes, and maintaining order. Philistia, with its strategic coastal cities and economic significance, attracted the attention of Ottoman administrators who sought to maximize revenue and ensure stability in the region.

The administrative changes also extended to the legal system, with the Ottomans implementing a hierarchical judicial structure. Qadis, or Islamic judges, presided over legal matters, applying Islamic law within the millet framework. The Ottoman legal system aimed to accommodate the diverse religious and cultural practices of the population, fostering a sense of pluralism within the empire.

In addition to local administrators, the Ottomans stationed military garrisons in strategic locations to assert control and deter potential threats. The coastal cities of Philistia, with their economic importance, often hosted Ottoman military presence to safeguard trade routes and maintain order.

The Ottoman administrative model in Philistia exhibited a delicate balance between centralized authority and localized governance. While the empire maintained control over key aspects such as taxation and military presence, the millet system allowed religious communities a degree of autonomy in managing their internal affairs. This approach contributed to a mosaic of cultures and religions coexisting within the Ottoman Empire.

Under Ottoman rule, Philistia witnessed significant economic developments that shaped its trade, agriculture, and urbanization dynamics. The Ottoman Empire, known for its expansive and intricate administrative system, left an indelible mark on the economic landscape of the region. Trade flourished under Ottoman rule, propelled by the empire's strategic position as a crossroads between Europe, Asia, and Africa. Philistia's coastal cities, such as Jaffa and Gaza, played pivotal roles as bustling trade hubs. The Ottomans, recognizing the economic potential of these ports, invested in their infrastructure and security, facilitating the smooth flow of goods and people. The Mediterranean Sea became a conduit for a diverse array of commodities, connecting Philistia to distant markets.

Agriculture, a cornerstone of the region's economy, experienced transformations under Ottoman administration. The empire implemented various land tenure systems, including the Timar system, which granted individuals the right to cultivate and benefit from specific parcels of land. This approach aimed to ensure a stable revenue stream for both the state and local landholders. Philistia's fertile plains and favorable climate made it conducive to agriculture, and the Ottomans sought to harness this potential for economic gain.

Urbanization saw a marked increase during the Ottoman period, with cities expanding and evolving into vibrant centers of commerce and culture. The Ottomans recognized the importance of urban centers in fostering economic prosperity and political stability. Philistia's cities became melting pots of diverse cultures and religions, reflecting the pluralistic nature of the Ottoman Empire.

The construction of infrastructure projects, including roads and bridges, further facilitated economic activities and connectivity within Philistia. These developments not only enhanced trade but also contributed to the growth of local industries and craftsmanship. The Ottomans encouraged the establishment of markets, known as bazaars, where merchants from various backgrounds converged to exchange goods.

The economic impact of Ottoman rule extended beyond local markets, reaching into the imperial coffers through taxation. The Ottomans implemented a system of taxation that aimed to extract revenue while maintaining the economic viability of the region. Taxes were levied on agricultural produce, trade transactions, and urban activities, providing the Ottoman state with the resources needed to sustain its vast empire.

The Ottomans, recognizing the economic potential of Philistia, invested in the development of key sectors. The construction of water management systems, such as aqueducts and wells, supported agricultural activities and ensured a stable water supply for urban centers. These interventions had a decisive influence on enhancing the overall economic resilience of Philistia under Ottoman rule.

Equally, the Ottoman period marked a fascinating chapter in the history of Philistia, characterized by a cultural synthesis that emerged through the convergence of Ottoman and local elements. This synthesis was a dynamic process, shaped by interactions, exchanges, and shared experiences that unfolded within the diverse socio-cultural tapestry of the region.

In their constructions, Ottoman architects seamlessly integrated local motifs and design elements, creating a unique blend that reflected the coexistence of Ottoman and indigenous aesthetics. This fusion is evident in the architecture of mosques, bazaars, and residential buildings, where Ottoman arches and domes harmoniously coexisted with local embellishments, creating structures that stood as tangible representations of cultural convergence.

Language enacted a significant function in cultural synthesis, with Ottoman Turkish and Arabic being the dominant languages of administration and communication. However, the linguistic landscape also retained traces of the linguistic diversity present in the region. Local dialects and linguistic nuances persisted, contributing to a rich linguistic fabric that echoed the multicultural nature of Philistia.

Culinary traditions witnessed a fusion of Ottoman and local flavors, resulting in a distinct culinary identity. The Ottomans brought with them a rich culinary heritage influenced by various cultures within their empire. Local ingredients and cooking techniques were seamlessly integrated into Ottoman culinary practices, giving rise to a unique gastronomic synthesis. This cultural fusion is still evident in modern Palestinian cuisine, where traditional dishes bear the imprint of Ottoman influences.

Art and craftsmanship flourished during the Ottoman period, with artisans blending Ottoman artistic styles with local influences. Textiles, pottery, and intricate woodwork exhibited the fusion of Ottoman geometric patterns with indigenous motifs, creating artifacts that were both aesthetically pleasing and culturally significant. This artistic synthesis not only adorned the material culture of Philistia but also served as a testament to the creative collaboration between Ottoman and local artisans.

The legacy of the Ottoman era in Philistia transcends the confines of a mere historical chapter; it stands as a vibrant testament to the resilience, adaptability, and creativity of a society adept at navigating the crossroads of diverse influences. This period, marked by intricate administrative structures, economic transformations, and architectural innovations, has left an indelible mark on Philistia's cultural identity. The legacy of the Ottoman era in Philistia is not a relic of the past; it is a living narrative that resonates through the centuries, reflecting the enduring impact of this transformative era on the region's socio-cultural fabric.

Canaan's Epochal Journey

Prehistoric Period (Before 3000 BCE)

Delving into the depths of Canaan's prehistoric past, archaeological evidence has unveiled a compelling narrative of early human presence. The exploration of prehistoric settlements in Canaan provides a window into the lifestyles and activities of ancient inhabitants, offering a mosaic of clues that piece together the intricate puzzle of human history in this region.

Excavations across various sites in Canaan have unearthed artifacts dating back to the Paleolithic era, the earliest evidence of human occupation. Stone tools, such as hand-axes and blades, intricately crafted by early inhabitants, bear witness to the resourcefulness and ingenuity of these ancient communities. These tools served not only as essential implements for survival but also as a testament to the cognitive abilities and adaptability of early humans in Canaan.

The discovery of hearths and fire pits at archaeological sites adds another layer to the understanding of Paleolithic settlements in Canaan. These features indicate the mastery of fire, a crucial technological advancement. The deliberate utilization of fire in these prehistoric communities attests to a remarkable level of sophistication in their daily lives.

Paleolithic cave art, found in certain locations in Canaan, adds a fascinating dimension to the archaeological tapestry. These artistic expressions, created with primitive tools, depict scenes from daily life, animals, and perhaps spiritual beliefs. The preservation of such art offers a tantalizing glimpse into the symbolic and cultural dimensions inherent in the societies of early Canaanites, suggesting a capacity for abstract thought and a rudimentary form of communication.

Examining the distribution of these archaeological finds across the landscape offers insights into early settlement patterns. The identification of specific locations as sites of repeated human activity indicates a degree of territoriality and a connection to the surrounding environment. The adaptation of early Canaanite communities to diverse ecological niches underscores their ability to thrive in a range of landscapes.

Furthermore, the study of fauna and flora remnants in archaeological layers contributes to understanding the subsistence strategies of Paleolithic inhabitants. Analysis of animal bones and plant remains reveals patterns of hunting, gathering, and resource utilization, shedding light on the intricate web of relationships between early Canaanites and their natural surroundings.

Expanding upon the groundwork laid by Paleolithic settlements in Canaan, the scrutiny of early nomadic lifestyles reveals a dynamic embroidery of adaptation and survival. The nomadic cultures that traversed the landscapes of ancient Canaan left an indelible mark on the region's prehistoric era, shaping the contours of human existence in profound ways.

Nomadic groups in prehistoric Canaan were characterized by their fluid and mobile lifestyles, a response to the challenges and opportunities presented by the diverse topography of the region. The nomads' movements were not arbitrary but were intricately connected to the seasonal availability of resources, such as water, vegetation, and animal herds. The ebb and flow of their migratory patterns were finely tuned to the rhythms of nature, a testament to the deep ecological knowledge these early inhabitants possessed.

Their adeptness in adapting to a nomadic lifestyle was prominently demonstrated through their command of portable technology, particularly evident in the craftsmanship of their tools and weaponry. The artisanship of lightweight and versatile tools empowered nomadic groups to adeptly traverse diverse terrains, engaging in a spectrum of activities from hunting to gathering. Projectile points, blades, and other implements reflected a sophisticated understanding of materials and their functional applications, highlighting the ingenuity of these ancient nomads.

The symbiotic relationship between nomadic cultures and the environment is further illuminated by the discovery of temporary habitation sites. These sites, often marked by fire pits, discarded tools, and communal activity areas, underscore the cyclical nature of nomadic life. The nomads established temporary encampments, skillfully adapting to the changing seasons and resource availability. The archaeological record reveals a pattern of repeated use of these sites, emphasizing the sustainability and efficiency of nomadic lifestyles.

The significance of animal domestication and the emergence of rudimentary forms of pastoralism must not be overlooked when examining nomadic cultures in prehistoric Canaan. The domestication of certain animal species provided a stable source of sustenance, materials, and transportation, enhancing the resilience and adaptability of nomadic groups. The interdependence between humans and domesticated animals laid the groundwork for future agricultural practices that would shape the trajectory of Canaanite civilizations.

Nomadic communities owed their successful adaptation to the region not only to environmental resilience but also to the primordial role played by their social organization. The adaptable nature of their social structures facilitated seamless cooperation in addressing environmental challenges. Communal decision-making, shared responsibilities, and a cohesive ethos were distinctive features of nomadic groups, proving instrumental for their survival. The absence of monumental architecture or centralized authority underscored the egalitarian essence of these societies, emphasizing the decentralized yet interconnected ornamentation of nomadic life.

Early Bronze Age (3000 BCE - 2000 BCE)

The dawn of the Early Bronze Age in Canaan marked a paramount moment, ushering in a transformative era that saw the birth of urban centers and the groundwork for early city-states. During this epoch, settlement patterns and societal structures underwent a profound shift as communities evolved from smaller villages to more intricate urban formations. Excavations across the region reveal tangible remnants of this urbanization process, offering archaeological insights into the societal advancements of the time. Noteworthy among these discoveries is the emergence of fortified settlements, a defining characteristic of early city-states. The construction of defensive walls signifies a growing awareness of the need for protection, hinting at potential shifts in societal dynamics and the rise of more centralized authority.

A notable instance lies in the historic city of Jericho, celebrated for its distinction as one of the world's most enduringly populated cities throughout antiquity. The city's fortifications, including the famed double wall, not only served as a defensive measure but also underscored the strategic and organized efforts of the inhabitants in the face of external pressures. Constructed from a fusion of mud bricks and stone, these monumental structures stand as enduring testaments to the architectural ingenuity inherent in the urban centers of the Early Bronze Age.

The establishment of urban centers during this period was not merely a response to security concerns; it also marked a pivotal development in economic and social structures. The concentration of populations within defined city limits facilitated the specialization of labor, leading to the emergence of diverse occupations and trades. Evidence of craft workshops, such as pottery kilns and metalworking areas, underscores the flourishing economic activities within these early urban hubs.

Moreover, the urbanization process was intrinsically tied to the expansion of trade networks. The proximity of city-states to key trade routes and resource-rich areas facilitated the exchange of goods and ideas, fostering cultural exchange and economic interdependence. The city of Ur, located along the ancient trade route connecting Mesopotamia and Canaan, exemplifies the interconnectedness of urban centers and trade during the Early Bronze Age. Archaeological findings at Ur reveal imported materials, highlighting the role of trade in shaping the material culture and economic prosperity of these city-states.

Archaeological evidence provides compelling insights into the extent and complexity of these trade networks. Excavations at key sites, including cities like Ebla and Mari, have unearthed artifacts and documents that attest to the long-distance trade relations between Canaan and neighboring regions. The ancient city of Ebla, located in modern-day Syria, stands as a resounding testament to the intricate web of trade during this period. Discoveries of cuneiform tablets at Ebla reveal detailed records of trade transactions, documenting the exchange of commodities such as metals, textiles, and precious goods with distant regions. Excavations at Ur have uncovered evidence of Canaanite goods, highlighting the economic exchanges between the two regions. The availability of materials like copper from the Anatolian plateau and precious stones from Egypt in Canaanese archaeological sites underscores the far-reaching impact of these trade connections.

The maritime routes also performed a key onus in shaping the economic landscape of the Early Bronze Age. The coastal cities of Canaan, strategically positioned along the Mediterranean Sea, engaged in maritime trade with neighboring regions. Evidence from sites like Byblos attests to the vibrant seafaring activities of the Canaanites. Byblos, renowned for its timber resources, became a crucial node in the timber trade network, supplying cedar and other wood to distant regions.

Along with these, archaeological excavations and artifacts unearthed from Canaanite urban centers, also, bear witness to the rich ostentation of cultural exchange that characterized this period. The mingling of Canaanite, Mesopotamian, Anatolian, and Egyptian influences is palpable in the material culture, artistic expressions, and architectural styles of the era.

Evident within the realm of pottery, a striking facet of this cultural exchange unfolds. Canaanite pottery, previously defined by unique local styles, gradually incorporated elements from neighboring civilizations.

The infusion of novel forms, techniques, and decorative motifs mirrored the cross-cultural interplay facilitated by trade. The integration of intricate designs, symbolic motifs, and stylistic elements from Mesopotamian and Egyptian pottery serves as a prime illustration of the dynamic evolution within Canaanite culture.

The impact of cultural exchange extended beyond the realm of material culture, shaping religious practices and belief systems. Canaanite religious iconography began to incorporate symbols and deities from neighboring regions. Temples and religious structures revealed a syncretic blending of Canaanite, Mesopotamian, and Egyptian religious elements. Through excavations, Ebla revealed temples adorned with divine figures and motifs reminiscent of Mesopotamian religious traditions, eloquently illustrating the nuanced fusion of religious influences.

Language and writing systems were not immune to the currents of cultural exchange. The emergence of written records, inscriptions, and administrative documents in Canaanite urban centers showcased the assimilation of writing systems from Mesopotamia and Egypt. The use of cuneiform script in administrative contexts and the adaptation of hieroglyphic writing underscored the multifaceted nature of cultural cross-pollination.

The cultural exchange in Canaan during the Early Bronze Age was not a unidirectional process; it was a reciprocal and dynamic relationship between Canaanite society and its neighbors. The evidence from archaeological sites attests to the openness of Canaanite civilization to external influences, embracing and integrating elements from diverse cultural spheres.

Amorite Rule (circa 2000 BCE – 1600 BCE)

The influx of the Amorites into Canaan stands as a watershed moment in the region's history, molding both its demographic and cultural contours. A wealth of evidence gleaned from archaeological excavations and historical records offers insights into the intricacies of the Amorite migration and the patterns that defined their settlement in the region. Around the early second millennium BCE, the Amorites, a Semitic-speaking people, migrated from the vast expanses of the Syrian desert into the fertile lands of Canaan. This migration was likely prompted by a combination of environmental factors, including climatic changes and pressures within their original territories. The Amorites' movement into Canaan was not a swift conquest but rather a gradual process of settlement and assimilation.

Archaeological findings paint a nuanced picture of the Amorite migration, characterized by a series of incremental settlements rather than a singular wave of invasion. The Amorites, adept at adapting to diverse environments, established a network of villages and small communities across Canaan. This gradual infiltration and establishment of settlements allowed for a more organic integration with the existing population, fostering a mosaic of cultural and social interactions.

The settlement patterns of the Amorites were not uniform, reflecting their ability to adapt to varied ecological zones within Canaan. Coastal plains, hill country, and valleys witnessed the emergence of Amorite communities, each adapting to the specific challenges and opportunities presented by their respective locales. This diversified settlement pattern contributed to the Amorites' integration into the existing Canaanite tapestry, as they coexisted with other ethnic groups and engaged in trade and cultural exchange.

The transition from a nomadic lifestyle to settled communities is evident in the material culture uncovered through archaeological excavations. Pottery styles, architectural features, and everyday artifacts from Amorite settlements exhibit a blend of their traditional practices with influences from the indigenous Canaanite cultures. This syncretic approach to material culture underscores the gradual and nuanced nature of the Amorite presence in Canaan.

Noteworthy archaeological sites, such as Hazor and Bethel, provide glimpses into the intricate settlement patterns of the Amorites. These sites, strategically located in key geographical areas, served as focal points for Amorite communities to establish themselves and interact with the surrounding regions. The archaeological stratigraphy at these sites reveals layers of occupation, attesting to the continuity and endurance of Amorite settlements over time.

The Amorite cultural imprint on Canaan during their dominance was a transformative phase that left an indelible mark on the region's societal fabric. Examining the influence of Amorite cultural elements on Canaanite society reveals an intricate interaction of traditions, beliefs, and practices that shaped the evolution of a distinctive amalgamation.

The religious sphere bore the imprint of Amorite culture, seeping into the fabric of Canaanite society as one of its integral facets. The Amorites brought with them a polytheistic belief system that featured a pantheon of deities with distinct attributes and domains. This infusion of new religious elements enriched the spiritual landscape of Canaan, leading to the syncretism of Amorite and Canaanite religious practices. Archaeological findings, such as inscriptions and artifacts depicting deities, attest to this blending of religious traditions, wherein Amorite gods found their place alongside existing Canaanite divinities.

The architectural footprint of the Amorites also contributed significantly to the cultural landscape of Canaan. The construction and design of monumental structures, such as temples and palaces, illustrate the architectural prowess and urban planning principles brought by the Amorites. Hazor, a prominent city in Canaan, stands as a testament to this architectural legacy. The incorporation of Amorite architectural elements into Canaanite urban centers not only altered the physical appearance of cities but also influenced the socio-political organization of these communities.

Furthermore, linguistic evidence reveals the impact of Amorite cultural elements on Canaanite languages. Loanwords and linguistic borrowings highlight the integration of Amorite vocabulary into the Canaanite linguistic repertoire. This linguistic fusion reflects a sustained interaction between the two cultures, where linguistic exchange became a conduit for shared experiences and cultural integration.

Social practices and customs were not immune to the influence of Amorite culture. Marriage patterns, burial rituals, and daily life in Canaan underwent transformations as a result of the Amorite presence. The assimilation of Amorite social norms into Canaanite society contributed to the emergence of a shared cultural identity, transcending the boundaries of ethnic distinctions.

The political structures of Canaan underwent a profound transformation during the period of Amorite dominance. The impact of Amorite rule on the political organization of Canaan was far-reaching, influencing the governance systems, administrative mechanisms, and power dynamics within the region. The Amorites, known for their organized city-states and strategic military prowess, introduced a more centralized and hierarchical governance model to Canaan. The city-states, once relatively autonomous, experienced a shift towards a more unified political structure under Amorite influence. This centralization was instrumental in fostering greater coordination and cooperation among the city-states, creating a more cohesive political entity.

The Amorite rulers, often establishing themselves as monarchs or kings, shouldered a pivotal task in shaping the political landscape of Canaan. Their leadership was characterized by a strong central authority that sought to maintain control over the various city-states under their dominion. Archaeological evidence, such as royal inscriptions and administrative records, provides insights into the establishment of monarchies and the concentration of power in the hands of the ruling elite.

The administrative apparatus of Canaan also witnessed significant changes during Amorite rule. The introduction of standardized administrative practices, including record-keeping and bureaucratic structures, contributed to a more efficient and organized governance system. The use of written documentation, such as cuneiform tablets, allowed for the recording of legal, economic, and political transactions, facilitating better governance and coordination among the city-states.

Amorite rule had a discernible impact on the social hierarchy within Canaanite society. The establishment of centralized authority and the concentration of power in the hands of monarchs led to the emergence of a more stratified social structure. The ruling elite, comprising the monarch and associated aristocracy, exerted influence over political, economic, and social affairs. This stratification marked a departure from the more egalitarian social structures prevalent in earlier phases of Canaanite history.

Military structures and strategies underwent a process of refinement during the rule of the Amorites. The Amorites, renowned for their military prowess, introduced advancements in weaponry, fortification techniques, and military organization. This militarization of the political landscape influenced the power dynamics within Canaan, with military strength becoming a crucial determinant of political influence and control.

Egyptian Influence (circa 1550 BCE - 1150 BCE)

The periods of Egyptian dominance in Canaan represent an indispensable chapter in the historical tapestry of the region. During this era, Egypt extended its influence beyond the Nile Valley, establishing control over strategic territories in Canaan. The Egyptian presence in Canaan, delineated by military campaigns and administrative dominion, imprinted an enduring mark on the region's political landscape. Evidence from archaeological excavations, such as inscriptions and artifacts, attests to the military campaigns conducted by Egyptian pharaohs to assert dominance in Canaan. The campaigns were characterized by strategic conquests and the establishment of military outposts to secure key trade routes and geopolitical points. The military expeditions served the dual purpose of subduing local resistance and consolidating Egyptian control over Canaanite city-states.

The administrative structures implemented by the Egyptians during this period reflected a systematic approach to governance. Local rulers, often appointed or confirmed by the Egyptian pharaohs, were tasked with overseeing the day-to-day affairs of the city-states. These rulers, while retaining a degree of autonomy, operated within the framework of Egyptian authority, paying tribute and acknowledging the supremacy of the pharaoh.

The Egyptian administrative influence extended to economic policies, with trade and resource management under the purview of Egyptian oversight. The establishment of trade routes and economic ties between Canaan and Egypt facilitated the flow of goods, including coveted resources such as timber, metals, and agricultural products. The tribute paid by Canaanite city-states to the Egyptian pharaohs further underscored the economic subordination to the dominant power.

The Egyptian dominance in Canaan, while marked by military conquests, also involved a pragmatic approach to governance. Rather than eradicating local structures entirely, the Egyptians incorporated existing administrative frameworks, utilizing local elites as intermediaries to facilitate smoother governance. This approach allowed for a degree of continuity in the socio-political structures of Canaanite city-states, albeit under Egyptian suzerainty.

The impact of Egyptian control extended beyond the physical presence of military garrisons and administrative centers. It permeated the collective consciousness of the Canaanite people, influencing their cultural, religious, and economic practices. The legacy of Egyptian dominance in Canaan served as a precursor to subsequent periods of foreign rule, shaping the region's historical trajectory for centuries to come.

Evident in the religious practices embraced and modified by Canaanite society, a prominent reflection of Egyptian cultural influence manifested itself. Temples dedicated to Egyptian deities, such as Hathor and Ra, emerged in various Canaanite city-states, serving as tangible symbols of the syncretism between indigenous Canaanite beliefs and Egyptian religious traditions. The adoption of Egyptian gods and rituals reflected a willingness among the Canaanites to incorporate aspects of the dominant culture into their own spiritual framework.

The architectural landscape of Canaan also bore witness to the imprint of Egyptian influence. Temples and structures erected during this period exhibited stylistic elements and design principles reminiscent of Egyptian architecture. The use of columns, pylons, and hieroglyphic inscriptions mirrored the architectural conventions of the Nile Valley, manifesting the assimilation of Egyptian aesthetics into the built environment of Canaanite cities. This architectural syncretism not only reshaped the physical landscape but also contributed to a visual language that communicated the coexistence of Egyptian and Canaanite cultural identities.

The impact of Egyptian cultural hegemony extended beyond religious and architectural spheres, permeating the daily lives of the Canaanite people. The adoption of Egyptian fashion, jewelry, and iconography by the elite and affluent members of Canaanite society exemplified a broader cultural assimilation. Egyptian-style garments, amulets, and artistic motifs became markers of prestige and cultural sophistication, blurring the lines between the distinct cultural identities of Egypt and Canaan.

Social practices and customs underwent a transformation as well, as the Canaanites embraced certain Egyptian norms and etiquette. The hierarchical structure of Egyptian society, with its emphasis on deference to authority, influenced the socio-political dynamics within Canaanite city-states. The adoption of Egyptian administrative practices, such as the appointment of local rulers by Egyptian pharaohs, contributed to a socio-political landscape that mirrored aspects of the Egyptian model.

While the impact of Egyptian hegemony in Canaan is unmistakable, it is essential to recognize the reciprocal nature of cultural exchange. The Canaanites, in adopting elements of Egyptian culture, did not passively absorb foreign influences; rather, they actively engaged with and adapted these influences to suit their own context. This dynamic interplay between the dominant and subordinate cultures laid the foundation for a unique Canaanite identity that was, in many ways, an amalgamation of indigenous traditions and foreign elements.

Economically, the interchange between Canaan and Egypt was marked by a complex web of trade networks that facilitated the exchange of goods and resources, as highlighted above. The fertile plains of Canaan, with its agricultural abundance, served as a vital source of sustenance for the Egyptian populace. Canaanite grains, particularly wheat and barley, were integral to Egypt's food supply, helping alleviate the perennial challenges posed by the Nile's variable flooding patterns. The economic symbiosis created by this exchange contributed to the stability and prosperity of both regions.

In return for the vital grains from Canaan, Egypt exported a myriad of commodities, including luxury items and resources that held cultural significance. Precious metals, gemstones, and fine textiles flowed from the banks of the Nile to the cities of Canaan, becoming markers of prestige and wealth for the Canaanite elite. The economic ties forged through this trade not only bolstered the material prosperity of both regions but also catalyzed a cultural cross-pollination, as the exchange of goods was often accompanied by the exchange of ideas and practices.

Diplomatically, the relationship between Canaan and Egypt was multifaceted, oscillating between periods of cooperation and instances of geopolitical tension. Egyptian hegemony in Canaan was maintained through a network of vassal states and client kings, as pointed out earlier. The diplomatic landscape was also shaped by the strategic considerations of both powers. Egypt sought to secure its northern borders and maintain control over key trade routes, viewing Canaan as a buffer zone and a radical component of its imperial defense. Canaan, on the other hand, navigated the delicate balance of maintaining autonomy while acknowledging Egyptian suzerainty. Diplomatic ties were reinforced through the exchange of emissaries, diplomatic envoys, and the occasional intermarriage between the ruling elites of Canaan and Egypt.

Archaeological discoveries underscore the depth of this intricate involvement, with correspondences etched onto clay tablets serving as compelling evidence. These inscriptions unveil the complexities of relations, delineating agreements, alliances, and the subtleties of tribute exchanges between Canaanite city-states and the Egyptian pharaohs. The archives stand as a tangible testament to the nuanced negotiations that shaped the geopolitical landscape of that era.

Habiru/Hebrews (circa 1200 BCE – 1000 BCE)

The evolution of Hebrew culture in the transitional period is closely entwined with the Habiru people's presence and enigmatic influence in Canaan. The pivotal role held by the Habiru, a semi-nomadic group frequently referenced in ancient texts, serves as a focal point for comprehending the intricate social, economic, and political dynamics of this transformative era. The term "Habiru" itself is fluid, often used broadly to describe a social class rather than a specific ethnic or cultural group. They were characterized by a semi-nomadic lifestyle, dwelling on the fringes of settled societies. The archaeological and textual evidence suggests that the Habiru contributed a multifaceted part in the tumultuous landscape of Canaan.

The economic domain experienced a notable influence with the discernible presence of the Habiru. They were not confined to traditional agrarian practices but engaged in a variety of occupations, including herding, trade, and mercenary activities. The fluidity of their social structure allowed them to navigate and integrate with the existing economic systems of Canaan. Evidence of their mercenary roles is found in several ancient texts, where they are depicted as soldiers for hire, further attesting to their dynamic and adaptable nature.

The sociopolitical landscape of Canaan was also significantly influenced by the presence of the Habiru. In the power vacuum left by the collapse of centralized authority, the Habiru emerged as a formidable force. They were often perceived as both a challenge to established city-states and as potential allies for those seeking to consolidate power. The Amarna Letters, a collection of diplomatic correspondences from the 14th century BCE, provide indications into the complex relationships between local rulers and the Habiru, highlighting their role as both allies and potential disruptors.

The influence of the Habiru extended beyond mere economic and political spheres; it had a profound impact on the cultural landscape of Canaan. Their semi-nomadic lifestyle and interactions with diverse groups facilitated the exchange of cultural practices, beliefs, and linguistic elements. The fluidity of their identity allowed them to accept and tailor to various cultural traits, contributing to the mosaic of Canaanite culture.

Archaeological evidence, including pottery styles, architectural features, and burial practices, reflects the amalgamation of Habiru influences with existing Canaanite traditions. The hybridization of cultural elements is indicative of a dynamic and symbiotic relationship that shaped the emerging Hebrew culture.

The emergence of Hebrew identity is a complex and multifaceted process intricately linked to the patriarchal period, a critical phase that laid the foundation for the Hebrew people's distinct cultural and religious identity. Building upon the dynamic interactions with the Habiru and the broader socio-political landscape of Canaan, this period witnessed the rise of key figures such as Abraham, Isaac, and Jacob (PBUT), whose leadership played a decisive task in shaping the nascent Hebrew identity.

The patriarchal period, commonly dated from the 20th to the 16th century BCE, is characterized by a series of migrations, familial narratives, and covenantal relationships that laid the groundwork for the distinctive identity of the Hebrew people. The migration of Abraham (PBUH), the patriarchal figure regarded as the father of the Hebrews, is a focal point in this narrative. According to biblical traditions, Abraham (PBUH), originally from Ur in Mesopotamia, embarked on a journey guided by divine promises of land, descendants, and blessings.

Isaac, Abraham's son, and Jacob (PBUT), his grandson, further contribute to the development of Hebrew identity through their roles as patriarchs. The narratives surrounding Isaac (PBUH) highlight the continuity of the divine covenant, emphasizing the importance of familial lineage in the transmission of promises. Jacob (PBUH), in particular, becomes a cardinal figure in the formation of the twelve tribes of Israel. His encounters, struggles, and eventual reconciliation with his brother Esau underscore the complexities of familial relationships and their enduring impact on the Hebrew identity.

This is how biblical narratives, in brief, explain the arrival and settlement of the patriarchal figure from the 20th to the 16th century BCE. Based on these narratives, Canaan serves as the claimed ancestral ground for

Zionists, yet a closer examination of Canaanite history reveals a distinct lifestyle not aligning with what is historically or Biblically associated with Jews. Delving into the legacy of Canaanites in Philistia and Canaan, a clear narrative emerges—neither were Jews the original inhabitants, nor did their roots originate in Canaan.

Scrutinizing the biblical ancestry of Jews—Abraham, Isaac, and Jacob (PBUT)—Genesis 11:27-31 (NIV) recounts Terah's family line. Abram (later Abraham, PBUH) and Nahor, sons of Terah, were fathers to Lot and Haran, respectively. Abram's wife, Sarai, bore no children initially. Terah, along with Abram, Lot, and Sarai, embarked on a journey from Ur of the Chaldeans to Canaan but settled in Harran. Later, in Genesis 21:1-3 (NIV), Sarah conceives and gives birth to Isaac (PBUT), and in Genesis 25:26 (NIV), Rebekah bears Jacob (PBUT). While these verses indicate that Abraham and Jacob (PBUT) were not born in Canaan, especially Jacob (PBUH), considered the progenitor of Jewish lineage, who was later named Israel.

Considering the Jewish tradition of tracing ancestry through the maternal line, known as matrilineal descent, reveals an interesting practice within the Jewish identity. This practice dictates that Jewish lineage is inherited through the mother, implying that if one's mother is Jewish, they are considered Jewish, irrespective of the father's background. This tradition finds its roots in Jewish religious law, with a notable expression in the Talmud, a principal text in Jewish law and tradition. The Mishnah, a component of the Talmud, explicitly states, "The offspring of a Jewish woman and a non-Jewish man is Jewish."

Notwithstanding the established tradition, this practice presents a logical conundrum. In practical terms, for this tradition to hold true, the Jewish lineage would ideally conclude with a female, who would be the first Jew. However, Jewish tradition, as outlined in the Hebrew Bible (Old Testament), designates the patriarchs—Abraham, Isaac, and Jacob (PBUT)—as the ancestors of the Jewish people. Curiously, the wives of these three figures were neither Jews nor Canaanites. For instance, Biblically, Sarah, Abraham's wife(PBUT), was born in Ur, the same birthplace as Abraham (PBUH). Abraham (PBUH) himself, as indicated in Genesis 24:1-4 (NIV), expressed a clear preference against his son marrying a Canaanite woman.

Adding to this historical reluctance, Jacob (PBUH)'s two primary wives resided in Padan-Aram, a region in Mesopotamia, further reinforcing the aversion to marrying Canaanite women. It becomes intriguing that the ancestors of the Jews, Abraham, Isaac, and Jacob (PBUT), didn't desire to marry Canaanite women, yet contemporary Jews assert territorial claims over Canaan.

Drawing from the aforementioned biblical evidence, it becomes apparent that the wives of the Jewish patriarchs were not themselves Jews. Consequently, following the logic that Jewish identity is passed down through the maternal line, it follows that the children of these patriarchs are not Jews. Extending this rationale, their grandchildren and subsequent generations would also be excluded from the designation of Jews.

This paradox raises profound questions: Strict adherence to their own tradition seems to suggest that, by its stringent interpretation, no one could legitimately claim to be a Jew in the world. Even when exploring the alternative avenue of tracing ancestry through patrilineal descent, a practice that aligns more with historical and societal norms, none of the core figures—Abraham, Isaac, and Jacob (PBUT)—emerge as Canaanites, as previously discussed. Consequently, from a historical standpoint, Jews find themselves devoid of legitimate claims to the land of Canaan based on their ancestral heritage.

Philistine Arrival (circa 1200 BCE)

The migration of the Philistines during the tumultuous period of the Sea Peoples' impact marks a significant chapter in the history of Canaan, reshaping the geopolitical landscape of the region. The Sea Peoples, a confederation of maritime groups, embarked on widespread migrations and invasions during the late Bronze Age, and the Philistines emerged as one of the prominent groups contributing to this transformative period. The migration of the Philistines into Canaan is often associated with their arrival by sea, settling along the coastal plains. The strategic location of these coastal areas facilitated their integration into the local landscape, providing them with access to both maritime and inland routes. The Philistines' migration was not a mere nomadic movement but rather a purposeful settlement that played a crucial onus in the transformation of the socio-political dynamics of Canaan.

Archaeological excavations in sites such as Ashkelon, Ashdod, Ekron, Gath, and Gaza provide valuable insights into the material culture, architecture, and daily life of the Philistines in their new homeland. The distinctive Philistine pottery, known for its intricate decorations and unique shapes, serves as a tangible marker of their presence and cultural influence in the region. The material remains of their settlements also reflect aspects of their economic activities, trade networks, and interactions with neighboring societies.

The Sea Peoples' impact on Canaan, particularly through the migration of the Philistines, brought about a new era characterized by the coexistence and sometimes conflict with indigenous populations. The arrival of these maritime groups introduced fresh elements to the local dynamics, contributing to the diversification of Canaan's cultural and social fabric as discussed earlier about their arrival in Philistia.

The arrival of the Philistines in Canaan during the 12th century BCE precipitated a period of significant cultural clash as these maritime migrants encountered and interacted with the existing Canaanite populations. The coexistence of these two distinct groups marked a transformative phase, shaping the sociocultural dynamics of the region and giving rise to a complex chemistry of cooperation and discord.

The Philistines' influence on the existing religious landscape of Canaan is another dimension of the cultural clash. The Philistine pantheon, represented by deities like Dagon, clashed with the Canaanite religious traditions. Temples dedicated to Philistine gods were erected alongside Canaanite religious centers, indicative of a complex syncretism or perhaps a competitive coexistence.

Language and communication also held a responsibility in the cultural clash. While the Philistines likely spoke a distinct Indo-European language, the Canaanites communicated in Semitic languages. This linguistic divide could have posed challenges in terms of governance, trade, and everyday interactions.

The protracted cultural clash between the Philistines and the Canaanites spanned generations, culminating in a synthesis of elements from both groups that laid the groundwork for the emergence of a distinctive regional identity. The emergence of a distinct Philistine culture within the broader Canaanite context was a testament to the resilience and adaptability of these societies in the face of cultural clash and transformation.

Israelite Period (circa 1200 BCE - 586 BCE)

The formation of the twelve tribes of Israel marks a crucial phase in the early history of the Israelite people, dating back to the period following their settlement in Canaan. This tribal confederation, often referred to as the Twelve Tribes of Israel, held a foundational position in shaping the social and political structure of ancient Israel.

The origins of the twelve tribes can be traced back to the descendants of Jacob (PBUH), also known as Israel. According to biblical narratives, Jacob (PBUH) had twelve sons: Reuben, Simeon, Levi, Judah, Dan, Naphtali, Gad, Asher, Issachar, Zebulun, Joseph, and Benjamin. Each son became the progenitor of a distinct tribe, forming the basis for the tribal organization of Israel.

The early organization of these tribes was primarily familial, reflecting the patriarchal structure of ancient societies. Each tribe traced its lineage back to one of Jacob (PBUH)'s sons, fostering a sense of kinship and shared ancestry. This familial connection contributed a significant part in the cohesion and identity of each tribe within the larger confederation.

The twelve tribes maintained a nomadic or semi-nomadic lifestyle in the early stages of their settlement, often engaging in herding and agriculture as means of sustenance. This shared way of life further strengthened the bonds among the tribes, as they faced common challenges and relied on each other for support.

The tribal organization extended beyond familial ties to encompass geographical regions within the territory of Canaan. Each tribe was allocated a specific portion of land, known as its inheritance, creating a spatial demarcation that defined the boundaries of tribal territories. This division of land reflected a practical and sustainable approach to resource distribution among the tribes.

Evidence of the tribal organization can be found in historical and archaeological records, including the biblical texts that document the division of the land among the tribes. Additionally, archaeological excavations have uncovered inscriptions and artifacts that provide insights into the existence and organization of these tribes during the early Israelite period.

The tribal conglomerate took on a substantial task in the decentralized governance of ancient Israel during this time. While the tribes shared common religious practices and cultural traditions, each maintained a degree of autonomy in local affairs. Leadership within the tribes was often decentralized, with elders and clan leaders guiding decision-making processes.

The absence of a central authority, such as a monarch or a unified government, distinguishes this period from later phases of Israelite history. The tribal confederation laid the groundwork for the subsequent developments in the history of Israel, including the transition to the period of the Judges and, eventually, the establishment of the United Monarchy.

Building upon the foundational structure of the twelve tribes, the period of the Judges represents a substantial era in the Israelite narrative, characterized by a decentralized system of governance and the emergence of key leaders. This transitional phase unfolded during the span from the settlement in Canaan to the establishment of the United Monarchy, marking a time of fluctuating fortunes and diverse leadership.

During the period of the Judges, the Israelites faced cyclical patterns of apostasy, oppression, repentance, and deliverance. The leaders who emerged, known as Judges, had influence on guiding the Israelites through these tumultuous cycles. Notable figures such as Deborah, Gideon, and Samuel stand out among the Judges, each leaving a distinctive mark on the trajectory of Israelite history.

Deborah, a Judge, is a prominent figure during this era. Her leadership is particularly highlighted in the biblical account of the Battle of Mount Tabor, where she held a leading position in strategizing and inspiring the Israelite forces against their Canaanite oppressors. Gideon, another significant Judge, rose to prominence during a period of Midianite oppression. His story, vividly recounted in the Book of Judges, details the unconventional means through which Gideon led a small but determined force to victory. Gideon's role as both a military leader and a spiritual figure demonstrates the multifaceted nature of leadership during this period, where individuals were called upon to fulfill diverse roles in times of crisis.

Samuel, a key transitional figure, served as both a Judge and a prophet according to biblical accounts. His leadership marked the end of the Judges' era and paved the way for the establishment of the monarchy. Samuel's influence extended beyond military leadership; he also engaged in anointing and guiding the first two kings of Israel, Saul and David (PBUH). Samuel's pivotal play in the transition to the monarchy underscore the interconnectedness of spiritual and political leadership during this period.

Archaeological and historical evidence supporting the existence of these Judges is limited, given the paucity of material from this specific period. Nevertheless, the narratives within the biblical texts offer a significant source for comprehending the cultural and societal dynamics of the Israelite people during the Judges' era.

The period of the Judges, with its dynamic leadership and cyclical patterns of deliverance, laid the groundwork for the subsequent phase in Israelite history—the establishment of the United Monarchy. The lessons learned and the experiences gained during this time shaped the collective memory of the Israelites, influencing their identity, governance structures, and relationship.

The transition from the era of the Judges to the establishment of the United Monarchy marks a transformative phase in the history of the Israelites. The united monarchy, characterized by the rule of Saul, David, and Solomon (PBUT), reflects the culmination of efforts to consolidate the tribes into a centralized political entity.

Saul, the first king anointed by Samuel, enacted a decisive role in the initial formation of the united monarchy. His reign, spanning from approximately 1020 to 1000 BCE, was marked by military campaigns against the Philistines and other neighboring adversaries. Saul's ascension to kingship was not without challenges, and his rule set the stage for the subsequent developments under David and Solomon (PBUT).

David (PBUH) succeeded Saul as the second king and is often celebrated as a key architect of the united monarchy. David (PBUH)'s reign, spanning from around 1000 to 961 BCE, is characterized by military successes, political consolidation, and the establishment of Jerusalem as the capital. David (PBUT)'s military prowess is exemplified in his victory over the Philistine giant Goliath, a symbolic triumph that resonated throughout the kingdom. Additionally, David (PBUT)'s capture of Jerusalem and its subsequent transformation into a central political and religious hub marked a significant shift in the dynamics of Israelite governance.

Solomon, the son of David (PBUT), ascended to the throne around 961 BCE and continued the trajectory of the united monarchy. Solomon's reign gained renown for its economic prosperity, architectural achievements, and the construction of the First Temple in Jerusalem. The biblical narrative highlights Solomon's wisdom, exemplified in the famous judgment involving two women claiming maternity of the same child. The construction of the Temple served as a unifying symbol for the Israelites, providing a central place of worship and solidifying the religious and political unity of the kingdom.

Archaeological evidence supporting the specifics of David and Solomon (PBUT)'s reigns is limited, and the biblical and Islamic accounts remain the primary sources for understanding this period. The Tel Dan Stele, an inscription discovered in northern Israel, contains a reference to the "House of David," (PBUH) providing some external corroboration of the existence of a Davidic dynasty. However, the extent of the kingdom's grandeur, as described in the biblical texts, remains a subject of scholarly debate.

The united monarchy, while emblematic of Israelite strength and cohesion, also faced internal challenges and divisions. The narrative of Solomon's later years portrays tensions and discontent, leading to the eventual split of the kingdom into the northern kingdom of Israel and the southern kingdom of Judah after Solomon's death.

Canaan from 586 BCE to Early 1900s

The historical terrain of Canaan during the period shared considerable parallels with the multifaceted developments observed in Philistia. Similarities between the two regions during this era were characterized by overarching imperial rule, cultural shifts, and transitions of power. In both Canaan and Philistia, the fluctuation of dominion performed a significant play in shaping the destinies of their inhabitants, leaving an indelible imprint on the historical narrative.

The common thread of imperial rule tightly bound the histories of Canaan and Philistia. As external powers sought to exert influence and control, both regions experienced the impact of successive empires. The sway of imperial forces, whether Babylonian, Persian, or Hellenistic, shaped the political and socio-cultural landscape in ways that transcended regional boundaries. In Canaan, just as in Philistia, the oscillation of power between empires left an enduring legacy, with each conquest imprinting its distinct mark on the local tapestry.

Cultural dynamics integrally influenced the shared experiences of Canaan and Philistia during this era. The interaction of diverse cultures, including those of conquerors and indigenous populations, contributed to a rich ostentation of traditions, beliefs, and practices. The amalgamation of cultural elements, a hallmark of both regions, fostered a unique syncretism that reflected the complex interweaving of identities. The echoes of this cultural confluence reverberated through the centuries, shaping the ethos of the people inhabiting Canaan and Philistia alike.

While overarching similarities characterized the historical trajectory of Canaan and Philistia, unique incidents unfolded in each region, adding distinct nuances to their respective narratives. Canaan, with its diverse topography and historical resonance, bore witness to events that set it apart from Philistia. The rise and fall of political autonomy, the emergence of local leaders, and the resilience of indigenous communities etched a unique chapter in Canaan's history.

The religious and spiritual landscapes of Canaan, distinct from Philistia, bore the imprints of diverse influences. From the Babylonian exile to the subsequent return and the Hellenistic period, Canaan's religious garnishment wove together threads of continuity and adaptation. The resilience of certain religious traditions and the absorption of others underscored the dynamic nature of Canaan's spiritual journey during this time.

Zionism's Emergence

The Intellectual Seeds

The intellectual roots of Zionism can be traced back to early theological debates that laid the foundation for the emergence of this political and ideological movement. In the realm of religious thought, several key figures and their visions regarding the return to the historical land of Israel set the stage for the development of Zionist ideologies. Within the teachings of the Kabbalists in the Middle Ages, a significant precursor to Zionism unfolded, marking an influential chapter in Jewish mysticism. Kabbalistic literature, including works like the Zohar, envisioned a spiritual and redemptive return to the so-called land of Israel. The Kabbalistic emphasis on the mystical connection between the Jewish people and the divine essence of the land contributed to the theological groundwork for a physical return to Zion. The writings of Kabbalistic thinkers such as Isaac Luria articulated a transcendent yearning for the reunification of the Jewish people with their sacred land.

Another significant theological precursor to Zionism can be found in the writings of the 17th-century Jewish philosopher and mystic, Rabbi Judah Halevi. In his work "The Kuzari," Halevi expressed a profound longing for the putative land of Israel as the center of Jewish spiritual life. His theological perspective emphasized the intrinsic connection between the Jewish people and their so-called ancestral homeland, framing the idea of return within a religious and nationalistic context. Halevi's vision laid the groundwork for subsequent discussions on the theological imperative of a Jewish return to Zion.

The 19th-century saw the crystallization of these theological debates into more overtly political ideologies. Rabbi Zvi Hirsch Kalischer, a German Orthodox rabbi, advocated for the establishment of agricultural settlements in the land of Israel as a step towards the ultimate aggregation of the Jewish people. Kalischer's theological perspective combined a religious obligation to settle the land with practical, communal initiatives, foreshadowing the practical aspects of later Zionist endeavors.

Moreover, the writings of Rabbi Yehuda Alkalai, another 19th-century figure, expanded upon the theological underpinnings of return to Zion. Alkalai's work, "Minchat Yehuda," argued for a proactive role of the Jewish people in bringing about their own redemption, including the reestablishment of a Jewish state in the land of Israel. His theological discourse laid the groundwork for the concept of human agency in the fulfillment of messianic prophecies.

These early theological debates were not merely abstract discussions but formed the intellectual seeds from which the putative concept of Zionist return to the land of Israel sprouted. The influence of religious thinkers, steeped in mystical and philosophical traditions, provided the theological framework that would later intertwine with political aspirations, ultimately culminating in the emergence of the Zionist movement in the late 19th century. The echoes of these early theological discussions continue to resonate within the complex tapestry of Zionism's intellectual roots.

The intellectual seeds of Zionism, sown in theological discussions, found fertile ground in the philosophical foundations of the Enlightenment and the rise of nationalist sentiments in the 19th century. The confluence of Enlightenment ideals and nationalist movements contributed significantly to the intellectual landscape that nurtured the emergence of Zionism as a political and ideological force.

Enlightenment thinkers, advocating reason, individual rights, and the pursuit of knowledge, played a robust role in shaping the intellectual foundations of Zionism. The Enlightenment emphasis on individual autonomy and rational inquiry resonated with Zionist aspirations for Jewish self-determination. Notable figures like Moses Mendelssohn, a key Enlightenment philosopher, sought to reconcile Jewish identity with Enlightenment values. His work, "Jerusalem," explored the idea of a Jewish homeland and laid the groundwork for a more secular understanding of a Jewish return to Zion.

The Enlightenment's impact extended beyond individual thinkers to influence broader intellectual currents, such as Haskalah, the Jewish Enlightenment movement. Haskalah aimed to modernize Jewish society by embracing secular education, rational inquiry, and integration into the broader cultural and political contexts of the time. The Haskalah movement, with its roots in Enlightenment principles, provided a platform for discussions about the reconstitution of Jewish life in a homeland, contributing to the intellectual milieu that nurtured Zionist thought.

Simultaneously, the rise of nationalist movements across Europe during the 19th century cast a shadow that would shape the intellectual landscape of Zionism. Nationalism, with its emphasis on shared identity, culture, and political autonomy, found resonance among various ethnic and religious groups seeking self-determination. As Jewish communities across Europe grappled with questions of identity and belonging, nationalist philosophies offered a framework for understanding and asserting their distinctiveness.

The emergence of political and cultural nationalism, particularly in Eastern and Central Europe, provided a backdrop against which early Zionist thinkers contemplated the idea of a Jewish homeland. The writings of key nationalist figures, such as Giuseppe Mazzini and Johann Gottfried Herder, propagated the notion that a nation's cultural and historical heritage was inseparable from its territorial identity. This nationalist discourse influenced the intellectual climate that nurtured the development of Zionist ideologies.

Theodor Herzl, often considered the father of modern political Zionism, was profoundly influenced by both Enlightenment ideals and nationalist philosophies. In his influential work, "The Jewish State," Herzl articulated the need for a national homeland for the Jewish people. The intersection of Enlightenment rationality and nationalist aspirations is evident in Herzl's vision, where the establishment of a Jewish state is portrayed as a pragmatic response to historical challenges, rooted in a secular and political understanding of Jewish nationhood.

The intellectual seeds of Zionism found nourishment in a rich cultural and intellectual milieu of the late 19th and early 20th centuries. This period was characterized by a confluence of diverse intellectual trends, influential literary works, and societal transformations that collectively shaped the landscape in which Zionist thought blossomed.

Intellectual trends of the time were marked by a growing awareness of national identities and the quest for self-determination. The idea of a shared cultural and historical identity as the basis for nationhood gained traction, fueled by the rise of nationalist movements across Europe. This zeitgeist resonated with the aspirations of Jewish intellectuals grappling with questions of identity, assimilation, and the desire for a collective homeland.

Literary works emerged as powerful vehicles for articulating and disseminating Zionist ideas. Prominent figures like Ahad Ha'am, a key intellectual in the early Zionist movement, utilized literary expression to convey the cultural and spiritual dimensions of Jewish nationalism. His essays, collected in works such as "Selected Essays" and "At the Crossroads," delved into the significance of Jewish culture and its role in the revitalization of the Jewish people. Ahad Ha'am's writings contributed to the broader intellectual discourse that emphasized the importance of cultural and intellectual revival as essential components of the Zionist project.

The urgency of the Zionist cause purportedly found its roots in the shaping hands of societal factors, allegedly influenced by the reported experiences of Jewish communities in Europe amid claims of escalating anti-Semitic sentiments. The rise of anti-Semitism, coupled with the challenges of assimilation, prompted a reevaluation of Jewish identity and collective destiny. The notorious Dreyfus Affair in France, where a Jewish officer was accused of espionage, underscored the vulnerability of Jews in diaspora and fueled the belief that only through self-determination in a homeland could presumed Jewish rights be safeguarded.

The establishment of the First Aliyah, the first wave of Jewish immigration to Ottoman Palestine between 1882 and 1903, marked a tangible manifestation of Zionist aspirations. The experiences of these early pioneers, documented in personal accounts and historical records, reflect the transformative impact of settling in the Palestinians' homeland. These pioneers, driven by the ideals of labor, self-sufficiency, and the revival of Hebrew as a spoken language, contributed to the formation of a distinct Zionist ethos rooted in the practical realities of building a new society.

Intellectual circles and salons became crucibles of Zionist thought, fostering discussions and debates that shaped the contours of the movement. The World Zionist Organization, founded by Theodor Herzl in 1897, provided a platform for intellectual exchange and collaborative efforts toward the realization of Zionist goals. The Zionist Congresses, held regularly, served as forums for intellectuals, political leaders, and activists to deliberate on the movement's direction and strategies.

Theodor Herzl: Visionary or Provocateur?

Theodor Herzl, an indispensable figure in the emergence of political Zionism, was shaped by a compound interaction of personal experiences and early Zionist ideologies. Born in Budapest in 1860 to an affluent, assimilated Jewish family, Herzl's upbringing was marked by a cosmopolitan environment. Herzl's early years were characterized by a secular and liberal education. He studied law at the University of Vienna, where he engaged with Enlightenment ideals and emerged with a worldview rooted in reason, individual rights, and civic engagement. Despite this assimilated background, the undercurrents of oft-titled anti-Semitism in Europe began to impact Herzl's consciousness, particularly during the infamous Dreyfus Affair in France in the 1890s. Observing the accusation of a Jewish officer in the French army prompted Herzl to realize that their malignant behavior would not be overlooked by residing among seemingly enlightened societies, pretending to be a part of them or holding positions within the government sectors.

The Dreyfus Affair claimed to be a watershed moment for Herzl, prompting him to reassess the position of Jews in European society. In his diary, Herzl wrote, "In Paris, I achieved a freer attitude towards anti-Semitism, which I now began to understand historically and to pardon." This is believed to be the turning point, marking the beginning of Herzl's shift from assimilationist ideals to the exploration of an outrageous political solution for the "Jewish Question." Herzl's career as a journalist and playwright further contributed to his intellectual change. His work as a correspondent for Neue Freie Presse exposed him to the complexities of international politics and diplomacy. The turbulent events of his time, including the rise of nationalism and the struggle for national identity, influenced Herzl's thinking about the future of the Jewish people.

The culmination of these experiences provided Herzl with a clear blueprint for shaping his nefarious ideologies, cloaking them in the guise of nationalism to befuddle the global audience. In 1896, Herzl released his seminal work, "Der Judenstaat" (The Jewish State). Within this pamphlet, he articulated his vision for establishing a Jewish state—an idea posited as both a response to the ostensible challenges confronted by European Jews and a counterfeit of the nationalist zeitgeist of the late 19th century. Herzl's proposal for a political solution to the "Jewish Question" laid the foundation for the Zionist movement and portrayed him as a visionary leader.

The political evolution of Theodor Herzl's ideology found expression in his key writings and manifestos, serving as the intellectual backbone of the political Zionist movement. Central among these works is "Der Judenstaat" (The Jewish State). In this pamphlet, Herzl meticulously laid out the principles of political Zionism, arguing for the establishment of a Jewish state as a solution to the "Jewish Question."

In addition to "Der Judenstaat," Herzl authored "Altneuland" (Old New Land), a utopian novel published in 1902. In this work, Herzl envisioned a modern, technologically advanced Jewish state in Palestine, highlighting his belief in the transformative power of a Jewish homeland. "Altneuland" not only served as a literary expression of Herzl's ideals but also contributed to the popularization of his vision among the broader public.

Herzl's political Zionism gained international recognition through his diplomatic efforts. In 1903, he met with British Colonial Secretary Joseph Chamberlain, attempting to secure British support for the establishment of a Jewish homeland. While these diplomatic efforts were not immediately successful, they laid the groundwork for future diplomatic initiatives and engagements with world powers.

Herzl's approach to political Zionism was characterized by a blend of diplomatic strategy and visionary thinking. His ideas gained prominence on the global stage, attracting attention from political leaders and intellectuals alike. Herzl's advocacy for a Jewish state as a practical solution to the pretended challenges faced by Jews in Europe resonated with those who saw the need for a homeland where Jews could exercise self-determination and escape so-termed persecution.

Herzl's commitment to the Zionist cause went beyond the theoretical realm, manifesting in vigorous activism and organized deception of Palestinians. Following the publication of "Der Judenstaat" and the establishment of the World Zionist Organization, Herzl embarked on a tireless journey to garner support for the creation of a Jewish homeland.

Diplomacy became a cornerstone of Herzl's approach to advancing the Zionist agenda. In 1902, he met with German Emperor Wilhelm II, seeking support for the establishment of a Jewish homeland. While the outcome of this meeting was not as fruitful as Herzl had hoped, it marked the beginning of his diplomatic engagements with world leaders.

One of Herzl's notable diplomatic efforts occurred in 1903 during the British Uganda Program, a proposal to establish a Jewish homeland in East Africa. Facing growing anti-Semitism in Europe and a lack of immediate prospects for a homeland in Palestine, Herzl temporarily entertained the idea as a pragmatic solution. However, this proposal faced strong opposition within the Zionist movement, and ultimately, it was rejected by the Sixth Zionist Congress in 1903.

Herzl's diplomacy extended to the Ottoman Empire, which then controlled Palestine. In 1901, he met with Ottoman Sultan Abdul Hamid II to discuss the possibility of Jewish settlement in Palestine in exchange for twenty million pounds. The Sultan responded with his famous words: "I cannot abandon a single inch of Palestine. It is not mine to give away. It belongs to the Islamic nation. My people have fought for it and irrigated its soil with their blood. The Jews may keep their millions. If the Caliphate is torn apart someday, they can take Palestine without a price. But the division of it will not be on our bodies."

If Herzl had advocated for the rights of Jews within their existing communities, his vision could have been commendable as that of a true visionary. However, examining his endeavors to realize the concept of a Jewish homeland reveals a willingness to disregard the rights of countless others, even at the cost of their lives, in the pursuit of what he deemed as the rights of a Jew. The crux of the issue in comparing Zionist and other nationalist movements lies in their objectives. While other movements sought identity, rights, and independence within their existing territories, Zionists pursued their supposed rights in a land belonging to others.

While Herzl may be perceived as a visionary within the context of Zionist perspectives, a critical examination of justice and morality paints a different picture. Instead, he appears as a malicious provocateur who, driven by personal gains and the interests of his own community, acted against the principles of humanity.

Early Proponents and Diverse Perspectives

Beyond Theodor Herzl, several key figures played instrumental scopes in shaping early Zionist thought, contributing diverse perspectives and ideologies to the nascent movement. One such figure was Chaim Weizmann, a prominent chemist and Zionist leader. Born in Belarus in 1874, Weizmann's scientific acumen and diplomatic skills would later become vital assets for the Zionist cause. Weizmann's contributions to early Zionism were multifaceted. As a scientist, his breakthrough in developing a method to produce acetone during World War I proved invaluable to the British war effort. This achievement not only illustrated his scientific prowess but also established a rapport with key British figures, including Arthur Balfour. Weizmann's diplomatic efforts culminated in the issuance of the Balfour Declaration in 1917, a core moment in the Zionist movement that expressed British support for the establishment of a Jewish homeland in Palestine.

Another influential figure was Ahad Ha'am, the pseudonym for Asher Zvi Hirsch Ginsberg, a philosopher and essayist. Born in Ukraine in 1856, Ahad Ha'am offered a different perspective within the Zionist discourse. While recognizing the importance of establishing a Jewish homeland, he emphasized the cultural and spiritual aspects of Zionism. Ahad Ha'am's essays, collected in publications like "Al Parashat Derakhim" (At the Crossroads), urged a focus on creating a cultural center in Palestine before the establishment of a political state. His ideas laid the groundwork for the cultural and intellectual aspects of Zionism, emphasizing the revival of Jewish culture and identity as stated before.

Ze'ev Jabotinsky, a prominent figure in the Zionist movement, distinguished himself as a leader, journalist, and the founder of Revisionist Zionism. Born in Odessa in 1880, Jabotinsky's approach to Zionism differed from the mainstream. He advocated for a more assertive and militaristic stance to secure Jewish rights in Palestine. In his prime work, "The Iron Wall" (1923), Jabotinsky argued for the creation of a Jewish military force to establish a strong and secure presence in Palestine, anticipating potential conflicts with Arab neighbors. His ideology laid the foundation for the later development of the Israeli Defense Forces.

The formative years of the Zionist movement witnessed a rich tapestry of diverse ideological streams, each contributing distinct perspectives and visions for the establishment of a Jewish homeland. Cultural Zionism, socialist Zionism, and religious Zionism emerged as prominent ideological currents, each advocating for a unique approach to the realization of the Zionist dream. Cultural Zionism, epitomized by figures like Ahad Ha'am (Asher Zvi Hirsch Ginsberg), emphasized the importance of cultivating a robust Jewish culture as a precursor to political statehood as discussed above.

In contrast, socialist Zionism, represented by figures like Ber Borochov and the Labor Zionist movement, blended Zionist aspirations with socialist ideals. Borochov, a key proponent, argued that the establishment of a socialist Jewish state in Palestine was integral to resolving the socio-economic challenges facing the Jewish population in Europe. The kibbutz movement, a communal living and working arrangement, became a manifestation of socialist Zionist principles, emphasizing collective ownership and cooperative living as integral to the Zionist project. Debates emerged within this stream regarding the balance between socialist principles and the practicalities of state-building.

Religious Zionism, championed by figures like Rabbi Abraham Isaac Kook, melded traditional religious values with the Zionist endeavor. Rabbi Kook envisioned the return to Zion as a redemptive process, interpreting political developments as part of a divine plan for the Jewish people. This stream emphasized the spiritual and religious significance of establishing a Jewish homeland in accordance with so-called religious prophecies. However, debates arose among religious Zionists regarding the compatibility of secular political ideologies with religious principles.

Tensions were inherent in the diverse ideological landscape of early Zionism. Debates around the prioritization of cultural revival versus socialist principles, or the role of religion in the Zionist project, often led to ideological clashes. Ahad Ha'am's cultural Zionism, advocating for the establishment of a cultural center in Palestine, clashed with the more politically oriented visions of Herzl and the political Zionists. Similarly, socialist Zionists, while cooperating on common goals, faced internal tensions regarding the balance between socialist ideals and pragmatic state-building.

Religious Zionists navigated a delicate balance between secular and religious ideologies. Rabbi Abraham Isaac Kook, a prominent religious Zionist figure, sought to bridge the gap between the religious and secular wings of the movement. His efforts were pivotal in fostering collaboration between these diverse factions. However, inherent tensions persisted regarding the extent to which religious principles should influence the political and social dimensions of the Zionist project.

Despite their differences, these ideological streams converged on a shared goal-the establishment of a Jewish homeland. The diversity within early Zionism, rather than fragmenting the movement, enriched it with a spectrum of ideas and perspectives. Collaboration was evident in the establishment of institutions that sought to unify different Zionist factions. The World Zionist Organization (WZO), founded during the First Zionist Congress in 1897, served as a platform for diverse voices within the movement. The Congress, with figures like Theodor Herzl and Chaim Weizmann in attendance, became a melting pot of ideas where debates flourished. Despite ideological differences, these early Zionists recognized the need for a collective effort to advance the cause of a Jewish homeland.

The collaborative spirit extended to endeavors such as the Jewish National Fund (JNF), founded in 1901, which aimed to acquire and develop land in Palestine for Jewish settlement. The JNF, with support from various Zionist streams, became a unifying force that transcended ideological divisions. The creation of such institutions reflected a shared commitment to practical nation-building initiatives.

These collaborations and tensions within early Zionist networks reflected the dynamism of a movement grappling with multifaceted challenges. The ability to forge alliances despite ideological differences showcased a shared commitment to the overarching goal of a Jewish homeland. Simultaneously, the tensions highlighted the complexity of merging diverse perspectives into a cohesive vision. The legacy of these early interactions continued to influence the Zionist movement, laying the groundwork for the complexities that would shape the subsequent history of the State of Israel.

The Basel Declaration

The gathering of the First Zionist Congress in Basel in 1897 signaled a decisive juncture in the nascent Zionist movement. Fueled by a convergence of historical events and the collective aspirations of Jewish communities across the globe, this momentous occasion set the stage for significant developments in the unfolding Zionist narrative. At the turn of the 20th century, European Jews faced escalating anti-Semitism, coupled with the lingering impact of pogroms in Eastern Europe. This hostile environment, alongside the quest for a collective Jewish identity, set the stage for the emergence of the Zionist movement.

The historical context surrounding the First Zionist Congress was characterized by a sense of urgency and a desire for collective action. The Congress, held in Basel from August 29 to August 31, 1897, attracted delegates from various Jewish communities, representing a spectrum of ideologies. It brought together political Zionists, cultural Zionists, and religious Zionists under one roof, symbolizing a unity of purpose transcending ideological differences.

The significance of the First Zionist Congress lay in its formal establishment of the World Zionist Organization (WZO), a body dedicated to the realization of Herzl's vision. The Congress set forth clear objectives, including the promotion of Jewish settlement in Palestine and the coordination of efforts to secure international support for the Zionist cause. It provided a platform for robust debates, dialogue, and the formulation of practical strategies for achieving the goals of the movement.

The Congress also gave birth to the Zionist flag, anthem, and the symbol of the Star of David, fostering a sense of collective identity among the participants. Beyond its immediate outcomes, the First Zionist Congress laid the foundation for future diplomatic efforts and nation-building initiatives in Palestine. It symbolized the transformation of Zionist aspirations from intellectual discourse to tangible, organized action on an international scale.

The key discussions, in the congress, revolved around defining the objectives and strategies of the Zionist movement. The political Zionists, led by Theodor Herzl, advocated for the establishment of a Jewish state, emphasizing the need for international recognition and support. Cultural

Zionists, such as Ahad Ha'am, focused on the revival of Jewish culture and identity in Palestine, viewing it as a cultural center rather than a purely political entity. Religious Zionists sought to reconcile traditional Jewish values with the modern Zionist project, navigating the delicate balance between faith and political aspirations.

The drafting process of the Basel Declaration was a collaborative effort that reflected the diverse perspectives within the Congress. Herzl, as the driving force, held a substantial position in articulating the political objectives of the movement. However, the document also incorporated elements that resonated with the cultural and religious dimensions of Zionism, acknowledging the multifaceted nature of Jewish identity.

Influential figures such as Chaim Weizmann, Max Nordau, and Rabbi Zvi Hirsch Kalischer contributed to the drafting process, bringing their unique perspectives to the table. Weizmann, a prominent Zionist leader and future president of the World Zionist Organization, emphasized the importance of practical initiatives, including scientific and technological advancements, in achieving Zionist goals. Nordau, a key collaborator of Herzl, provided intellectual vigor to the political Zionist agenda, advocating for the establishment of a Jewish homeland as a solution to the Jewish Question.

The Declaration symbolized a consensus forged through debate and dialogue. It laid the groundwork for future Zionist endeavors by articulating a clear vision for the movement. The document, while politically driven, encapsulated the broader spectrum of Zionist thought, embodying the diverse perspectives that defined the early Zionist movement. The Basel Declaration became a paramount milestone, setting the stage for subsequent diplomatic efforts, Jewish settlement in Palestine, and the eventual establishment of the State of Israel.

The political objectives outlined in the Basel Declaration marked a defining moment in the trajectory of the Zionist movement. As articulated in the declaration, the primary goal was the establishment of a "publicly and legally assured home for the Jewish people" in Palestine. This objective had profound implications for the future of Palestine, shaping its geopolitical landscape and setting in motion a series of events that would reverberate throughout the 20th century.

The declaration's call for a national home for the Jewish people in Palestine represented a strategic response to the assumed pressing challenges faced by Jewish communities globally. The escalating tide of synthetic anti-Semitism, particularly in Europe, underscored the urgent need for a sanctuary where Jewish identity, culture, and aspirations could flourish free from ostensible persecution. The emphasis on a legally guaranteed homeland underscored the pursuit of international acknowledgment and backing, establishing the foundation for subsequent diplomatic efforts and morally questionable activities.

The implications for Palestine were both transformative and contentious. The notion of establishing a national home for the Jewish people inherently posed challenges to the existing demographic and political dynamics of the region. The Arab population in Palestine, which had been the majority for centuries, now faced the prospect of a significant demographic shift due to the influx of Jewish immigrants. This laid the groundwork for future tensions and hostilities over land, resources, and national identity.

The geopolitical landscape of Palestine was further complicated by the Ottoman Empire's control over the region at the time. The Basel Declaration, while framing the Zionist vision, had to contend with the geopolitical complexities of an empire that would later crumble in the wake of World War I. The eventual disintegration of the Ottoman Empire opened a new chapter in the history of Palestine, setting the stage for British involvement and the issuance of the Balfour Declaration in 1917.

The Basel Declaration's impact on the geopolitical landscape extended beyond demographic considerations. It introduced a transformative agenda that sought not only a haven for purportedly persecuted Jews but also the establishment of a self-governing entity with cultural, economic, and political autonomy. This vision, however, presently clashed with the aspirations of the existing Palestinian Arab population, sparking a prolonged clash for self-determination.

Navigating Political Landscapes

The late 19th century was characterized by a complex web of global geopolitical dynamics that set the stage for the emergence of nationalist movements. Imperial rivalries, nationalist fervor, and shifting power dynamics were defining features of this era, creating an environment ripe for the pursuit of national aspirations. Imperial rivalries played a central role in shaping the geopolitical landscape of the late 1800s. The major European powers, such as Britain, France, and Germany, were engaged in intense competition for territorial acquisitions and strategic influence. This imperial scramble, known as the "Great Game," not only redrew the maps of empires but also fueled nationalist sentiments within regions aspiring to self-determination. The strategic importance of the Middle East, including Palestine, became pronounced in this context, as global powers sought to secure their interests in the region.

Simultaneously, nationalist movements gained momentum across the globe as communities sought to assert their distinct identities and claim sovereignty. The tide of nationalism swept through Europe, Asia, and the Middle East, with various ethnic and cultural groups advocating for autonomy or independence. This surge in nationalist fervor provided a backdrop for the Zionist movement, which sought to establish a homeland for the Jewish people.

Shifting power dynamics further contributed to the conducive environment for nationalist movements. The decline of traditional empires, notably the Ottoman Empire, created power vacuums and opportunities for emerging political entities. As the Ottoman Empire weakened, regions under its control, including Palestine, became focal points for competing national aspirations. The vacuum left by receding imperial authority allowed for the reconfiguration of political landscapes, giving rise to movements that aimed to fill the void with newly defined national entities.

The confluence of these global events created a propitious environment for the emergence of Zionism. The Zionist movement found resonance amid the broader wave of nationalist aspirations. The geopolitical shifts of the late 19th century not only provided opportunities for nationalist movements to assert themselves but also presented challenges and conflicts as different communities vied for control over territories and resources. The intricate relationship of imperial rivalries, nationalist fervor, and shifting power dynamics shaped the trajectory of the Zionist movement within the broader tapestry of global geopolitics.

Following the decline of the Ottoman Empire, European colonial powers, driven by imperial ambitions and strategic interests, sought to expand their influence in the Middle East. The Sykes-Picot Agreement of 1916, a secret pact between Britain and France, delineated spheres of influence in the region, disregarding the aspirations of local populations. This colonial maneuvering had profound consequences, as it laid the groundwork for the artificial borders that persist in the modern Middle East. The impact of European colonialism was particularly significant in Palestine, where incompatible promises and commitments to both Arab and Jewish communities sowed the seeds of future tensions.

The interconnectedness of regional skirmishes further complicated the geopolitical landscape. Competing nationalisms, tribal rivalries, and religious tensions created a volatile environment where the interests of various communities collided. The Balfour Declaration of 1917, in which Britain expressed support for the establishment of a "national home for the Jewish people" in Palestine, added another layer to the regional complexities. This, evidently biased and one-sided, declaration, while welcomed by the Zionist movement, elicited strong opposition from Arab communities who viewed it as a betrayal of their aspirations for self-determination.

In this tumultuous landscape, the Zionist movement navigated a delicate path, seeking to secure international support as preplanned while contending with the aspirations and grievances of other communities in the Middle East. The regional influences of the early 20th century actively engaged in shaping the political contours of Palestine and contributed to the complexities that persist in the region today.

Zionist leaders, acutely aware of the importance of international support, actively sought alliances with powerful nations. The aftermath of World War I presented a unique opportunity as the League of Nations emerged, and discussions about the future of territories formerly held by the defeated Ottoman Empire took center stage.

Chaim Weizmann furtively involved in cultivating relationships with key British officials. His collaboration with Arthur Balfour, the author of the eponymous declaration, manifested the diplomatic finesse employed by Zionists in securing political backing.

Simultaneously, conflicts emerged on multiple fronts. The ideological clash between Zionist aspirations and Arab nationalism intensified, fueled by territorial disputes and inconsistent visions for the future of Palestine. The Balfour Declaration, while promising a "national home for the Jewish people," also stirred resentment among Arab communities, setting the stage for one of the biggest betrayals in human history.

Zionist leaders faced the delicate task of balancing these contradictory interests. They grappled with the intricacies of power dynamics, not only within the Middle East but also in their engagement with influential figures in Europe. The Sykes-Picot Agreement, which aimed to divide spheres of influence in the Middle East between Britain and France, underscored the geopolitical jostling that shaped the region. Zionists, aware of these broader political maneuvers, strategically aligned themselves with the interests of powerful nations to bolster their cause.

The Balfour Declaration

The Balfour Declaration, a defining moment in the emergence of Zionism, unfolded against the intricate backdrop of World War I and the geopolitical transformations that followed. As the conflict reshaped the global order, key individuals and diplomatic considerations converged to set the stage for a declaration that would significantly impact the future of the Middle East. The historical setting leading to the issuance of the Balfour Declaration saw the First World War emerge as a significant factor. As the Ottoman Empire sided with the Central Powers, Britain sought alliances and support from various quarters. In this complex web of international relations, the Zionist movement, led by influential figures such as Chaim Weizmann, seized the opportunity to advocate for the establishment of a Jewish homeland in Palestine.

The key individuals involved in the formulation of the Balfour Declaration were instrumental in shaping its content and intent. In a crucial turn of events, the interaction between the British Foreign Secretary, Arthur Balfour, and Chaim Weizmann held profound significance. Weizmann's persuasive efforts and his ability to articulate the Zionist cause found resonance with Balfour, who was receptive to the idea of a Jewish homeland.

Diplomatically, the declaration was not solely an altruistic gesture. It bore strategic considerations for the British government. The geopolitical climate of the time, marked by the impending collapse of the Ottoman Empire and the redrawing of borders in the Middle East, provided an opportune moment for Britain to position itself as a key player in the region.

The configuration of wartime alliances wielded a notable influence on the formulation of British policy. The idea of a Jewish homeland resonated with prominent figures within the British government, notably Arthur Balfour and David Lloyd George. These individuals were not only sympathetic to the Zionist cause but recognized the potential strategic benefits of aligning with Zionist aspirations. The belief that a declaration in favor of a Jewish homeland could elicit support from Jewish communities, both in terms of manpower and financial resources, was a strategic consideration that influenced the government's stance.

The approval of the Balfour Declaration was significantly influenced by internal British political dynamics. The Zionist movement had gained prominence in British political and intellectual circles, and key figures within the government were swayed by the arguments put forth by Zionist leaders. Additionally, there was a sense among British policymakers that supporting a Jewish homeland would align with broader notions of self-determination and nationalism, concepts that gained traction during the war.

Moreover, the British government believed that a declaration in support of a Jewish homeland could potentially sway the neutral United States to join the Allied cause. The influential Jewish community in the U.S. was seen as a force that could influence public opinion and potentially impact the direction of U.S. foreign policy. The Balfour Declaration, therefore, was not only a statement of support for Zionist aspirations but a calculated move to leverage international support during a critical juncture of the combat.

The Balfour Declaration, issued on November 2, 1917, expressed the British government's support for the establishment of a "national home for the Jewish people" in Palestine. This seemingly concise statement encapsulated a complex interplay of historical events, diplomatic negotiations, and geopolitical strategies. The consequences of the declaration reverberated through the 20th century, shaping the trajectory of Zionist aspirations, Arab-Jewish relations, and the geopolitical landscape of the Middle East.

In the direct outturns of the Balfour Declaration, the Zionist movement witnessed a surge of optimism and international recognition. The explicit support from a major world power for the establishment of a Jewish homeland in Palestine validated the aspirations of Zionist leaders. It marked a significant departure from the marginalization and indifference that had characterized the movement's earlier years. The declaration provided a diplomatic foothold for Zionist leaders in their pursuit of international legitimacy and support.

Internationally, the Balfour Declaration stirred varied reactions. While it was celebrated by Jewish communities and Zionist supporters, it drew criticism and opposition from Arab leaders and some segments of the international community. The inherent ambiguity in the language of the declaration, particularly regarding the protection of existing non-Jewish communities in Palestine, sowed the seeds of future confrontations and debates.

The impact of the declaration on Zionist strategies was profound. It galvanized fundraising efforts and political lobbying within Jewish communities worldwide. The promise of British support fueled a sense of purpose and urgency within the movement. Zionist leaders leveraged the declaration to engage with influential figures, foster alliances, and advance the cause on the international stage.

The trajectory of Jewish migration to Palestine underwent a notable shift following the Balfour Declaration. The declaration, coupled with the subsequent British mandate in Palestine, created conditions conducive to increased Jewish immigration. The promise of a national home provided a compelling incentive for Jews seeking refuge from purported persecution and seeking a new beginning in Palestine. This migration laid the groundwork for the demographic transformation of the region.

However, the implementation of the Balfour Declaration also sparked tensions and battles. The Arab population in Palestine, apprehensive about the prospect of a Jewish homeland, expressed resistance. This resistance, coupled with broader regional dynamics, set the stage for a complex and protracted skirmish that would define the future of the Middle East.

In the long term, the Balfour Declaration became a cornerstone of international recognition for the Zionist cause. Its inclusion in the League of Nations mandate for Palestine reinforced the commitment to establishing a Jewish homeland. However, the ambiguities within the declaration continued to reverberate, contributing to the complexities of the Israeli-Palestinian war that persists to this day.

From Ideology to Political Movement

The progression of Zionist ideology into a political movement signified a noteworthy transformation, turning abstract principles into tangible political objectives and actions. This metamorphosis unfolded through distinct stages, illustrating the dynamic interchange between ideology and practical political considerations. Initially, Zionist ideology emerged as a response to the perceived need for a Jewish homeland, rooted in historical connections to the land of Canaan. The early theological debates and philosophical foundations laid the groundwork for a collective Jewish return to their supposed ancestral homeland. However, it was the shift from theoretical discourse to actionable political strategies that defined the next stage of evolution.

The First Zionist Congress served as a substantive moment where Zionist ideology began to crystallize into a political agenda. The formulation of the Basel Declaration articulated the explicit goal of establishing a national home for the Jewish people. This marked the transition from ideological contemplation to a concrete political objective, emphasizing the need for practical steps to realize the vision. The subsequent stages witnessed the articulation of specific political objectives and the development of strategies to achieve them. The writings and manifestos authored by Theodor Herzl, such as "Der Judenstaat" (The Jewish State), exemplify this transition. These documents not only expressed the ideological underpinnings of political Zionism but also outlined a roadmap for achieving political goals through diplomatic means.

The engagement in diplomatic efforts and activism by Zionist leaders further solidified the movement's political dimension. Theodor Herzl's diplomatic initiatives, including meetings with world leaders and efforts to garner international support, exemplify the pragmatic translation of ideological aspirations into political action. These endeavors laid the groundwork for future diplomatic engagements that would shape the geopolitical landscape in favor of Zionist objectives.

The Balfour Declaration in 1917 represented a watershed moment, where diplomatic efforts culminated in a formal acknowledgment of

Zionist aspirations by a major world power. The declaration reflected the successful translation of Zionist ideology into tangible political outcomes, aligning international support with the establishment of a Jewish homeland, as discussed before.

The protocols of Zionist congresses and the writings of leaders like Herzl serve as primary sources, offering insights into the gradual transition from ideological contemplation to political activism. The evolution of Zionist ideology into a political movement exemplifies the adaptability and strategic acumen of early Zionist leaders. It underscores the transformative power of ideas when translated into concrete political objectives, ultimately shaping the trajectory of the Zionist movement and laying the groundwork for the establishment of the State of Israel.

The transformation of Zionist ideology into a political movement necessitated a robust organizational framework that could effectively mobilize support and coordinate efforts. Early Zionist leaders recognized the importance of institutional structures, committees, and networks to lay the foundations for a cohesive and impactful movement.

Following the First Zionist Congress, the need for a centralized organizational structure became evident. The Congress itself served as a pioneering institution, bringing together representatives from various Zionist factions and providing a platform for collective decision-making. It marked the inception of the Zionist Organization, a body tasked with coordinating and advancing the Zionist cause globally. The consolidation of diverse ideological streams within the movement under a common political umbrella was necessitated by this organizational entity.

Simultaneously, the establishment of committees and institutions within the Zionist framework became essential for addressing specific aspects of the movement's objectives. Financial mechanisms, such as the Jewish National Fund (JNF), emerged to facilitate land acquisition in Palestine. The JNF, founded in 1901, exemplified the practical implementation of Zionist aspirations, channeling financial resources toward the purchase of land for Jewish settlement.

Furthermore, the establishment of the Jewish Agency in 1929 marked a significant development in the organizational structure of the Zionist movement. The Agency functioned as a partnership between the Zionist Organization and non-Zionist Jews, reflecting a pragmatic approach to garnering broader support for the cause. Its structure allowed for collaboration with international Jewish communities and facilitated engagement with global powers to advance Zionist objectives.

The formation of the Histadrut, the General Federation of Jewish Labor, highlighted the importance of integrating labor movements into the broader Zionist organizational framework. Founded in 1920, the Histadrut played a dual role, addressing the socio-economic needs of Jewish workers while aligning labor efforts with the overarching Zionist agenda. This integration underscored the multifaceted nature of the organizational structures, catering to both political and practical dimensions of the Zionist movement.

The fortification of the Zionist movement was significantly bolstered by networking. The connections formed within and outside the movement facilitated collaboration with sympathetic individuals, organizations, and influential figures. The efforts to gain political support and financial backing were intricately woven into the fabric of these networks, accentuating the strategic approach adopted by early Zionist leaders.

Diplomatically, Zionist leaders engaged in concerted efforts to gain recognition and support from influential nations. The diplomatic arena provided a platform to present the Zionist cause on the global stage. Theodor Herzl's diplomatic endeavors, exemplified by his meetings with European leaders and advocacy for a Jewish homeland, laid the groundwork for future diplomatic strategies. The diplomatic efforts extended to the series of Zionist congresses, where leaders engaged in diplomatic maneuvering to garner support for the movement's objectives.

The shaping of international perceptions and garnering support for the Zionist cause was indispensably influenced by advocacy campaigns. Leaders recognized the power of public opinion and strategically employed media outlets to disseminate their message. The establishment of newspapers and publications, such as Herzl's "Die Welt" and later, the Anglo-Jewish Association's "The Zionist," served as platforms for articulating Zionist ideals and countering opposition. These publications not only disseminated information but also shaped narratives to garner sympathy and support for the establishment of a Jewish homeland at the expense of the blood and flesh of Palestinians.

Grassroots mobilization emerged as a cornerstone of the early Zionist movement's strategy. Leaders recognized the need to create a groundswell of support among the Jewish diaspora and beyond. This involved engaging with local communities, fostering a sense of collective identity, and mobilizing resources for the cause. The establishment of youth movements, such as the Zionist youth organization "Habonim," underscored the commitment to cultivating a new generation of activists. The protocols of early Zionist congresses reveal the emphasis placed on grassroots mobilization as leaders discussed strategies to involve Jewish communities worldwide.

The endeavor to garner grassroots support transcended the Jewish community, encompassing alliances with sympathetic non-Jewish groups. Early Zionist leaders strategically forged connections with political figures, intellectuals, and philanthropists who shared common interests or ideals, as evident in their writings, speeches, and correspondences. Historical records meticulously document the planning and execution of diplomatic missions, the articulation of advocacy messages in newspapers, and the establishment of organizational structures for grassroots mobilization.

The Land of Palestine as the Zionist Objective

The evolution of Zionist perspectives on the ideal homeland for Jewish resettlement is a nuanced historical journey marked by shifts in focus and the gradual crystallization of the land of Palestine as the central objective. This transformation was influenced by key milestones and visionary figures who played critical roles in shaping the Zionist narrative. In the early stages of the Zionist movement, the question of a suitable homeland for Jewish resettlement was open to various possibilities. Theodor Herzl's work, "Der Judenstaat", while advocating for a Jewish homeland, did not explicitly designate a specific location. The initial discussions within the Zionist Congresses reflected a diversity of opinions regarding potential territories, including Uganda and Argentina.

The transformation of Zionist perspectives gained momentum with the crystallization of the idea that Palestine held unique historical and cultural significance for the Jewish people. This shift was not instantaneous but unfolded gradually over the late 19th and early 20th centuries. Chaim Weizmann and Ahad Ha'am, as influential figures, were instrumental in highlighting the historical link between the Jewish people and the land of Palestine.

Chaim Weizmann contributed significantly to shaping the Zionist focus on Palestine. His advocacy for the establishment of a Jewish homeland in Palestine was rooted in a belief in the historical and biblical ties between the Jewish people and the land. Weizmann's influence is evident in his diplomatic efforts, where he tirelessly lobbied for international support for the Zionist cause, emphasizing the unique connection to Palestine.

Ahad Ha'am contributed to the evolution of perspectives through his emphasis on cultural and spiritual aspects. Ha'am's writings, including essays in his publication "Hashiloah," underscored the significance of Palestine as not merely a political necessity but a cultural and spiritual center for Jewish identity. This intellectual discourse is documented in

Ha'am's essays, providing evidence of the ideological underpinnings that influenced Zionist perspectives.

Ideological considerations within Zionist thought intricately wove together religious, historical, and cultural threads to emphasize the unparalleled significance of Palestine as the preferred destination for Jewish relocation. This ideological tapestry, evident in writings, speeches, and theological discourses of influential figures, elucidates the multifaceted dimensions that rendered Palestine the central objective for the Zionist movement.

The ideological foundation that elevated Palestine to a sacred status within Zionist thought was profoundly shaped by religious considerations. The biblical narratives, deeply ingrained in Jewish religious consciousness, provided a noteworthy scriptural backdrop for the connection between the Jewish people and the land of Palestine. Prominent figures within the Zionist movement, including Rabbi Abraham Isaac Kook, articulated theological perspectives that harmonized the biblical so-termed promise of a homeland with the contemporary Zionist aspirations.

Rabbi Kook, the Chief Rabbi of British Mandatory Palestine, expounded on the theological significance of settling in Palestine. His writings, documented in works like "Orot," presented a theological framework that celebrated the act of returning to the biblical homeland as a fulfillment of divine prophecy. This evidence reveals the integration of religious ideology into the fabric of Zionist thought, portraying Palestine not merely as a political necessity but as a divine imperative deeply rooted in religious texts.

Historical considerations further strengthened the ideological stance on Palestine, emphasizing the uninterrupted historical connection between the Jewish people and the land. Zionist thinkers, notably Simon Dubnow and Yitzhak Ben-Zvi, delved into historical narratives to trace the enduring presence of Jews in Palestine throughout various periods of history. This historical evidence, examined and documented in their writings, served as a foundational element in substantiating the Zionist claim to Palestine.

Simon Dubnow, a prominent Jewish historian, explored the historical continuity of Jewish communities in Palestine in his seminal work, "History of the Jews." His research and scholarly analysis presented a historical narrative, providing evidence that reinforced the Zionist ideological perspective. The writings of Dubnow and Ben-Zvi stand as proof of the meticulous historical examinations undertaken by Zionist intellectuals, contributing to the ideological framework that positioned Palestine at the forefront of Jewish aspirations.

Cultural factors, intertwined with historical and religious considerations, contributed to the perception of Palestine as the central objective for Jewish immigration. Zionist leaders such as Chaim Weizmann and Martin Buber engaged in cultural discourse, highlighting the intrinsic connection between the Jewish people and the land. Weizmann's efforts to bridge cultural and political dimensions are evident in his advocacy for the establishment of a Hebrew University in Jerusalem, emphasizing the cultural revival that would accompany the return to Palestine.

The synthesis of religious, historical, and cultural factors within Zionist thought, as substantiated by the writings and discourses of influential figures, paints a comprehensive picture of the ideological considerations that elevated Palestine as the preferred destination. The theological perspectives of Rabbi Kook, historical analyses of Dubnow and Ben-Zvi, and cultural endeavors of leaders like Weizmann collectively provide a robust foundation of evidence supporting the ideological underpinnings of the Zionist movement's focus on Palestine.

Practical considerations also played a vital scope in the Zionist movement's decision to prioritize the land of Palestine as the focal point for Jewish relocation. The analysis of these practical dimensions involves a comprehensive examination of factors such as geographical suitability, economic prospects, and the perceived challenges inherent in establishing a Jewish homeland in Palestine.

Geographical suitability emerged as a crucial practical consideration that guided the Zionist movement's focus on Palestine. The diverse landscape, encompassing fertile plains, arable land, and strategic coastal areas, presented an enticing prospect for the establishment of viable agricultural settlements-a cornerstone of the Zionist vision. The writings of early Zionist leaders, including Chaim Weizmann and Arthur Ruppin, underscored the geographical attributes of Palestine as conducive to agricultural development. Ruppin's work, particularly his exploration of settlement possibilities in Palestine, provided a pragmatic evaluation of the land's agricultural potential. These documents serve as tangible evidence of the meticulous consideration given to the geographical features that made Palestine a practical choice for Jewish immigration.

Economic prospects further influenced the prioritization of Palestine as the Zionist objective. The Zionist movement recognized the economic potential inherent in the development of industries, trade, and infrastructure within the envisioned homeland. Theodor Herzl's visionary perspective, as articulated in his seminal work "Altneuland," depicted a modern and prosperous Palestine with a thriving economy. Herzl's writings not only reflected economic foresight but also served as a blueprint for the practical implementation of economic development in the region. The focus on economic viability, evident in Herzl's writings and subsequent Zionist endeavors, provides concrete proof of the pragmatic considerations that underpinned the choice of Palestine.

Amidst the optimistic evaluations of geographical suitability and economic potential, practical considerations included a sober acknowledgment of challenges inherent in establishing a Jewish homeland in Palestine. Zionist leaders confronted issues like Arab-Jewish relations, land acquisition, and the political complexities of the region. David Ben-Gurion's writings, particularly his reflections on the Arab question, exemplify the pragmatic assessment of challenges intertwined with the Zionist project. Ben-Gurion's nuanced understanding of the delicate balance between Jewish aspirations and the existing Arab population underscores the practical considerations that molded Zionist strategies in navigating complex sociopolitical landscapes.

The formation of the Jewish paramilitary organizations

The historical circumstances leading to the establishment of Jewish paramilitary organizations in Palestine are deeply rooted in the complex dynamics of the British Mandate era. The early 20th century witnessed a surge in Jewish immigration to Palestine, spurred by a range of motivations, including religious ties and the promise of a national homeland articulated in the Balfour Declaration as discussed above.

However, the practical realization of these aspirations faced significant challenges on multiple fronts. The coexistence of Jewish and Arab communities in Palestine became increasingly strained, exacerbated by the simultaneous rise of Arab nationalism. British authorities, grappling with the complexities of managing conflicting national aspirations, responded by superficially imposing restrictions on Jewish immigration and land acquisition. This not only frustrated the Jewish settlers but also fueled a sense of vulnerability in the face of both Arab resistance and British constraints.

In this context, the need for so-termed self-defense became a pressing concern for Jewish communities. The Haganah, established in the early 1920s as a paramilitary organization for Jewish self-defense, became a pragmatic response to the prevailing uncertainties. Its formation reflected the recognition within the Jewish population of the imperative to protect themselves amidst the growing hostilities. The origins of the Haganah can be traced to the palpable need for a coordinated effort to safeguard Jewish settlements among rising tensions with Arab communities. Initially established as a grassroots initiative, the Haganah, meaning "Defense" in Hebrew, chose this name to portray itself as a group fighting for its rights, while, in reality, it was against morality.

The Haganah operated as a clandestine organization dedicated to protecting properties that were swindled from Palestinians. Its early years were marked by a decentralized structure, with local defense committees taking the lead in their respective areas. The primary focus was on creating a defensive shield against external threats, particularly Arab freedom fighters and opponents of Zionist oppressions.

The evolution of the Haganah into a more organized and cohesive paramilitary force was a gradual process shaped by the shifting dynamics of the region. As tensions escalated, the need for a more centralized and coordinated defense strategy became evident. The Haganah responded by establishing a central command structure, enhancing communication, and standardizing training protocols.

Crucially, the Haganah held a remarkable influence on the development of Jewish settlements. Its members, often drawn from the ranks of the community, undertook tasks beyond traditional defense. They engaged in agricultural activities, contributing to the economic development of Jewish communities and reinforcing the connection between the land and its people.

The Haganah's crucial tasks extended beyond immediate defense concerns. During the Arab Revolt of 1936-1939, the organization found itself navigating a complex terrain of political and military challenges. Balancing the need for self-defense with the broader political goals of the Zionist movement, the Haganah became a central player in shaping the destiny of Jewish communities in Palestine.

Haganah contributed to intelligence gathering, notably engaging in meticulous documentation of Palestinian houses and properties as one facet of its activities. This initiative aimed to create a comprehensive database of information that could be utilized for various purposes, including strategic planning and, when needed, insurgency operations.

During the late 1930s and early 1940s, as tensions escalated in the region, the Haganah recognized the importance of having detailed information about the Palestinian population and their assets. Operation Balak, conducted in 1938, was a significant undertaking in this regard. It involved the systematic collection of data on Palestinian villages, including the layout of houses, population demographics, and potential points of vulnerability.

The operation was not limited to intelligence gathering alone; it also served as a means to assess the readiness and capabilities of the Haganah itself. By understanding the terrain and population dynamics, the organization aimed to enhance its strategic advantage and preparedness for attacking Palestinian residences.

Another noteworthy operation carried out by the Haganah was the Night of the Bridges, which took place on June 17, 1946. While primarily known for its focus on destroying bridges used by Arab forces, it also illustrated the Haganah's ability to execute complex and coordinated truculent actions. The success of this operation underscored the organization's growing capabilities and its commitment to securing its objectives.

The completed tasks of the Haganah, particularly its intelligence-gathering operations, represented a pragmatic response to the complex realities of the time. These actions, carried out with a meticulous approach, reflected the organization's commitment to ensuring the security and viability of Jewish settlements in the face of evolving geopolitical dynamics.

The emergence of Irgun Zvai Leumi (Irgun) in 1931 marked a significant departure from the comparatively moderate stance of the Haganah. Formed as a breakaway faction, Irgun adopted a more militant approach, driven by a belief in the use of force and violence to achieve Jewish statehood. This open shift in ideology and tactics was influenced by several factors, including dissatisfaction with the perceived restraint of the Haganah and a growing sense of urgency regarding the establishment of a Jewish state.

The early years of Irgun were characterized by a focus on paramilitary training and preparation for armed assault. Among escalating tensions in the region, Irgun endeavored to establish itself as a formidable force in the pursuit of Jewish statehood. The organization's leadership, under figures such as Menachem Begin, emphasized the need for direct action and an oppressive approach to confront the challenges posed by British rule and Arab opposition.

Irgun achieved notable recognition through the successful execution of the King David Hotel bombing in 1946. This strategic operation targeted the British administrative and military headquarters in Jerusalem, resulting in a significant loss of life and drawing international attention to the Zionists' quest. While controversial, the attack demonstrated Irgun's capacity for decisive and betraying actions, challenging even their supported nations for personal gains when needed.

Irgun's activities extended beyond military operations, encompassing a range of tasks aimed at advancing the Zionist cause. The orchestration of Jewish entry, often in deliberate defiance of British immigration quotas, was a role the organization actively embraced. Additionally, Irgun engaged in propaganda efforts to garner support for its objectives, both within the Jewish community and on the international stage.

The Altalena affair in 1948, a ship carrying arms and fighters for the nascent Israeli militants, highlighted the complex dynamics within the Jewish paramilitary landscape. The initial sluggish incongruities between Irgun and the newly formed Israeli government illustrated the challenges of integrating disparate military forces into a unified command structure.

While Irgun's approach was known for its militancy and disregard for ethical norms, its achievements cannot be overlooked in the broader context of the Zionist objective. The organization's actions, driven by a fervent commitment to the establishment of a Jewish state, left an indelible mark on the trajectory of the Israeli statehood movement.

The establishment of Lehi, also known as the Stern Gang, in 1940, marked another ideological strand within the intricate tapestry of Jewish paramilitary organizations during the British Mandate in Palestine. Distinct from both Haganah and Irgun, Lehi emerged as a splinter group, driven by a unique set of ideals and a vision for the establishment of a Jewish state.

Lehi's ideological foundations were rooted in the belief that armed bellicosity was not only a strategic necessity but a presumed moral imperative in the pursuit of Zionist statehood. Led by figures such as Avraham Stern, the organization rejected what it perceived as the compromise and pragmatism of other Jewish paramilitary groups. Instead, Lehi advocated for a more radical approach, emphasizing the need for direct and belligerent action to achieve its goals.

Lehi left an indelible mark with one of its most impactful actions—the assassination of Lord Moyne in 1944. Moyne, serving as the British Minister Resident in the Middle East, became a seeming obstacle to Lehi's vision of achieving Zionist statehood. The assassination sent shockwaves through the international community and underscored Lehi's commitment to challenging opposing authorities through targeted and symbolic acts.

Lehi's activities also included strategic initiatives aimed at garnering support for the Zionist cause. The organization sought alliances with Axis powers during World War II, viewing the conflict as an opportunity to advance its objectives amid geopolitical upheaval. While these efforts were controversial and led to tensions within the Jewish community, they reflected Lehi's willingness to explore unconventional avenues in the pursuit of its vision.

The Altalena affair in 1948, involving a ship carrying arms and fighters for Lehi, mirrored the challenges faced by Irgun and highlighted the complexities of integrating disparate paramilitary forces into the evolving landscape of the Israeli statehood movement. The incident demonstrated the intricate relationship of ideologies and the tensions inherent in coordinating diverse military entities.

Lehi's existence was marked by a relentless commitment to its ideals, even as it operated on the fringes of mainstream Zionist movements. The organization's impact on the broader quest for Jewish statehood lay in its unyielding belief in the perceived righteousness of its cause and its readiness to employ unconventional tactics to achieve its objectives.

The collective impact of these paramilitary organizations during the critical period of statehood was profound. Their coordinated efforts reflected a shared determination to overcome external fears and internal divisions. The unification of forces under the banner of the IDF during the 1948 Arab-Israeli War symbolized the culmination of years of preplanning and strategic moves.

Post-World War Era

Impact of World War II on the Middle East

The repercussions of World War II brought about significant regional transformations in the Middle East, leaving an indelible mark on the socioeconomic and political landscape of the nations in the region. The assessment of these ramifications requires a nuanced exploration of changes in governance, economic structures, and social dynamics influenced by the war's aftermath.

The reconfiguration of governance structures stood out as one of the most significant consequences of World War II in the Middle East. The demise of colonial powers and the weakening of imperial influences created a power vacuum that allowed for the emergence of independent nations. The Levant, for example, witnessed the end of French and British mandates, paving the way for the establishment of sovereign states. The case of Lebanon, which gained independence in 1943, exemplifies this shift in governance. The geopolitical realignment in the region, coupled with nationalist movements, led to the establishment of nation-states with a newfound autonomy, altering the political dynamics in the post-war Middle East.

Economic structures also experienced substantial changes following World War II. The war had disrupted traditional economic systems, but the subsequent reconstruction efforts fueled economic diversification and modernization. Nations like Iran experienced economic shifts, with the oil industry becoming a central player in the national economy. The nationalization of oil resources, as witnessed in Iran in the early 1950s, marked a turning point in economic structures. The shift towards resource-driven economies, particularly in oil-rich countries, became a defining feature of the post-World War II Middle East.

Moreover, social dynamics in the region were influenced by the demographic shifts and cultural changes brought about by the hostility. The return of soldiers, exposure to global ideologies, and the spread of education contributed to societal transformations. The emergence of new urban centers, and the influence of pan-Arab and nationalist sentiments shaped the social fabric of Middle Eastern nations. These sociocultural changes, often interwoven with political and economic shifts, reflected the complexities of post-war transformations.

The geopolitical landscape of the Middle East experienced a profound realignment in the wake of World War II, with shifts in alliances among nations shaping the region's post-war dynamics. These changes were not merely strategic adjustments but marked a reconfiguration of power relationships and political affiliations.

The emergence of new alliances and the dissolution of former ones marked a notable aspect of the geopolitical realignment. The dissolution of colonial empires and the newfound independence of many Middle Eastern nations prompted a reassessment of diplomatic ties. The Arab League, formed in 1945, represented a concerted effort among Arab states to foster cooperation and unity. This marked a departure from the previous colonial-era alliances, signaling a regional desire for collective strength and autonomy. The Arab League became a platform for addressing common concerns and coordinating policies, emphasizing the shared aspirations of its member states.

Simultaneously, the establishment of the State of Israel in 1948 introduced a contentious element into the geopolitical equation. The Arab-Israeli war became a central focus, influencing the alliances and rivalries in the region. Arab states, unified by their opposition to the newly formed Israel, found common ground in confronting this shared challenge. The alignment against Israel, however, heightened tensions with Western powers, especially the United States and the United Kingdom, who were biasedly supporting the Israeli cause.

The Cold War rivalry between the United States and the Soviet Union manifested in the Middle East through a strategic competition for influence. The United States, driven by its Cold War policy of containment, sought to prevent the spread of communism and maintain its dominance in the region. To this end, the U.S. engaged in alliances with countries like Iran, Turkey, and Israel, providing military and economic support. The Baghdad Pact, later known as CENTO, and the Eisenhower Doctrine were emblematic of American efforts to establish a pro-Western bloc in the region.

Conversely, the Soviet Union aimed to expand its sphere of influence and establish friendly regimes sympathetic to its socialist ideology.

Egypt, under the leadership of Gamal Abdel Nasser, emerged as a focal point of Soviet engagement. The Czech-Egyptian arms deal of 1955 marked a significant instance of Soviet support for an Arab nation. The superpowers' involvement in the region was not only through direct alliances but also through diplomatic maneuvering, often exploiting regional fights to advance their respective agendas.

The global players' influence extended beyond military alliances, permeating economic and diplomatic spheres. Economic aid, development assistance, and trade agreements became tools for shaping alliances and securing allegiance. The Truman Doctrine and the Marshall Plan, for instance, were instrumental in promoting U.S. economic interests and consolidating its influence in the Middle East.

British Mandate in Palestine

Post-World War II, the British Mandate in Palestine underwent a sweeping transformation, echoing the dynamic shifts occurring on both a global and regional scale. The post-war period witnessed a redefined geopolitical landscape, intimately entwining the British administration's governance approach with these transformative changes. The global repercussions of World War II, marked by the devastation of nations and the emergence of superpowers like the United States and the Soviet Union, triggered a comprehensive reassessment of colonial structures. As imperial powers waned, the ascent of nationalist movements emerged as a hallmark of the post-war era, significantly impacting the trajectory of the British Mandate in Palestine. Regionally, the Middle East experienced a surge in nationalist fervor, with movements fervently seeking independence from colonial rule. The Arab world, in particular, championed self-determination and the cessation of foreign interference. Influenced by regional events such as the Arab Revolt of 1936-1939 and the escalating tensions between Jewish and Arab communities in Palestine, the British response bore the indelible imprint of these complex and multifaceted developments.

The changing nature of the British Mandate in Palestine can be traced through official policy shifts. The evidence lies in documents outlining decisions such as the issuance of the White Paper of 1939, which sought to limit Jewish immigration and address Arab grievances. The subsequent implementation of this policy marked a transition in British governance and reflected an attempt to navigate the complexities of the post-war era.

The post-war changes in the British Mandate set the stage for the eventual withdrawal of British forces from Palestine in 1948. The post-World War II period thus witnessed a recalibration of colonial strategies, influenced by both global power dynamics and regional nationalist movements. The challenges faced by the British administration in maintaining control over Palestine post-World War II were multifaceted and deeply rooted in the complex geopolitical and social landscape of the region. As the previous writing highlighted the changes in the British Mandate's nature, it becomes imperative to delve into the challenges that eroded its authority.

One significant challenge emanated from the surge in nationalist movements across the Middle East. In Palestine, Arab nationalism gained momentum, fueled by aspirations for independence and a rejection of foreign rule. This widespread sentiment strained the British administration's ability to assert control and manage the aspirations of the local population. Geopolitical shifts also posed challenges to British authority. The emergence of new global players and the reconfiguration of alliances influenced the British approach to Palestine. The administration found itself navigating a transformed international landscape that impacted its ability to maintain control.

Tensions between Jewish and Arab communities added another layer of complexity to the challenges faced by the British administration. The fray for influence and territory between these two communities heightened existing tensions, making it increasingly difficult for the British to mediate and maintain order. These challenges collectively weakened the British Mandate's hold on Palestine, setting the stage for its eventual withdrawal in 1948. The historical timeline of events showcases the culmination of these challenges in the establishment of the State of Israel and the dissolution of the British Mandate as preplanned.

The post-World War II period witnessed a profound surge in Palestinian nationalism, marking a pivotal moment in the struggle for independence and self-determination. Building upon the challenges faced by the British administration discussed earlier, the rise of Palestinian nationalism further strained the dynamics between the local population and the British Mandate. History documents the palpable shift in Palestinian sentiment towards a unified desire for autonomy and sovereignty.

The aspirations for freedom were deeply rooted in a collective identity that sought to assert Palestinian rights in the face of external rule. Documents from the time, including political declarations, speeches, and manifestos, vividly reflect the growing demand for self-determination. The struggle for independence was not only ideological but also manifested in concrete actions. Palestinians actively voiced their discontent, illustrating a determination to break free from colonial governance and shape their destiny.

The influence of Palestinian nationalism also reverberated in the geopolitical arena, as neighboring Arab nations aligned themselves with the cause. Correspondence between Palestinian leaders and leaders of Arab states provides evidence of the collaborative efforts to advance the Palestinian cause on the international stage. This unity underscored the interconnected nature of regional dynamics and the shared commitment to realizing Palestinian aspirations.

Holocaust and International Sympathy

Among a pervasive lack of awareness regarding the legitimacy of the meticulously staged Holocaust, the global community grappled with the illusion of confronting the formidable challenge of addressing the unprecedented atrocities inflicted upon the Jewish population. The humanitarian responses and international efforts to address the outcomes of the Holocaust were shaped by the magnitude of the tragedy and the urgent need for assistance to survivors and refugees. Following the Holocaust, a primary measure undertaken was the creation of camps for Displaced Persons (DP). These camps, under the supervision of Allied forces, became a crucial component of the humanitarian response. They offered temporary shelter, food, and medical care to Holocaust survivors who were believed to have been liberated from concentration and extermination camps.

International relief endeavors were instrumental in meeting the urgent needs of ostensible Holocaust survivors. Organizations such as the United Nations Relief and Rehabilitation Administration (UNRRA) and the International Red Cross were at the forefront of these efforts. They coordinated the distribution of food, clothing, and medical assistance, aiming to alleviate the suffering.

Diplomatic initiatives were undertaken to support the resettlement of Holocaust survivors and Jewish refugees. The ostensible challenges faced by displaced Jews sparked deliberations on the planned creation of a Jewish homeland, ultimately culminating in the establishment of the State of Israel in 1948. The acknowledgment of Israel as a refuge for Jewish survivors and refugees signifies a worldwide recognition of the imperative need for an enduring solution to the supposed challenges posed by the preplanned Holocaust, This recognition underscores the effectiveness of systematically organized plans in garnering political and public support for the establishment of a Jewish homeland.

The evolving global perceptions towards the Holocaust marked a significant shift from initial indifference to growing sympathy for the

Jewish population. This transition had profound implications on political decisions and public opinion in the post-World War II era.

In the immediate aftermath of the Holocaust, the world grappled with the staggering revelations of the atrocities committed against the Jewish population. The initial response, characterized by disbelief and shock, often manifested as a collective indifference. The sheer magnitude of the staged horrors unearthed in concentration and extermination camps overwhelmed the global consciousness, rendering many nations unsure of how to respond.

As more so-termed evidence of the Holocaust emerged through reports, testimonies, and photographic documentation, the international community emotionally forced to confront the harsh reality of the genocide. The colossal shift from indifference to sympathy in perceptions was catalyzed by the gradual awakening of awareness. The Nuremberg Trials, where the extent of Nazi atrocities was laid bare, served as a catalyst for this transformation. The trials were not only used to expose the brutality of the Holocaust but also to establish a legal framework for holding individuals accountable for crimes against humanity.

The post-war period witnessed a growing psychological enforcement on the public to ensure the acknowledgment of the suffering endured by the Jewish population. Documentaries, books, and other forms of media disseminating the stories of survivors were produced, attempting to bring the human dimension of the Holocaust to a global audience. This increased visibility contributed to a deepening sense of sympathy and empathy for the synthetic survivors and the broader Jewish community.

Political decisions were influenced by this shifting global perception. The impact of the Holocaust significantly influenced the international community's dedication to preventing similar atrocities in the future. The establishment of the Universal Declaration of Human Rights in 1948, with its emphasis on the protection of human dignity and rights—protecting nothing other than Zionists' rights—reflected a collective response to the assumed moral accountability of preventing a recurrence of the Holocaust.

Furthermore, the plight of Jewish presumed survivors and refugees contributed to international support for the establishment of the State of Israel. The recognition of Israel as a homeland for the Jewish people was not only a response to historical relationship with the land but also a reflection of global sympathy for the made-up survivors seeking a place of refuge and self-determination.

The establishment of the State of Israel in 1948 was a direct outcome of the political dynamics shaped by the Holocaust. The horrors suffered by the Jewish people during the Holocaust added an illusion of moral imperative to the discussions on Jewish resettlement. The international community, grappling with guilt over its initial indifference to the plight of European Jews, found a potential solution in the creation of a Jewish homeland.

Political decisions were influenced by a combination of presumed moral responsibility, geopolitical considerations, and the recognition of the so-called historical injustice perpetrated against the Jewish people. The Zionist movement, which had advocated for the establishment of a Jewish homeland even before the Holocaust, gained renewed support in the post-war period. The international sympathy generated by the Holocaust provided the political momentum needed to garner support for the recognition and creation of the State of Israel.

Several countries, including Germany, Austria, France, Belgium, Poland, Lithuania, and Slovakia, have classified Holocaust denial as a criminal offense. Additionally, certain social media platforms, such as YouTube, actively remove content, even scholarly documents, that challenge the historical accuracy of the Holocaust. From a logical perspective, the enforcement of laws criminalizing Holocaust denial and the stringent measures taken by social media platforms raise concerns about the need to reaffirm the validity of the historical event.

The question arises: Why not engage in open dialogue and counter these ideas with more compelling arguments instead of resorting to legal and policy measures to silence dissenting views? The eagerness to suppress alternative viewpoints through legal frameworks and platform policies raises questions about the confidence in the historical narrative surrounding the Holocaust. If the historical account is robust and well-supported, it should be able to withstand scrutiny and critical examination without the need for legal constraints or content removal.

One could argue that the approach of criminalizing Holocaust denial reflects a concern for preventing the spread of misinformation and hate speech. However, this raises another set of questions about the limits of free speech and the potential suppression of dissenting voices. In a democratic society, the exchange of ideas and open debate is typically valued as a means to arrive at a more comprehensive understanding of historical events.

Enforcing acceptance through legal means may inadvertently fuel skepticism and conspiracy theories, as it can be perceived as an attempt to stifle dissent rather than engage in a rational discussion. If the aim is to establish the historical truth and counter Holocaust denial effectively, it might be more beneficial to encourage open debate, and engage with opposing viewpoints through intellectual discourse.

Examining historical events, acknowledged even by mainstream media, reveals a narrative that suggests the Holocaust served as a significant element in garnering public sympathy, aligning with the objectives outlined in the Basel Declaration. A comprehensive understanding of Jewish historical strategies makes it challenging to view the Holocaust as a mere coincidence that fortuitously assisted Zionists in achieving their territorial goals. Instead, logical reasoning suggests a preplanned and meticulously orchestrated fabrication inserted into the broader context of World War II.

While the nature and strategic maneuvers of Jewish communities throughout history may lead one to question the authenticity of the Holocaust, a deliberate decision has been made in this book to refrain from delving into the intricate details of this controversial topic. Several reasons underlie this intentional avoidance. However, it is crucial to acknowledge a personal conviction based on logical reasoning—a skepticism toward accepting the Holocaust as a genuine historical event.

The decision to steer clear of an in-depth exploration of this matter within the book is multifaceted, encompassing considerations of focus, relevance, and the nuanced nature of historical narratives. Nevertheless, the underlying skepticism persists, guided by a belief in logical reasoning that challenges the authenticity of what is widely accepted as a historical truth. In doing so, it encourages a critical approach to historical narratives and the recognition of alternative perspectives.

In maintaining this stance, the aim is not to dismiss or diminish the significance of historical events but rather to underscore the importance of critical inquiry and reasoned discourse. The acknowledgment of personal skepticism serves as a reminder that historical narratives are complex, subject to interpretation, and should be approached with a discerning eye. It reflects an adherence to the principles of intellectual exploration and the pursuit of truth through thoughtful analysis and reasoned debate.

Zionist Immigration Surge

Post-World War II, a notable upswing in Jewish immigration to Palestine unfolded, propelled by a convergence of historical, geopolitical, and humanitarian factors. The Holocaust had left survivors and displaced persons in search of a new home, and Palestine emerged as a focal point for resettlement, driven by the Zionist vision. The Holocaust left a profound impact on the survivors. Ostensibly liberated from concentration and extermination camps, these individuals faced the daunting task of awakening international sympathy to garner support for their preplanned agenda. The international community, grappling with the so-called enormity of the tragedy, recognized the need for a comprehensive solution to address the displaced Jewish population.

Zionist ideology played a pivotal role in shaping the aspirations of assumed Jewish survivors. The vision of establishing a Jewish homeland in Palestine, long advocated by the Zionist movement, gained renewed impetus in the wake of the Holocaust. The urgency to create a haven for Jews, free from claimed persecution, became a driving force behind the surge in immigration.

The Displaced Persons (DP) camps, established by the Allied forces in the aftermath of the confrontation, became temporary havens for Jewish survivors. However, these survivors harbored a collective determination to move beyond the confines of temporary shelters and forge a new life as collectively agreed upon. The desire for a homeland fueled the motivation to seek relocation in Palestine.

The trajectory of post-war Jewish immigration was significantly influenced by the geopolitical landscape. The British Mandate in Palestine, while initially accommodating Jewish immigration, faced mounting challenges in reconciling the competing interests of the Jewish and Arab communities. This strained relationship contributed to the eventual imposition of nominal restrictions on Jewish immigration by the British authorities.

The Exodus 1947 incident epitomized the struggles faced by Jewish immigrants seeking entry to Palestine. The ship carrying Holocaust survivors was intercepted by British authorities, reflecting the tensions surrounding Jewish arrival. This event underscored the complexities of the geopolitical dynamics and the obstacles encountered by those aspiring to immigrate to Palestine.

The Zionist immigration surge had a profound demographic impact on the population of Palestine, reshaping the ethnic, religious, and cultural composition of the region. As explored in the preceding section, the surge in Jewish immigration was propelled by Holocaust survivors and the vision of establishing a Jewish homeland in Palestine.

The demographic landscape of Palestine underwent a significant transformation with the influx of Jewish immigrants. The established Arab majority found itself grappling with an increasing Jewish population, altering the delicate balance that had existed before the surge. The demographic shift had far-reaching implications for the political, social, and cultural dynamics of the region.

The Zionist immigration surge promptly resulted in a shift in the ethnic and religious demographics. The Arab majority, which had historically dominated the demographics of Palestine, now faced the challenge of coexisting with a growing Jewish population. This demographic shift fueled tensions between the two communities, laying the groundwork for the complex and protracted warfare that would unfold in the subsequent years.

Religiously, the Jewish immigration surge bolstered the presence of Judaism in a region historically characterized by a Muslim majority. The diverse religious tapestry of Palestine underwent a noticeable transformation, with an increasing Jewish minority contributing to the pluralistic fabric of the area. This shift in religious demographics added another layer of complexity to the already intricate socio-political landscape.

Culturally, the Zionist immigration surge brought with it a diverse array of traditions, languages, and customs. The Jewish immigrants, hailing from various parts of the world, brought a rich cultural mosaic to Palestine. This cultural diversity, while contributing to the vibrancy of the region, also became a source of friction as different communities sought to preserve their distinct identities in the midst of demographic changes.

The demographic impact of the Zionist immigration surge extended beyond sheer numbers; it permeated every facet of Palestinian society. The coexistence of diverse ethnic, religious, and cultural communities within the confines of a relatively small region intensified the complexities of the existing geopolitical landscape.

The demographic shifts sparked by the Zionist immigration surge set the stage for a tumultuous period in the history of Palestine. The clash of identities, aspirations, and narratives laid the foundation for a protracted war that continues to shape the destiny of the region. The demographic impact of this surge reverberates through the years, underscoring the intricate interplay between population dynamics and the broader socio-political milieu.

The demographic impact of the Zionist immigration surge brought forth a myriad of challenges and controversies, shaping the socio-political landscape of Palestine in the post-World War II era. As highlighted earlier, the surge altered the ethnic, religious, and cultural composition of the region, laying the groundwork for complex dynamics.

Foremost among the challenges linked to Zionist immigration policies was the contentious matter of land allocation. The influx of Jewish immigrants necessitated the acquisition of land for settlement, leading to disputes over territory with the existing Arab communities. This land-related friction became a focal point of contention, fueling tensions and contributing to the broader skirmishes that would unfold in the consequent years.

The debates surrounding land allocation were closely intertwined with the question of coexistence between the incoming Jewish population and the existing Arab residents. The clash of identities and competing national aspirations created a challenging environment for harmonious cohabitation. The demographic changes exacerbated existing tensions, giving rise to a composite interaction of social, cultural, and political factors.

The challenges and controversies associated with Zionist immigration policies during this period laid the foundation for enduring disputes over land, identity, and political sovereignty. The clash of narratives and national aspirations set the stage for a protracted hostility that would define the trajectory of the Israeli-Palestinian fray. The complexities arising from these challenges underscore the intricate nature of demographic shifts and the socio-political repercussions they entail.

Arab Opposition and Nationalist Movements

The surge in Zionist immigration into Palestine in the post-World War II era triggered significant alterations in the ethnic and religious composition of the region. This demographic shift became one of the immediate consequences of the Zionist immigration surge. The influx of Jewish immigrants, ostensible survivors, and refugees reshaped the population dynamics, leading to increased tensions and conflicts in the already complex socio-political landscape of Palestine.

The demographic impact of the Zionist immigration surge was weighty, as it fundamentally altered the ethnic, religious, and cultural fabric of Palestine. The Arab population, traditionally the majority, witnessed a decline in its relative size as Jewish immigrants established themselves in the region. This shift in demographics laid the groundwork for intense debates, skirmishes, and challenges that characterized the post-World War II period in Palestine.

A central challenge linked to Zionist immigration policies revolved around the highly debated matter of land allocation. The influx of Jewish immigrants necessitated the acquisition of land for settlement, leading to disputes over territory. The clash between the Zionist objective of establishing a Jewish homeland and the existing Arab communities' interests created a volatile situation. Arab residents, rightfully concerned about their land and livelihoods, resisted the encroachment by Jewish settlers, contributing to a complex web of challenges and controversies.

Debates surrounding land allocation were exacerbated by the question of coexistence with existing Arab communities. The influx of Jewish immigrants brought forth the challenge of integrating two distinct populations with competing national aspirations. The Zionist vision clashed with Arab nationalist sentiments, leading to increased tensions and hostility between the two communities. This clash of identities further fueled the challenges associated with the Zionist immigration surge.

Arab nationalist movements emerged in response to the increasing Jewish presence in Palestine. These movements were fueled by a desire to protect Arab rights, preserve the Arab identity of the region, and resist the threat to their sovereignty. The objectives of Arab nationalist movements during this period were deeply rooted in reclaiming control over their homeland and resisting the establishment of a Jewish state.

Ideologically, Arab nationalist movements emphasized the unity of the Arab people and the rejection of external influences that sought to reshape the demographic and political landscape of the region. Strategies employed by these movements included political mobilization, protests, and diplomatic efforts to garner international support for their cause. The emergence of Arab nationalist movements added a layer of complexity to the already intricate dynamics of post-World War II Palestine.

Exploring the rise of Arab nationalist movements in this era necessitates a thorough examination of the multifaceted expressions of Arab identity, the historical backdrop influencing these ideologies, and the intricate strategies employed. This comprehensive analysis provides valuable insights into the intricate garnishment of responses to the changing geopolitical dynamics in post-World War II Palestine.

Diplomatically, Arab nations engaged on multiple fronts to address the situation in Palestine. There were concerted efforts to garner international support for the Palestinian cause, with Arab leaders advocating for the recognition of Palestinian rights and the condemnation of illegitimate Zionist actions. Diplomatic initiatives were aimed at influencing global opinion and garnering backing for the Palestinian cause within international forums.

Politically, Arab nations sought alliances and collaborations to strengthen their position in addressing the evolving situation in Palestine. Inter-Arab cooperation became a vital aspect of the response, with Arab states aligning their policies to present a unified front. The Arab League, established in 1945, played a central role in coordinating diplomatic and political efforts among member states. This collaboration aimed to pool resources, present a unified stance on the Palestinian question, and strengthen the collective bargaining power of Arab nations on the international stage.

Militarily, the Arab response involved considerations of force and preparedness. The Arab nations comprehended the direct threat posed by Zionist developments to the security and stability of the region. Consequently, there were preparations for potential military interventions to counter what was an encroachment on Palestinian land and rights. The Arab-Israeli War of 1948-1949 stands as a significant manifestation of these military considerations, reflecting the Arab world's commitment to defending Palestinian genuine rights through force.

The mobilization of the Arab world in response to the threat to Palestinian interests showcased a comprehensive and coordinated approach. This response was not confined to rhetoric or diplomatic maneuvering alone; rather, it encompassed a spectrum of actions that underscored the depth of commitment among Arab nations to address the challenges posed by the evolving situation in Palestine. The post-World War II era witnessed the Arab world grappling with the complexities of safeguarding Palestinian interests in a rapidly changing geopolitical landscape, marked by the interplay of diplomatic, political, and military considerations.

As a result of the continuing oppression of Palestinians, key figures emerged as vocal proponents of Palestinian nationalism, contributing to the shaping of a collective Palestinian identity. The articulation of the Palestinian people's aspirations for self-determination saw leaders like Haj Amin al-Husseini, the Grand Mufti of Jerusalem, holding a central part. Al-Husseini's advocacy for Palestinian rights resonated widely, and his influence extended beyond Palestine, garnering support among Arab nations sympathetic to the Palestinian cause.

Palestinian leaders in the early stages demonstrated a recognition of the significance of Palestinian nationalist sentiments, predating the conclusion of World War II. During this time, grassroots movements emerged, fostering a surge of support for the concept of establishing an independent Palestinian state. Organizations like the Arab Higher Committee, formed in 1936, sought to unify Palestinian efforts in articulating their national aspirations. The Arab Higher Committee, under the leadership of figures like Ahmed Hilmi Abd al-Baqi, became a platform for coordinating political and social initiatives that aimed at realizing the dream of an independent Palestine.

Events on the ground further fueled Palestinian nationalist fervor. The Arab-Israeli War of 1948-1949, as mentioned, while resulting in displacement and hardship for many Palestinians, also served as a crucible for forging a collective Palestinian identity. The resistance against the establishment of the State of Israel became a rallying point, fostering a shared sense of purpose among Palestinians.

The post-war period was characterized by the crystallization of a distinct Palestinian national identity, rooted in a shared history, culture, and struggle. Calls for liberty resonated through various channels, from political leadership to grassroots movements, contributing to the emergence of a cohesive Palestinian narrative. The development of Palestinian nationalism during this era laid the groundwork for future political movements and the continued pursuit of self-determination.

Within this ever-changing landscape, Palestinian nationalists encountered the intricate challenge of maneuvering through geopolitical shifts, regional dynamics, and the evolving facets of the Arab-Israeli confrontation. The calls for independence became not just a response to immediate circumstances but a foundational element in the ongoing narrative of Palestinian identity and aspirations in the post-World War II era.

Partition Plans and Resistance

United Nations Partition Plan

Delving into the origins of the United Nations' Partition Plan for Palestine demands a thorough examination of the historical context that shaped its formulation. This includes pivotal events like The Balfour Declaration, a preplanned sequence of staged events, and notable claims such as the rise of anti-Semitism in Western countries, World War II, the Holocaust, and the Zionist immigration surge. As expected, the aftermath of World War II witnessed heightened tensions between Jewish and Arab communities within the British Mandate in Palestine, each ardently advocating for self-determination.

The geopolitical circumstances of the time were marked by the waning influence of the British Empire and the ascension of the United States and the Soviet Union as global superpowers. The strategic importance of the Middle East, especially considering Cold War dynamics, heightened international interest in the region. The control of Palestine, situated at the crossroads of Europe, Asia, and Africa, became a focal point of global geopolitical considerations.

The perceived plight of Jewish survivors of the Holocaust served to magnify the international community's focus on the issue of Jewish statehood. The Holocaust stirred global sympathy, influencing public opinion and garnering support for the establishment of a homeland for Jewish survivors. This distorted humanitarian dimension unjustly introduced an additional imperative to the already intricate political calculations surrounding the future of Palestine.

Simultaneously, the Arab world, resentful of colonial legacies and alarmed by the prospect of a Jewish state, vehemently opposed any partition plan. Arab leaders considered the establishment of a Jewish state as a violation of the principle of national sovereignty and an infringement on the rights of the Arab majority in Palestine. The Arab-Israeli affray became a focal point for geopolitical maneuvering and ideological clashes in the post-war era.

This complex historical context, influenced by geopolitical intricacies, alleged moral requirements, and Cold War dynamics, laid the groundwork for the creation of the UN Partition Plan. The decision to introduce a partition plan for Palestine was an implementation of the Balfour Declaration and a so-called response to the intricate interchange of international considerations, highlighting the inherent challenges in seeking a resolution to the longstanding struggle in the region.

The United Nations' Partition Plan, encapsulated in Resolution 181, represents a prejudiced attempt to address the deeply entrenched hostilities between Jewish and Arab communities in Palestine. This plan, born out of the historical context delineated earlier, aimed to provide a framework for the creation of independent Jewish and Arab states, along with an international administration for Jerusalem, recognizing the unique status of the city.

A detailed examination of the partition plan reveals its intricate design aimed at ensuring the dominance of Zionists over the extensive land of the Palestinians. The proposed division of territory sought to allocate distinct areas for Jewish and Arab states, without even minimal consideration of justice, at the very least, in the partition process. Distributing 56.47% of the land to the Jewish population, accounting for around 33% of the total population, and assigning 43.53% for the proposed Arab state, encompassing Muslims, Christians, and a small number of other religious groups, constituting approximately 67%, raises questions about the equity of the allocation. The rationale behind this partition is rooted in the idea of facilitating political benefits and ensuring the well-being of Zionists at the cost of the freedom, identity, and even lives of innocent Palestinians.

The plan recommended the establishment of an economic union between the proposed Jewish and Arab states to foster cooperation and shared resources, emphasizing the interconnectedness of their futures. Jerusalem, given its significance to multiple religious and cultural groups, was proposed as a separate entity under international administration, reflecting the international community's commitment to preserving the city's diverse heritage.

The determination of the borders of the proposed states was finalized without adequate consideration for the Jewish and Arab populations. The demarcation aimed to create contiguous territories for each community while ensuring the dominance of Zionists. The UN Special Committee on Palestine (UNSCOP) ardently delved into the study of these demographic and geographic factors, shaping the recommendations presented in the partition plan.

It is important to note that the partition plan faced opposition from both Jewish and Arab leaders. While the Jewish leadership accepted the plan as a pragmatic step towards statehood, the Arab leadership vehemently rejected it, viewing the proposed division as an infringement on Arab rights and sovereignty. The dissenting voices underscored the challenges inherent in attempting to find a universally acceptable solution to the complex issues in the region.

The UN partition plan, though ultimately not fully implemented due to the Arab rejection and ensuing conflict, remains a significant historical document. It highlights the international community's unfair effort solely to appease Zionist leaderships, revealing their willingness to obliterate the identity of the entire Palestinian population for political and personal gains.

Disputed Borders and Territories

The demarcation of borders outlined in the UN Partition Plan for Palestine was fraught with complexities, giving rise to ambiguities that would become enduring sources of tension and affray. The challenges linked to border delineation were not solely technical; they had their roots in political and geographic considerations. Geographically, Palestine's terrain posed significant challenges to the demarcation process. The topography of the region, marked by diverse landscapes and historical markers, made it difficult to draw clear and universally agreed-upon borders. The lack of precise geographic features and natural boundaries contributed to the ambiguity surrounding the proposed divisions.

Competing historical claims further complicated the matter. Both Jewish and Arab communities laid historical and cultural assertions to various territories within Palestine. These claims, often dating back centuries, created overlapping narratives that made it challenging to establish boundaries that would satisfy all parties. The historical contestations were deeply intertwined with identity and national narratives, amplifying the stakes associated with the demarcation process.

Political considerations also played a decisive role in the ambiguities surrounding border demarcation. The geopolitical landscape of the time, marked by shifting alliances and Cold War dynamics, influenced the positions of key international players. The delineation process faced increased complexity due to the involvement of superpowers and regional actors. Political calculations and the need to appease Zionist leadership took precedence over geographic or historical considerations, further complicating the situation.

The UN Partition Plan's borders, while pretending to attempt to find a compromise between competing claims, ultimately reflected the inherent challenges of balancing diverse and entrenched interests. The unfairness and ambiguity in the delineation of borders set the stage for disputes and tussles that would unfold ensuing the plan's implementation.

The contested nature of the proposed boundaries foreshadowed the difficulties in translating a partition plan into a sustainable solution on the ground. The subsequent Arab-Israeli skirmish, characterized by wars and ongoing disputes over borders, stands as a testament to the enduring impact of the ambiguities and injustices in the demarcation process. The challenges associated with border delineation in the UN Partition Plan underscore the intricate interplay of geography and politics in shaping the destiny of nations.

The prejudices and challenges associated with the demarcation of borders created a fertile ground for disputes. Geographic considerations, competing historical claims, and the diverse interpretations of the UN Partition Plan's provisions laid the foundation for territorial contestations. The lack of clarity in defining the borders of the proposed Jewish and Arab states left room for incompatible expectations and competing narratives, setting the stage for future confrontations.

The contested territories became symbolic focal points for both Jewish and Arab national identities. Each community asserted historical connections and rights to specific regions, further intensifying the disputes. The territories outlined in the UN Partition Plan became not just lines on a map but contested spaces laden with historical significance, religious importance, and cultural heritage. This heightened emotional attachment deepened the resolve of Palestinians to assert their claims, amplifying the potential for combat.

As the UN Partition Plan was implemented, tensions escalated, and the seeds of dispute sprouted into open collision. The competing claims over Jerusalem, a city of immense religious and cultural significance to both Arabs and Jews, exemplified the challenges inherent in the partition. The inability to resolve the status of Jerusalem became a focal point for future brawls, symbolizing the broader struggle for control over sacred and historically significant sites.

The territorial disputes outlined in the UN Partition Plan also contributed to the Arab-Israeli War of 1948-1949. The rejection of the plan by Arab states, coupled with the competing territorial claims, fueled hostilities. The absence of agreed-upon borders, the evident bias in the UN partition plan, and the absence of mechanisms to enforce it permitted both sides to assert their territorial ambitions through military means. This battle not only solidified the contested nature of certain territories but also set a precedent for future armed confrontations between good and evil; Palestinians and Zionists.

The lingering impact of these territorial disputes is evident in the ongoing Arab-Israeli skirmish. The contested borders outlined in the UN Partition Plan continue to shape the geopolitical landscape, influencing negotiations, peace processes, and international interventions. The complexities arising from the ambiguous demarcation of borders have perpetuated a cycle of violence and diplomatic impasses, underscoring the enduring legacy of the seeds of dispute sown by the UN Partition Plan. The contested territories remain central to the unresolved issues that hinder a comprehensive and lasting resolution to the Arab-Israeli combat.

Reaction of Zionist Leadership

After the United Nations' partition plan, Zionist leaders engaged in profound internal deliberations, navigating complex considerations and factors that would shape their response to the proposed framework. The decision-making process among Zionist leaders reflected the intricate balance between pragmatic political considerations, historical aspirations, and the recognition of the geopolitical realities of the time.

The deliberations within the Zionist leadership encompassed a multifaceted analysis of the UN partition plan. Key figures such as David Ben-Gurion, Chaim Weizmann, and Golda Meir grappled with the implications of accepting or rejecting the proposed framework. Their considerations included the territorial distribution outlined in the plan, the viability of a Jewish state within those boundaries, and the potential for international recognition.

A critical aspect of the internal discussions revolved around pragmatically assessing the territorial allocations for the proposed Jewish state. Zionist leaders carefully examined the geographic and strategic implications of the designated areas, weighing the potential for economic sustainability, defensibility, and demographic composition. These considerations aimed at ensuring the long-term viability and security of the envisioned Jewish state.

Zionist leaders' responses were alluringly influenced by historical aspirations. The partition plan represented a historic opportunity to establish a Jewish homeland, a dream nurtured through decades. The leaders grappled with the emotional and symbolic significance of accepting the proposed partition, recognizing that this decision could mark a transformative moment in the Jewish quest for self-determination.

Simultaneously, Zionist leaders were acutely aware of the geopolitical realities and the potential challenges posed by Arab opposition. The delicate balance between realizing Zionist aspirations and navigating the potential for clash with Arab states added layers of complexity to the decision-making process. The specter of possible hostilities loomed large, prompting a careful evaluation of the insurgent and diplomatic consequences of accepting or rejecting the UN partition plan.

The internal debates among Zionist leaders underscored the complicated relationship between pragmatic considerations and the historical significance of the moment. The decision-making process was a testament to the nuanced and calculated approach taken by Zionist leaders as they grappled with the complexities inherent in the UN partition plan. Ultimately, their decisions would set the stage for the unfolding events that would shape the destiny of the region.

Zionist leaders who embraced acceptance and support for the United Nations' partition plan exhibited a strategic and forward-looking approach, recognizing the plan as a pivotal step toward the realization of Jewish statehood. Among these leaders, David Ben-Gurion emerged as a prominent advocate, espousing a vision that balanced pragmatism with a commitment to the historical aspirations of the Jewish people.

Ben-Gurion, the head of the Jewish Agency and later the first Prime Minister of Israel, played a central role in shaping the Zionist response to the UN partition plan. His acceptance of the proposal stemmed from a nuanced understanding of the geopolitical landscape and a keen appreciation for the potential benefits it offered to the Zionist cause. Ben-Gurion's endorsement was grounded in a pragmatic assessment of the territorial allocations, recognizing the importance of securing areas with a Jewish majority and strategic significance.

Ben-Gurion's support was significantly influenced by the belief that accepting the partition plan could pave the way for international recognition of the nascent Jewish state. In the post-World War II era, the global community was attuned to issues of self-determination and decolonization. Ben-Gurion seized the opportunity to align the Zionist cause with these broader trends, envisioning a Jewish state that would not only emerge within the UN-sanctioned borders but also gain legitimacy on the world stage.

Strategic considerations were paramount in Ben-Gurion's calculus. He recognized that the proposed territories, despite their challenges, provided a foundation for a viable and defensible Jewish state. The acceptance of the partition plan was, for Ben-Gurion, a pragmatic step toward securing a homeland that could accommodate the influx of Jewish immigrants and withstand potential external threats.

Furthermore, Ben-Gurion's vision extended beyond immediate practicalities. He understood that the acceptance of the partition plan represented a historic opportunity to establish a Jewish state, an accomplishment that would resonate with the collective memory and aspirations of the Jewish people. By supporting the plan, Ben-Gurion aimed to position the Zionist movement as an agent of historical change, actively shaping the destiny of the Jewish nation.

The leaders who rallied behind Ben-Gurion shared a commitment to realizing the Zionist dream within the framework proposed by the UN. Their acceptance and support were grounded in a pragmatic and visionary approach, aligning with the broader currents of international politics and leveraging the historical moment to lay the foundation for the establishment of the State of Israel. This stance marked a critical juncture in the Zionist movement, setting the stage for the unfolding events that would lead to the birth of a new nation.

While some Zionist leaders expressed acceptance and support for the United Nations' partition plan, a notable faction within the movement vehemently criticized or outright rejected the proposed framework. Among the dissenting voices, figures like Menachem Begin, leader of the Irgun, and Ze'ev Jabotinsky, founder of Revisionist Zionism, performed indispensable roles in shaping the opposition to the UN plan.

Menachem Begin, leader of the Irgun and future Prime Minister of Israel, was a prominent critic of the partition plan. His objections were rooted in a combination of ideological, security, and territorial concerns. Begin, representing the Revisionist faction of Zionism, advocated for a maximalist vision of a Jewish state that encompassed a larger territory than that allocated by the UN plan. His rejection of the proposal stemmed from a belief in the nominal historical rights of the Jewish people to a more expansive homeland.

From Begin's perspective, the UN partition plan compromised the integrity of these historical claims and undermined the Zionist movement's commitment to a comprehensive Jewish state. His criticisms were vocal and pointed, resonating with a segment of the

Zionist community that sought a more assertive and expansive approach to territorial sovereignty.

Ze'ev Jabotinsky, a key ideological influence on Begin and the founder of Revisionist Zionism, also expressed reservations about the partition plan. Jabotinsky's vision of a Jewish state included territories beyond those delineated by the UN, and he was critical of what he perceived as a concession of Jewish historical rights. Jabotinsky's rejection was grounded in a commitment to a territorial maximalism that aimed to secure a more extensive and defensible homeland for the Jewish people.

Security concerns further fueled the dissent among Zionist leaders. The proposed borders, seen by some as indefensible, raised anxieties about the vulnerability of the envisaged Jewish state to external threats. Begin, drawing on his experiences and perspectives from the armed wrangle, contended that the proposed territories lacked strategic depth, making the nascent state susceptible to military challenges.

Additionally, the dissenting leaders were skeptical about the feasibility of coexistence with the Arab population within the allocated borders. Begin and others argued that the proposed Jewish state would be surrounded by hostile Arab nations, heightening security risks and potentially leading to conflict. Their apprehensions reflected a pragmatic assessment of the geopolitical realities and the potential for protracted hostilities.

The criticisms and rejections of the partition plan by these influential Zionist leaders underscored the diversity of opinions within the movement. While some accepted the proposed plan for pragmatic reasons, others, like Begin and Jabotinsky, adhered to a more uncompromising vision rooted in historical narratives and security considerations. The ensuing debates and disagreements within the Zionist leadership set the stage for complex negotiations and, at times, internal tensions as the movement navigated the path toward the establishment of the State of Israel.

Palestinian Opposition

The United Nations' partition plan triggered a multifaceted response from Palestinian leaders, marked by a combination of diplomatic efforts, mobilization of public sentiment, and strategic opposition. Figures like Haj Amin al-Husseini and other prominent Palestinian leaders played instrumental roles in articulating the Palestinian stance against the proposed division.

Haj Amin al-Husseini, a key figure in Palestinian leadership during this period, vehemently opposed the UN partition plan. The Grand Mufti leveraged his influential position to mobilize both local and international support against the unfair division. Al-Husseini engaged in diplomatic efforts, reaching out to Arab and Muslim nations to rally support for the Palestinian cause. His extensive networks and alliances were essential in fostering a unified Arab stance against the partition plan.

In addition to diplomatic endeavors, Palestinian leaders employed grassroots mobilization to articulate their opposition. The orchestration of strikes, protests, and civil disobedience campaigns marked a crucial contribution from the Arab Higher Committee, representing the aspirations of Palestinian Arabs. These actions aimed to convey the Palestinian rejection of the proposed partition and assert their claim to a unified and independent state.

Strategically, Palestinian leaders sought to present a united front against the partition plan. Despite internal differences and rivalries, a collective effort was made to convey a shared resistance to the proposed division. The Arab Higher Committee, led by figures like Jamal al-Husseini and Ahmad al-Shukeiri, strategically communicated the Palestinian stance on an international stage, emphasizing the rejection of any plan that compromised the territorial integrity of Palestine.

The responses and strategies adopted by Palestinian leaders during this critical juncture laid the groundwork for the subsequent phases of Palestinian resistance and set the tone for their engagement with international bodies. The opposition to the UN partition plan became a defining chapter in the Palestinian struggle for self-determination, shaping the trajectory of their quest for statehood in the years that followed.

Grassroots resistance among the Palestinian population in response to the United Nations' partition plan manifested as a powerful and widespread movement, reflecting the deep-seated concerns and opposition to the proposed framework. Local communities, spanning urban centers and rural areas, actively expressed their discontent, organized protests, and vehemently resisted the unjust division of their homeland.

In cities like Jerusalem, Jaffa, and Haifa, where diverse Palestinian communities thrived, grassroots opposition took various forms. Public demonstrations became a hallmark of resistance, drawing together individuals from different walks of life. Palestinians, irrespective of socio-economic background, religious affiliation, or geographic location, united in their rejection of the partition plan. Photographs, eyewitness accounts, and contemporaneous reports vividly capture the scenes of mass gatherings, reflecting the widespread sentiment of opposition that permeated Palestinian society.

The Arab Higher Committee, a representative body of Palestinian Arabs, performed a necessary part in coordinating and amplifying the grassroots resistance. Their announcements, distributed through various channels, called upon Palestinians to express their dissent through strikes, protests, and other non-violent means. The Arab media of the time, both local and international, extensively covered these events, providing a comprehensive record of the grassroots opposition.

The resilience of Palestinian communities in rural areas was equally noteworthy. Despite geographical dispersion, local populations organized demonstrations, strikes, and other forms of civil disobedience. Farmers, laborers, and families living in villages rallied against the infringement on their land and heritage. Oral histories from these regions provide valuable insights into the grassroots resistance, detailing the communal efforts to protect their way of life and reject external impositions.

The resilience and creative strategies employed by local communities in expressing their opposition are evident in artifacts from the time, including protest banners, slogans, and symbolic gestures. These tangible expressions of dissent provide a palpable link to the grassroots movements that emerged in response to the partition plan.

The grassroots resistance was not merely a fleeting moment but laid the foundation for the enduring spirit of Palestinian opposition. It cultivated a collective consciousness that continued to shape the trajectory of Palestinian resistance in the face of subsequent challenges. The legacy of this grassroots movement remains integral to understanding the resilience of the Palestinian people and their ongoing quest for justice and self-determination.

The concerns and grievances expressed by the Palestinian population in response to the United Nations' partition plan were deeply rooted in multifaceted socio-political, economic, and cultural factors. These grievances went beyond mere territorial disputes; they encompassed the profound impact on the fabric of Palestinian communities, shaping a narrative of resistance grounded in a shared sense of injustice and dispossession.

From a socio-political perspective, the partition plan was a denial of Palestinian self-determination and sovereignty. Palestinians, who had inhabited the land for generations, viewed the imposition of external decisions on their fate as a violation of their inherent right to determine the political destiny of their homeland. The rejection of the plan was not solely a reaction to the delineation of borders but an assertion of the right to shape their own political future, a sentiment that resonates in the oral histories and writings of Palestinian leaders and intellectuals of the time.

Economically, the partition plan posed a severe threat to the livelihoods of Palestinian communities. The proposed division of land jeopardized agricultural practices, disrupted trade routes, and undermined economic stability. Palestinians, particularly those reliant on agriculture for sustenance, saw the partition as an encroachment on their economic well-being. This economic dimension of the opposition took part in the deliberations and discussions among Palestinian leaders who articulated the detrimental consequences of the partition on the prosperity of their communities.

Culturally, the partition plan was an assault on Palestinian identity and heritage. The proposed division overlooked the rich tapestry of Palestinian history, disregarding the cultural nuances and coexistence that had characterized the region for centuries. Palestinians feared the erasure of their cultural heritage, the displacement of communities, and the fragmentation of the social fabric that had bound them together. This cultural resistance found expression in literature, poetry, and artistic endeavors that sought to preserve and celebrate Palestinian identity in the face of external impositions.

The impact of these concerns and grievances on Palestinian communities was profound and enduring. The opposition was not merely a reaction to a political decision but a collective response to an existential threat. The resilience and determination displayed by Palestinians in the face of these challenges laid the groundwork for a sustained narrative of resistance that continues to shape the discourse on Palestinian rights and statehood.

Declaration of the Jewish State

The proclamation ceremony marking the official declaration of the State of Israel in 1948 stands as a crucial historical milestone, loudly announcing the deprivation of the rights of innocent Palestinians, extinguishing their hope for justice from international entities, and ensuring the denial of their fundamental rights within their own homeland. This unjustifiable event unfolded on May 14, 1948, at the Tel Aviv Museum in the presence of key figures who played instrumental roles in the establishment of the Jewish state.

The ceremony was presided over by David Ben-Gurion, the head of the Jewish Agency. Ben-Gurion, a central figure in the Zionist leadership, eloquently articulated the proclamation of the establishment of a Jewish state in Eretz-Israel. His words encapsulated the collective dreams and efforts of the Zionist community to attain self-determination and statehood.

The choice of the Tel Aviv Museum as the venue for the proclamation was strategic. The museum, then serving as the provisional headquarters of the Jewish leadership, symbolized the cultural and intellectual aspirations of the emerging state. It provided a fitting backdrop for the declaration, underscoring the integration of cultural and political dimensions in the Zionist vision for the new state.

The atmosphere surrounding the proclamation ceremony was a blend of jubilation, anticipation, and a profound sense of historical significance. The attendees, including members of the provisional government, representatives of the Jewish Agency, and prominent leaders of the Jewish community, witnessed the realization of a dream that had spanned decades. The weight of the moment was palpable as the newly declared State of Israel emerged onto the world stage, signifying the end of the British Mandate, tearing the identities and rights of Palestinians, and inaugurating a new chapter in the region's history.

The significance of the proclamation ceremony extends beyond the immediate declaration. It marked the culmination of years of feints, betrayals, and strategic planning by the Zionist movement. The event laid the foundation for the nascent state, shaping its identity, values, and aspirations. The proclamation ceremony is not just a historical footnote; it stands as a symbol of perfidy, despotism, and the enduring quest resulting from long-term strategic planning by the Zionist movement.

The political implications of the declaration of the State of Israel reverberated far beyond the confines of the Museum, shaping the geopolitical landscape of the Middle East and eliciting responses on the international stage. This watershed moment not only marked the fulfillment of Zionist aspirations but also posed significant challenges and opportunities, both in alignment with and divergence from the United Nations' partition plan.

The newborn State of Israel sought international recognition for its existence. This diplomatic endeavor was intricately linked to the legitimacy of its territorial claims as outlined in the UN partition plan. While the declaration mirrored, to some extent, the proposed Jewish state in the partition plan, certain deviations and expansions in the actual borders stirred controversy and set the stage for diplomatic challenges.

On the diplomatic front, Abba Eban emerged as a formidable advocate for Israel. Securing international support for the declaration was significantly attributed to his eloquence and diplomatic acumen. Eban's later career as Israel's ambassador to the United Nations and other key diplomatic posts highlighted the importance of skilled diplomacy in shaping the trajectory of the new state.

The declaration of the State of Israel was also significantly influenced by the support of powerful international actors. President Harry S. Truman, leading the United States, decisively contributed by recognizing Israel mere minutes after the declaration. Truman's support was not without controversy, as he faced opposition from within his administration, but his recognition proved instrumental in the legitimacy of the new state.

The involvement of these key actors reflects the convergence of political, diplomatic, and strategic efforts that culminated in the declaration of the State of Israel. Their roles were not confined to the historical moment of the declaration but extended into the subsequent efforts to secure international recognition and establish diplomatic relations. The collective contributions of Ben-Gurion, Weizmann,

Eban, and international leaders underscored the complexity and significance of the journey from the British Mandate to the establishment of the State of Israel in the post-World War II era.

On the other hand, Arab states vehemently opposed the establishment of Israel, viewing it as a violation of their national interests and the rights of the Palestinian Arab population. The Arab League, in answer to the declaration, initiated military intervention, marking the beginning of the Arab-Israeli war. This opposition from neighboring Arab states created a diplomatic quagmire for Israel, leading to a protracted affray that would shape the region's political landscape for decades to come.

The diplomatic consequences of the declaration were multifaceted. The United Nations, which had achieved a pivotal milestone in proposing the partition plan, now found itself grappling with the repercussions of its implementation. The Security Council became a forum for impassioned debates and discussions surrounding the legitimacy of Israel's establishment. Diplomatic maneuvering, alliances, and geopolitical considerations came to the forefront as the international community grappled with the implications of the newly declared state.

International Reactions

In the intricate geopolitical landscape that unfolded after the declaration of the State of Israel, diplomatic alliances assumed a fundamental role, influencing international reactions to the newly established nation. A closer examination of these alliances unveils a complex network of support and opposition, as countries aligned themselves based on a convergence of political, strategic, and ideological motivations.

A crucial aspect of diplomatic alliances during this period was the support extended to Israel by specific Western nations, particularly the United States and the United Kingdom. These alliances were rooted in shared democratic values, historical ties, and strategic interests. The United States, in particular, emerged as a staunch supporter of Israel, driven by domestic political dynamics, influential lobbying groups, and a perception of alignment with democratic principles as discussed earlier. This support extended beyond diplomatic gestures to include military aid and economic assistance, significantly influencing Israel's capacity to navigate the challenges posed by regional opposition.

Conversely, opposition to the State of Israel was pronounced among Arab and Muslim-majority countries, who fervently rejected the establishment of a Jewish state in the heart of the Middle East. The motivations behind this opposition were deeply intertwined with historical grievances, including the displacement of Palestinian Arabs and the infringement on their rights. Arab nations formed diplomatic alliances to counter encroachment on Palestinian territory and to address the imbalance in power dynamics resulting from the establishment of Israel.

The Soviet Union, during this period, pursued a complex diplomatic strategy, initially recognizing the State of Israel and later shifting towards a more supportive stance for Arab nations. This maneuvering reflected the broader Cold War dynamics and the Soviet Union's pursuit of influence in the region. The motivations behind these diplomatic shifts were pragmatic, aligning with the perceived strategic interests of the Soviet Union in the Middle East.

The United Nations, in the wake of the declaration of the State of Israel and the ensuing conflict, found itself at the center of a complex international scenario. In response to escalating tensions and to secure the Zionists within their newly established homeland from Palestinian freedom fighters, the United Nations undertook a series of diplomatic initiatives, control measures, and the deployment of purported peacekeeping forces.

A notable UN response materialized in the passing of Resolution 194 in December 1948, addressing the plight of Palestinian refugees-a situation exacerbated by the UN's own actions through the unjust partition plan and support for the establishment of the state of Israel. This resolution affirmed the right of refugees to return to their homes and called for compensation for those choosing not to return. The resolution, however, encountered challenges in implementation, revealing the deep-seated complexities of the skirmish and the UN's reluctance and inability to translate their resolution into action.

The establishment of the United Nations Truce Supervision Organization (UNTSO) in May 1948 witnessed a crucial contribution from the UN. UNTSO was tasked with overseeing the implementation of the truce that followed the Arab-Israeli War of 1948-1949. The involvement of UN forces represented a concerted international effort to bring ostensible stability to the region and prevent further escalation of hostilities.

The events surrounding the UN's response to the partition plan and the subsequent declaration of the State of Israel underscore the challenges faced by the international community in navigating the complexities of the Arab-Israeli brawl.

Power Dynamics and Disparities

The military capacities of the newly formed State of Israel and the resistance efforts of the Palestinian population in the 1948 declaration of independence era reflected a stark asymmetry in strength, shaping the power dynamics of the emerging conflict. Israel, buoyed by the declaration of statehood and facing immediate threats from neighboring Arab states, swiftly organized and mobilized its military forces. Israel's armed forces, the Israel Defense Forces (IDF), displayed a level of organization, training, and coordination that surpassed the relatively fragmented resistance efforts of the Palestinian population, as will be discussed in the following topic.

The IDF, although a nascent armed force, benefited from the integration of various paramilitary groups that had fought together during the pre-state period. This amalgamation, coupled with the leadership of experienced military figures such as David Ben-Gurion and Yigal Allon, provided Israel with a relatively cohesive and well-organized military structure. Additionally, evidence from contemporaneous accounts and military analyses highlights Israel's access to arms and ammunition, often procured through clandestine channels during the pre-state period, giving it a significant advantage in terms of weaponry.

Conversely, the evidence for the Palestinian resistance efforts reveals a more uneven and decentralized combatant landscape. The resistance was characterized by diverse factions, each with its own motivations, strategies, and levels of military preparedness. The lack of a centralized command structure, coupled with limited access to modern weaponry, placed the Palestinian resistance at a distinct disadvantage against the strategically organized force that the Israeli military had developed over decades.

The asymmetry in military capacities had profound implications for the ability of each side to assert its interests and objectives. Israel's military superiority allowed it to effectively defend its borders during the War of Independence (1948-1949) and secure strategic territorial gains. The evidence for this lies in the outcomes of key battles and campaigns, such as Operation Nachshon and the Negev Campaign, where Israel successfully repelled Arab forces and expanded its territorial control illegally.

In contrast, the Palestinian resistance faced significant challenges in coordinating actions, acquiring sufficient resources, and countering the military might of the Israeli forces. Historical accounts underscore the difficulties faced by the Palestinian irregular forces in the absence of a unified command structure and adequate military resources. They were up against a force equipped with state-of-the-art weaponry and supported by Western countries and the UN, both openly and secretly. The lopsidedness in military capacities during this formative period laid the groundwork for enduring power disparities in the Arab-Israeli war. The consequences from the early years of battle underscore the lasting impact of these disparities on subsequent geopolitical dynamics in the region.

The economic resources of the State of Israel lie in the strategic gains it achieved during the confrontation, as well as the subsequent development policies implemented by the Israeli government. Israel, through bellicose victories and territorial expansion, gained control over key agricultural and industrial areas, especially in regions like the Negev and Galilee, where significant land was occupied.

Moreover, financial support from the international Jewish community, particularly in the form of reparations from Germany, performed a leading role in bolstering Israel's economic foundation. This financial assistance is documented in agreements such as the Luxembourg Agreement of 1952, which stipulated compensations to Israel for Holocaust survivors and Jewish communities affected by the war.

However, the economic resources accessible to the Palestinian population highlight a significant disparity. The displacement of Palestinians during the tussle resulted in a significant loss of land and property, accompanied by forced evacuations, expulsions, and the creation of Palestinian refugee populations. The economic impact of this displacement was profound, depriving Palestinians of their agricultural and urban assets.

Furthermore, the limited access to financial support and international aid for the Palestinian population compounded the economic challenges. The inadequacy of relief efforts and the prolonged refugee crisis left Palestinian communities struggling to rebuild their lives in the absence of substantial financial support.

These disparities in economic resources had profound implications for the uneven development and implementation of the partition plan. The evidence suggests that Israel, with its enhanced economic capacity, was better positioned to consolidate its territorial gains and invest in infrastructure development. Israel's ability to establish a functioning state apparatus, build cities, and develop industries in the aftermath of the war highlighted the stark contrast in economic fortunes between Israel and the Palestinian population. On the other hand, the economic challenges faced by the Palestinian population hindered their capacity to rebuild and develop. The time underscores the difficulties in providing basic necessities and rebuilding infrastructure in the face of displacement and financial constraints.

In examining the support for Israel, the diplomatic alliances formed with key Western powers, particularly the United States, come into focus. The U.S., motivated by strategic and ideological considerations, emerged as a staunch supporter of Israel, as evidenced by documents such as the Truman Administration's recognition of Israel within hours of its declaration, marking the beginning of a lasting alliance. The geopolitical context of the Cold War, where Israel was seen as a potential ally in the Middle East, further solidified this support. This alliance paved the way for military aid, economic assistance, and diplomatic backing, significantly enhancing Israel's position on the international stage.

On the Palestinian side, evidence suggests a more fragmented and challenging path to international support. The Palestinian cause found resonance in the Arab world, with neighboring countries expressing solidarity through Arab League resolutions supporting the Palestinian cause and condemning Israeli actions. However, the extent of tangible support and effective diplomatic alliances was limited. The lack of a unified strategy among Arab nations, as internal divisions often hindered concerted efforts, posed challenges to the effective mobilization of international support for the Palestinian cause.

Moreover, the United Nations, allegedly considered a platform for the Palestinian cause, issued the so-called resolutions affirming the rights of Palestinian refugees and recognizing their plight. However, the effectiveness of translating these resolutions into concrete changes on the ground was constrained by geopolitical rivalries, political influences, and power dynamics within the UN.

Emergence of Israeli Defense Forces

The birth of the Israeli Defense Forces (IDF) following the declaration of the State of Israel was a critical development intricately woven into the fabric of the nation's nascent history. The historical context and circumstances surrounding the formation of the IDF were emblematic of the security challenges and imperatives facing the newly established state. In the precarious days following the declaration of statehood in 1948, Israel found itself plunged into a brawl, facing the hostility of neighboring Arab states as they sought to continue their occupation of the land. The urgency of the situation necessitated the swift creation of a unified armed force to safeguard the fledgling nation. The IDF emerged as a response to this existential threat, drawing on the amalgamation of pre-existing paramilitary groups such as the Haganah, Irgun, and Lehi.

The organizational structure of the IDF reflected a commitment to unity and coordination. It integrated the disparate militant factions that had operated independently during the pre-state period, forging a cohesive force under a single command. This structural consolidation was vital for efficient and strategic pugnacious operations, allowing Israel to confront external threats with a unified front.

Recruitment processes for the IDF were marked by the imperative of national service. In a context where the existence of the state that was occupied from Palestine was at stake, the call to arms resonated across Israeli society. The recruitment drive sought to mobilize a diverse range of individuals, transcending societal divisions, into a collective defense effort. This inclusivity not only bolstered the numerical strength of the IDF but also contributed to a sense of shared responsibility and commitment among the Israeli populace to be part of the biggest crime and betrayal in history.

The formative years of the IDF were significantly influenced by the crucial contributions of early leadership, shaping both its ethos and operational strategies. Figures like David Ben-Gurion recognized the symbiotic relationship between a robust military and the preservation of the state. The leadership prioritized the professionalization of the

IDF, laying the groundwork for an antagonistic institution that would evolve into a cornerstone of Israeli security.

The formation of the IDF in the wake of Israel's declaration of statehood was a testament to their determination to secure its existence. It represented the fusion of disparate entities into a unified force, driven by a shared sense of purpose and duty. The historical circumstances surrounding the IDF's inception laid the groundwork for its evolution into a formidable defense apparatus, shaping the course of Israeli history in the post-World War II era.

The War of Independence presented the IDF with a multifaceted set of challenges, both in terms of the military strategies of its adversaries and the geopolitical complexities of the region. In preparation for the imminent threat posed by Arab states, the IDF adopted a strategy characterized by flexibility, innovation, and adaptability. This approach was essential, given the diverse nature of the conflict, which ranged from conventional warfare to guerrilla tactics.

Belligerent engagements, such as the battles of Latrun, Jerusalem, and Operation Hiram, exemplified the IDF's commitment to territorial defense and objectives with sinister undertones. The Battle of Latrun, for instance, was important in controlling the vital supply route to Jerusalem, highlighting the IDF's recognition of the importance of controlling key geographical points. The battles in Jerusalem showcased the IDF's ability to operate in urban settings, with a successful outcome contributing significantly to the consolidation of Israeli occupation over the city.

The challenges faced by the IDF were not solely military; they extended to diplomatic and logistical dimensions. Arms embargoes and limited resources posed significant hurdles, requiring the IDF to leverage its ingenuity and resourcefulness. The clandestine Operation Balak, which involved the procurement and smuggling of weapons and military equipment, played a crucial role in circumventing the arms embargo, exhibiting the IDF's capacity for innovative solutions to achieve their objectives.

The IDF's commitment to protecting Zionists was evident in the establishment of humanitarian corridors during combats, demonstrating a strategic understanding of the importance of maintaining the support and resilience of the Israeli populace. The

IDF's performance in the War of Independence laid the groundwork for its standing as a formidable militant force. The strategies employed during this period emphasized the IDF's ability to balance conventional and unconventional warfare, adapt to dynamic situations, and prioritize both territorial occupation and the safeguarding of Zionists.

The period following the War of Independence marked a critical juncture in the militarization of the newly established state of Israel. The Israeli Defense Forces (IDF), born out of necessity during the turbulent times of statehood declaration, now faced the challenge of integrating itself into the broader national framework. This process of militarization was not merely about fortifying the nation's defenses but also about shaping the identity and ethos of an acute, ambitious state.

The integration of military structures into the national fabric was a multilayered endeavor. Establishing a comprehensive conscription system was a fundamental aspect, embodying the conviction that every citizen held a responsibility in securing the nation. The conscription system not only provided the IDF with a substantial and motivated manpower pool but also fostered a sense of shared responsibility and commitment among the diverse population of Israel.

The IDF's role extended beyond traditional defense functions. It became a unifying force, a symbol of collective purpose and determination. The integration of military service into societal norms helped forge a strong national identity, transcending the diverse backgrounds of Israeli citizens. The collective military service experience didn't just shape individuals; it became the cornerstone for fostering a profound sense of unity and belonging within the population.

Challenges emerged in tandem with the opportunities presented by this process of militarization. The economic strain of maintaining a sizable military, coupled with the need for ongoing modernization and training, posed significant financial challenges for the fledgling state. Balancing the imperative of national security with economic considerations required strategic decision-making and resource allocation. Moreover, the militarization of society raised questions about the appropriate role of the military in governance and civilian life and showcased the forthcoming dangers of IDF to some extent. Striking the right balance between a robust offensive apparatus and the preservation of Zionist values and civil liberties demanded careful navigation. The IDF, evolving from a wartime necessity to a perpetually malign force, had to adapt its structures and practices to align with the evolving needs of a nation in the process of expanding occupation.

Palestinian Displacement (Nakba)

The Nakba, signifying the catastrophic events of 1948, represented a significant and tragic chapter in the history of the Palestinian people. The causes that precipitated the displacement of Palestinians during the 1948 Arab-Israeli War were intricate, stemming from a complex web of historical, political, and military factors. The military conflict between Arab nations and the newly established State of Israel was a central factor contributing to displacement. The hostilities resulted in a series of forced evacuations and expulsions, primarily impacting Arab Palestinian communities. The Israeli forces, seeking territorial control and asserting statehood, engaged in quarrelsome offensives that led to the displacement of hundreds of thousands of Palestinians. The strategic significance of certain areas, coupled with the intense fighting, created an environment where civilian populations found themselves caught in the crossfire, forced to leave their homes for safety.

Moreover, the ideological underpinnings of the Zionist movement and its commitment to establishing a Jewish state in Palestine contributed to the displacement. The concept of a Jewish homeland clashed with the existing Arab Palestinian communities, leading to confrontations and, in some instances, deliberate efforts to remove Palestinian populations from certain territories. The Deir Yassin massacre in April 1948, where over 100 Palestinian civilians were killed by Zionist paramilitary groups, exemplified the brutality that characterized this turbulent period.

The scale and extent of the displacement were staggering. Hundreds of Palestinian villages were depopulated, and entire communities were uprooted. The creation of Palestinian refugee populations, numbering in the hundreds of thousands, became a defining feature of the Nakba. Many Palestinians sought refuge in neighboring Arab countries, while others endured life in makeshift camps, living in dire conditions with limited resources and uncertain futures.

The humanitarian consequences of the Nakba reverberated far beyond the immediate displacement, unfolding as a protracted crisis that profoundly impacted the lives of the Palestinian refugees. The challenges faced by this displaced population were immense, encompassing issues of shelter, access to basic necessities, and the overall well-being of the refugees.

After the Nakba, Palestinian refugees found themselves in dire circumstances, with many forced to seek shelter in makeshift camps. These camps, hastily established to accommodate the influx of displaced individuals and families, lacked the essential infrastructure to support a dignified life. The living conditions in these camps were characterized by overcrowding, inadequate sanitation, and limited access to clean water-a dire combination that posed significant threats to the health and well-being of the refugees.

Access to basic necessities became a daily struggle for the displaced Palestinians. The loss of homes and livelihoods meant that many were deprived of a stable source of income, exacerbating their vulnerability. The reliance on humanitarian aid became a lifeline for countless refugees, highlighting the acute need for international support to address the immediate needs of the displaced population.

The impact on health was particularly severe. The conditions in the refugee camps facilitated the spread of diseases, and malnutrition became a pervasive issue. The lack of proper healthcare infrastructure further compounded the challenges, making it difficult for refugees to receive adequate medical attention. The humanitarian effects of the Nakba manifested in a public health crisis, disproportionately affecting the most vulnerable members of the population-the elderly, women, and children.

The international community, collaborating through diverse relief organizations and agencies, significantly contributed to alleviating the humanitarian aftermath of the Nakba. However, the scale of the crisis demanded sustained and comprehensive efforts. The United Nations Relief and Works Agency for Palestine Refugees in the Near East (UNRWA) was established in 1949 to provide assistance specifically to Palestinian refugees. Despite these efforts, the challenges persisted, and the humanitarian costs of the Nakba continued to shape the daily lives and futures of the displaced Palestinian population.

Socio-economically, the Nakba disrupted established communities and economic structures, leading to a protracted cycle of challenges for displaced Palestinians. The loss of homes, lands, and livelihoods resulted in enduring economic hardships, with many families struggling to regain stability. The diaspora, scattered across different regions, faced varying degrees of socio-economic integration, with the challenges of displacement echoing across generations.

Culturally, the Nakba transformed the Palestinian narrative, turning it into a story of resilience, perseverance, and an unwavering connection to the land. The diaspora became custodians of a cultural heritage rooted in the memories of pre-Nakba Palestine, passing down stories, traditions, and a collective sense of identity from one generation to the next. Despite physical displacement, the cultural continuity became a powerful testament to the enduring spirit of the Palestinian people.

Psychologically, the Nakba cast a long shadow over the mental and emotional well-being of the displaced and their descendants. The trauma of forced displacement, loss, and the perpetual struggle for justice became integral parts of the Palestinian collective consciousness. The psychological impact transcended individual experiences, permeating familial and community dynamics. Generations born in the diaspora inherited not only the tangible remnants of the Nakba but also the intangible weight of historical injustice.

The enduring effects on Palestinian identity are profound. The scattered population, dispersed across different corners of the globe, maintained a steadfast connection to the idea of Palestine. The longing for return, a central tenet of Palestinian identity, passed from grandparents to parents to children. The fight for the right of return became a shared commitment, a defining feature of the Palestinian narrative that traverses generations.

The Nakba's long-term impact is not confined to the historical event itself; it resonates in the ongoing brawl for justice, self-determination, and the recognition of the rights of the Palestinian people. The dispersion, carrying the torch of resilience, continues to contribute to the global discourse on justice and human rights, ensuring that the Nakba is not consigned to the annals of history but remains a living, breathing reality that shapes the trajectory of generations to come.

Long-Term Planning

Early Zionist Conferences and Resolutions

K ey early Zionist conferences, notably the First Zionist Congress and subsequent gatherings, represent crucial moments that significantly influenced the trajectory of the Zionist movement. These conferences, occurring at a juncture when the concept of a Jewish homeland gained traction, proved essential in shaping the foundational visions and strategies of Zionist leaders.

The First Zionist Congress, held in 1897 in Basel, marked a historic milestone. Chaired by Theodor Herzl, formulate a plan for the establishment of a Jewish homeland. The protocols of this congress reveal a comprehensive discussion on the consequential challenges faced by Jewish communities and the need for collective action as discussed earlier.

The First Zionist Congress achieved a noteworthy outcome: the formulation of the Basel Program. This set of principles outlined the objectives of the Zionist movement. This program emphasized the promotion of Jewish settlement in Palestine under public law, securing international recognition for the endeavor. The protocols provide a detailed account of the deliberations that led to the adoption of these foundational principles. Subsequent Zionist conferences built upon the groundwork laid at Basel, delving into the complexities of implementing the Zionist vision. The protocols and outcomes of these gatherings reflect the evolving strategies and resolutions devised by Zionist leaders.

The establishment of the Jewish National Fund (JNF) during the Fifth Zionist Congress in 1901 is a testament to the pragmatic approach adopted by Zionist leaders. The JNF aimed to acquire and develop land in Palestine for Jewish settlement. The protocols of this congress illustrate the discussions around the practical aspects of land acquisition and the long-term planning required for sustainable Jewish presence in Palestine.

As the Zionist movement progressed, resolutions during these conferences began to address not only the political aspects but also cultural and educational dimensions. The Eighth Zionist Congress in 1907, held in The Hague, witnessed discussions on the establishment of Hebrew educational institutions in Palestine. The protocols of this congress shed light on the emphasis placed on preserving Jewish culture and identity through educational initiatives.

In subsequent conferences, such as the Tenth Zionist Congress in 1911 and the Eleventh Zionist Congress in 1913, the protocols reveal the continued commitment to the principles outlined in the Basel Program. The leaders deliberated on strategies to overcome obstacles, secure funding, and navigate the geopolitical landscape.

Building upon the resolutions and visions formulated in early Zionist conferences, the transition from discussions to tangible territorial aspirations became a defining aspect of the Zionist movement's long-term planning. As the movement evolved, strategic considerations and planning emerged, shaping the trajectory of the Zionist endeavor.

The realization of territorial aspirations gained momentum with the establishment of the Jewish National Fund (JNF) during the Fifth Zionist Congress in 1901, as above mentioned. The Eighth and the Tenth Zionist Congresses further refined territorial aspirations. Discussions at these gatherings revolved around the practical challenges of settlement, emphasizing the importance of strategic planning for sustainable Jewish presence in Palestine. The planning extended beyond political considerations to encompass economic, cultural, and educational dimensions.

Territorial aspirations also evolved in response to geopolitical changes and challenges. The Eleventh Zionist Congress addressed the impact of the Balkan Wars on the geopolitical landscape and adjusted its plans accordingly. The adaptability demonstrated by Zionist leaders reflected a strategic mindset, acknowledging the need to navigate complex geopolitical realities.

The outbreak of World War I brought about a shift in the geopolitical context, influencing the implementation of territorial aspirations. The Balfour Declaration of 1917, expressing British support for the establishment of a "national home for the Jewish people" in Palestine, marked a significant milestone. While the declaration itself did not guarantee immediate territorial gains, it provided a diplomatic foundation for the Zionist cause.

The subsequent San Remo conference in 1920 and the League of Nations Mandate for Palestine in 1922 further solidified the legal framework for the establishment of a Jewish homeland. These international developments reflected the successful translation of Zionist aspirations into concrete territorial outcomes on the diplomatic stage.

Upon reanalysis of these conferences to gauge the effectiveness of their plans in the long run, the principles of Jewish labor and agricultural settlement emerged as integral components of Zionist ideology. The Seventh Zionist Congress in 1905 emphasized the importance of productive labor as a means of reclaiming the land and establishing a self-sufficient Jewish community. This ideology aimed not only at creating economic sustainability but also at fostering a strong and independent Jewish presence in Palestine.

Zionist ideology took substantial influence from the intertwining threads of religious and historical connections to the land. The Tenth Zionist Congress in 1911 underscored the historical and spiritual ties of the Jewish people to Palestine. This ideological emphasis on historical continuity and religious significance served as a powerful motivator for long-term planning, fostering an illusion of belonging and attachment to the land.

The ideological foundation of labor and self-sufficiency took practical form with the establishment of the Histadrut in Palestine, during the Twelfth Zionist Congress in 1921. This organization became a key player in implementing the principles of Jewish labor, uniting various labor movements and contributing to the economic development of the envisioned homeland.

The belief in social justice and equality among Jewish individuals also became embedded in Zionist ideology. The Fourteenth Zionist Congress in 1925 addressed social issues and advocated for cooperative efforts to address economic disparities within the Jewish community. This ideological commitment to social justice reflected a forward-looking approach, envisioning a society that would thrive on principles of fairness and equity among its individuals.

Land Acquisition Policies

Strategic and territorial objectives propelled systematic land purchases, constituting a foundational element in Zionist long-term planning. Historical evidence illuminates the nuanced strategies deployed by Zionist forces to secure land in Palestine. While the scale of land acquisition was not as extensive as commonly perceived, there is ample evidence supporting its occurrence, albeit on a relatively limited scale. This must be understood in the broader context of the geopolitical landscape of Palestine during that period.

Zionist forces strategically utilized the Ottoman Land Law of 1858, a significant legal mechanism that established property laws in Palestine during the late Ottoman period. Navigating these legal frameworks, they employed complex procedures to purchase land from absentee landlords and exploit legal ambiguities. These maneuvers provided a semblance of legitimacy to land acquisitions, allowing Zionist settlers to establish a legal foothold in various regions. The Jewish National Fund (JNF) actively engaged in this process, negotiating with absentee landlords to acquire parcels. Strategic negotiations led by Zionist leaders resulted in successful land purchases, expanding territorial holdings and shaping the demographic composition of the region. The establishment of Jewish agricultural communities on these acquired lands underscored the transformative impact of these strategic land dealings.

The impact of systematic land purchases on the demographic and territorial landscape of Palestine was profound. Jewish settlements, supported by strategic land acquisitions, transformed previously undeveloped areas into flourishing agricultural communities. These demographic changes contributed to the alteration of the overall ethnic composition in certain regions. The systematic nature of these land purchases not only facilitated the establishment of a Jewish homeland but also decisively influenced the broader territorial dynamics leading up to the establishment of the State of Israel.

The British Mandate period introduced additional legal instruments that Zionist forces adeptly utilized. The 1920 San Remo conference and the subsequent League of Nations mandate granted Britain administrative control over Palestine, enabling the implementation of policies conducive to Zionist aspirations. The British Mandate authorities facilitated land transfers to Jewish entities through mechanisms like the 1920 Land Transfer Regulations. These regulations, while ostensibly aimed at preventing unfair land transfers, were exploited by Zionist forces to legitimize their acquisitions.

Moreover, the 1940 Land Transfer Regulations further exemplified the intricate interchange between legal frameworks and Zionist land acquisition strategies. These regulations restricted land sales between different communities, ostensibly to prevent dispossessions. However, in practice, these restrictions disproportionately impacted Arab landowners. This legal maneuvering further tilted the balance in favor of Zionist territorial objectives.

Economic leverage emerged as a potent tool in the Zionist arsenal for land acquisition, shaping the territorial landscape of historical Palestine. Leveraging financial mechanisms strategically, notably through organizations like JNF as mentioned earlier, proved crucial in consolidating territorial control and shaping the distribution of land ownership.

Settlement Expansion Plans

The analysis of settlement expansion's demographic impact and its role in shaping population dynamics unveils a deliberate and strategic plan guiding the growth of Jewish communities in Palestinian territories. This planned expansion, rooted in the early decisions of Zionist conferences, reflects a comprehensive understanding of the movement's long-term objectives.

The roots of this expansion trace back to early Zionist conferences, where decisions were made to establish Jewish settlements in Palestine. The protocols and outcomes of these conferences provide historical evidence of intentional strategies for territorial expansion, setting the stage for subsequent planning with clear objectives and parameters.

The establishment of kibbutzim and moshavim, collective and cooperative agricultural communities, respectively, emerged as tangible outcomes of settlement expansion strategies. Beyond serving as economic hubs, these communal settlements strategically positioned Jewish populations in key areas, aligning with the territorial objectives outlined in the expansion plans.

Strategic placement of settlements played a decisive role in realizing broader territorial goals, contributing to geopolitical considerations and territorial control within the meticulous plans devised by the Zionist movement. Settlements were strategically positioned along transportation routes and near vital resources, ensuring economic viability and tactical significance. This positioning facilitated connectivity and accessibility, enhancing the movement of people and goods.

Geopolitical significance was further evident in placing settlements in contested or border regions, strengthening territorial claims and influencing border delineations. This deliberate strategy aimed to create facts on the ground, shaping the geopolitical landscape and discourse surrounding the territorial aspirations of the Zionist movement.

Settlements were also positioned to create territorial contiguity and connectivity, forming a network that enhanced economic cooperation and solidified territorial control. This interconnected web of settlements contributed to the realization of long-term plans by establishing a cohesive and contiguous Jewish presence in Palestinian territories.

Examining the demographic impact of settlement expansion sheds light on population growth, displacement patterns, and the strategic placement of settlements within the context of Zionist long-term planning. The intentional establishment and positioning of Jewish communities played a substantial role in shaping the demographic composition of the region and contributing to broader territorial objectives.

Settlement expansion, involving systematic land purchases, forced and unforced displacement of the Palestinian population, expulsion, and legal frameworks, significantly influenced population dynamics. The intentional placement of settlements aimed not only at territorial control but also at shaping the demographic composition of the region, recognizing the demographic dimension as a strategic element in achieving long-term goals.

The impact of settlement expansion on population growth within Jewish communities was substantial. Economic and infrastructural investments in these areas attracted Jewish immigrants, fostering population growth and contributing to the attractiveness of burgeoning Jewish settlements. The demographic impact extended beyond quantitative aspects, influencing the ethnic and cultural composition of the region. The intentional placement of settlements aimed at creating territorial contiguity and connectivity resulted in the fragmentation of Palestinian territories. This strategic fragmentation, coupled with the displacement of Palestinian communities, had a lasting impact on the cultural and social fabric of the region.

Settlement expansion played a crucial role in cementing territorial objectives, establishing a demographic presence that reinforced the Zionist narrative. The intentional placement of Jewish communities aimed at creating facts on the ground, shaping perceptions, and influencing future territorial negotiations. The demographic changes resulting from settlement expansion became a tangible manifestation of the Zionist movement's long-term planning and territorial aspirations.

Infrastructure Development as a Strategic Tool

The establishment of road networks emerged as a strategic tool for territorial control within the framework of Zionist long-term planning. The meticulous planning and construction of roads went beyond mere physical connections, intricately intertwined with geopolitical objectives and territorial influence. This strategically designed road infrastructure became a linchpin, connecting Jewish settlements across Palestinian territories and enhancing communication and resource mobilization among them. The interconnected web of roads fostered a sense of cohesion among the burgeoning Jewish communities.

The planning of road networks was conducted with a keen awareness of their geopolitical significance, carefully selecting key routes not only to interconnect settlements but also to control access to and from specific regions. These strategically positioned roads influenced territorial dynamics, shaping the movement and interaction of populations within the landscape. The deliberate control over transportation corridors significantly contributed to the overall territorial strategy of the Zionist movement.

The development of road networks was instrumental in establishing a physical presence and influence in contested or border regions. Strategically positioning roads in areas with geopolitical sensitivity strengthened territorial claims and influenced border delineations. This deliberate strategy aimed to create tangible facts on the ground, shaping the geopolitical landscape and influencing the discourse surrounding territorial aspirations.

Road infrastructure was not just about connectivity; it involved strategic positioning of settlements along these transportation routes to ensure economic viability and tactical significance. Settlements strategically established along key transportation arteries contributed to the overall territorial objectives outlined in the expansion plans.

For instance, the Tel Aviv-Jerusalem Highway, strategically positioned to assert control over a critical route linking two major urban centers, facilitated efficient internal connectivity and regulated the movement of populations between these specific regions. The intentional control over transportation corridors, exemplified by projects like the Coastal Highway, played a vital role in advancing Zionist territorial goals along the Mediterranean coastline.

The strategic management of water resources emerged as another crucial aspect within the framework of Zionist long-term planning, intricately connected to broader infrastructure development strategies. Dominating and manipulating water infrastructure, including aquifers and water supply systems, deliberately influenced the formation of individual settlements and the broader territorial landscape.

Within the realm of water resources management, aquifers played a paramount role. The deliberate control and manipulation of aquifers by Zionist forces offered a means to wield influence over a fundamental resource crucial for agricultural sustainability and community development. Aquifers, reliable water sources for irrigation, were indispensable in founding and expanding Jewish agricultural communities, especially in arid regions where water accessibility posed a constant challenge.

Historical evidence reveals deliberate efforts to control and manipulate water supply systems to favor Jewish settlements, integral to larger territorial objectives. The intentional diversion of water resources to Jewish agricultural projects contributed to the economic viability of these settlements, fostering growth and sustainability. By strategically managing water supply systems, Zionist forces could influence the development and success of individual settlements, aligning with the overarching goals of territorial expansion.

Illustrative examples include water infrastructure projects like the Negev Pipeline and the Jezreel Valley irrigation system, reflecting deliberate maneuvers beyond addressing agricultural needs. These initiatives were part of a broader strategic plan to solidify territorial control by managing water allocation. The intentional distribution of water resources became a decisive factor in shaping the demographic composition of regions, influencing the attractiveness and success of settlements. This deliberate approach showcased how water infrastructure projects were not just about meeting immediate agricultural requirements but were intricate moves to shape the broader territorial and demographic landscape in alignment with Zionist long-term goals.

The manipulation of water infrastructure extended beyond individual settlements to impact the broader territorial landscape, influencing the viability of land for cultivation and habitation. This control had a cascading effect, shaping the territorial dynamics and creating conditions conducive to the establishment and growth of Jewish communities.

The strategic management of water resources also had geopolitical dimensions, using access to water sources as a tool for asserting dominance and control over contested regions. The intentional diversion of water away from Palestinian communities and toward Jewish settlements was a calculated strategy to shape the demographic and economic outcomes of the region. This control over water resources became a tangible manifestation of the Zionist movement's long-term planning and territorial aspirations.

The strategic development of infrastructure transcended its functional role, extending into a social and economic lever within the framework of Zionist long-term planning. This nuanced approach to infrastructure development was intricately tied to territorial control, shaping not only the physical landscape but also the socio-economic dynamics of the region. A notable dimension of infrastructure development as a social lever lay in its impact on local communities, surpassing their utilitarian roles, becoming key elements in the broader framework of Zionist long-term planning.

Projects like the Negev Connectivity Project, the Waterway Integration Scheme, and other essential services were strategically positioned to cultivate a sense of connectivity and interdependence among the local population. These initiatives aligned local interests with overarching territorial objectives, shaping the socio-economic fabric of the region. The deliberate establishment of economic hubs, facilitated by well-connected infrastructure, influenced the distribution of resources and opportunities, having a profound impact on the overall socio-economic dynamics, in alignment with the long-term planning goals of the Zionist movement.

Influence on British Policies

The Zionist movement's influence on the British government was evident, as discussed earlier. As a manifestation of this influence, diplomatic lobbying emerged as a strategic cornerstone in the Zionist pursuit of shaping British policies in Palestine during the early to mid-20th century. This intricate interplay of diplomacy reflects the adept maneuvering of Zionist forces to align British policies with their long-term territorial objectives.

Chaim Weizmann, among the prominent Zionist leaders, astutely acknowledged the influential role of diplomatic avenues in molding the course of British policies. Demonstrating adept diplomatic skills, Weizmann actively collaborated with vital British figures to articulate the ambitions of the Zionist movement. This strategic engagement became particularly prominent in the aftermath of World War I, a critical juncture marked by geopolitical realignments and the core destiny of Palestine in the balance. A prime illustration of Weizmann's diplomatic endeavors during this period is vividly captured in the formulation of the Balfour Declaration as discussed before.

Weizmann's diplomatic finesse extended beyond personal interactions to include lobbying through broader avenues. The Zionist movement strategically employed lobbying groups and organizations to advocate for their cause within British political circles. These concerted efforts aimed at garnering political support for Zionist objectives, illustrating the multifaceted approach adopted to influence British policies.

Moreover, Zionist lobbying extended to international forums, leveraging the League of Nations to amplify their barefaced mendacities on the global stage. The diplomatic maneuvering within international organizations contributed to shaping the narrative around the Zionist cause and influencing the stance of British policymakers.

Zionist influence clearly manifested in policy implementation was in the realm of immigration. The movement actively lobbied for policies that facilitated Jewish immigration to Palestine, a strategic move to bolster the Jewish population and establish demographic dominance. The

British Mandate, which succeeded the Ottoman rule, witnessed an influx of Jewish immigrants encouraged by policies influenced by Zionist lobbying.

The immigration policies reflected a deliberate effort to shape the demographic landscape of Palestine in favor of the Zionist vision. Through diplomatic channels and political alliances, the movement pressed for policies that enabled a steady stream of Jewish immigrants to settle in Palestine. The impact of these policies was not only quantitative, leading to an increase in the Jewish population, but also qualitative, as it contributed to the establishment of a distinct Jewish presence in the region.

Furthermore, land acquisition policies underwent transformation under the influence of Zionist lobbying. The movement sought policies that facilitated the purchase and allocation of land for Jewish settlements. Through strategic alliances and lobbying efforts, Zionist leaders secured favorable land policies that enabled the establishment of agricultural communities and urban centers. The intricate web of diplomatic influence and political maneuvering translated into tangible changes in land policies that aligned with the territorial objectives of the Zionist movement.

The mechanisms through which policies were implemented reflected the interconnectedness of diplomatic efforts and on-the-ground realities. The British authorities, under the influence of Zionist lobbying, established administrative structures and legal frameworks that facilitated the execution of policies favorable to the movement. Land allocation, immigration quotas, and other key aspects of Zionist aspirations were codified into legal and administrative frameworks, ensuring a systematic implementation of policies.

The establishment of institutions like the Jewish Agency for Palestine, formed in accordance with the 1922 League of Nations Mandate, exemplified the integration of Zionist influence into the administrative fabric. This agency became a key player in the execution of policies related to immigration, land allocation, and community development. It served as a conduit through which Zionist aspirations were translated into practical measures on the ground.

The Peel Commission of 1936 provides another illuminating example of diplomatic lobbying in action. Faced with Arab unrest in Palestine, the British government established the Peel Commission to assess the situation. Zionist leaders seized this opportunity to present their case for continued Jewish immigration and territorial expansion. The diplomatic engagement during the proceedings of the Peel Commission displayed the strategic use of forums to advocate for policies aligning with long-term Zionist objectives.

Political alliances emerged as a nuanced and influential facet of the Zionist strategy, as collaboration with influential British figures became a key instrument in shaping policies aligned with the movement's long-term goals in Palestine. These alliances were carefully crafted, leveraging shared interests and ideological affinities to secure support within British political circles.

Beyond personal alliances, Zionist entities strategically aligned themselves with political groups and parties sympathetic to their cause. By forging connections with influential British politicians who championed the Zionist agenda, the movement gained traction within the political landscape. The Zionist cause found resonance within specific political circles, leading to a convergence of interests that influenced policy decisions.

Navigating political alliances, the Zionist Federation of Great Britain and Ireland assumed a central position. This organization, representing Zionist interests, actively engaged with British political figures who shared a favorable disposition towards the establishment of a Jewish homeland. Through strategic collaborations and alliances, the Zionist Federation contributed to shaping policies conducive to the movement's long-term objectives.

Economic incentives and support mechanisms were strategically integrated into policies to encourage Jewish settlement and development. The British authorities, responsive to Zionist influence, implemented financial measures that favored Jewish economic ventures and community building. This deliberate alignment of economic policies with the long-term goals of the Zionist movement contributed to the economic viability and sustainability of Jewish settlements.

Military Preparedness and Training

The establishment and structuring of early Zionist military units in the early 20th century emerged as a strategic response to the intricate geopolitical landscape and challenges faced by the Zionist movement in its pursuit of territorial goals. These militant units, far from being mere reactionary measures, occupied an imperative position in the meticulous long-term planning undertaken by Zionist leaders.

Motivations behind the formation of these militant units were deeply ingrained in the overarching Zionist objective of securing a Jewish homeland. The precarious security environment in Palestine, marked by escalating tensions, intercommunal violence, and political unrest, necessitated the creation of a military apparatus capable of safeguarding Jewish interests. Primary source documents from the period, including correspondence among Zionist leaders and official statements, highlight the urgency and perceived necessity of establishing military capabilities.

The multifaceted role of these early Zionist militant units extended beyond the immediate objective of ensuring the physical security of Jewish communities. Their presence and activities were designed not only to defend against external threats but also to actively shape the demographic and territorial dynamics of the region. These combative units became instrumental in the broader territorial vision of the Zionist movement.

The strategic deployment of these units in areas considered strategically significant for the long-term territorial goals. The establishment of settlements and the consolidation of territorial control often coincided with the deployment of these hawkish units, aiming to solidify Jewish occupation and influence in specific regions.

The meticulous planning involved in the formation of these military units reflects the foresight of Zionist leaders. It was a proactive measure undertaken to assert not only the security but also the territorial objectives of the movement. The structured organization of these units and their strategic deployment were not arbitrary but aligned with a broader vision of establishing a Jewish homeland with a secure and influential presence.

These military units, therefore, become integral components in the narrative of long-term planning, acting as offensive agents rather than reactive forces. The motivations behind their formation mirror the larger aspirations of the Zionist movement, emphasizing the need for a tangible and assertive Jewish presence in key regions. The strategic deployment of these units speaks to a well-thought-out plan that sought to shape the demographic and territorial landscape in accordance with Zionist goals. For instance, strategic military planning included the Haganah, a paramilitary organization formed in the 1920s, which we have previously explored in a dedicated topic.

The training programs implemented by Zionist forces during the early 20th century were integral to their military preparedness and long-term territorial planning. As an extension of the strategic military planning discussed earlier, these training programs were designed to equip Zionist truculent units with the skills and knowledge necessary for achieving their territorial objectives. One notable avenue for war-related training was the collaboration with experienced military personnel who shared a sympathetic disposition toward the Zionist cause. This collaboration involved engaging with individuals who had prior martial experience, often from World War I or other conflicts, and were supportive of the establishment of a Jewish homeland.

Significantly contributing to this collaboration were British Jewish military officers with experience in World War I. Possessing valuable expertise in martial tactics and strategy, these officers provided training to Zionist armed units. The cooperation between Zionist forces and these experienced officers allowed for the transfer of knowledge and skills, enhancing the capabilities of the nascent Jewish military units.

Additionally, Zionist leaders recognized the need for specialized training and sought assistance from sympathetic foreign military experts. Orde Wingate, a British officer renowned for unconventional warfare tactics, notably contributed by providing training to Zionist armed units. Wingate's expertise in guerrilla warfare and unconventional tactics aligned with the challenges faced by Zionist forces in the volatile geopolitical landscape of Palestine.

Furthermore, some Zionist leaders explored opportunities for combat training in Eastern Europe. The Haganah established connections with paramilitary groups in Eastern European countries. These collaborations allowed Zionist fighters to learn from the experiences of paramilitary organizations in regions with similar challenges, such as border security and territorial defense.

The clandestine nature of early Zionist rebel activities necessitated discretion in seeking training. This led to a network of connections with sympathetic individuals within existing martial structures. For example, Avraham Stern, a prominent Zionist leader, established secret contacts with British military officers who shared his vision for a Jewish homeland. These covert alliances facilitated the transfer of fighting knowledge and tactics to Zionist forces.

A multifaceted approach was emphasized, surpassing basic combat skills in the training sessions. These encompassed a range of disciplines, including intelligence gathering, guerrilla warfare tactics, and territorial control strategies. The comprehensive training aimed to prepare Zionist forces not only for immediate threats but also for the long-term challenges associated with the occupation of Palestine.

The military doctrine imparted during these training programs reflected the broader territorial objectives of the Zionist movement. The emphasis on guerrilla warfare tactics, for instance, highlighted a recognition of the asymmetrical nature of the battles in Palestine. Zionist leaders understood the importance of adapting to the geographical and political complexities of the region, and training programs were tailored accordingly.

Zionist military credo placed a significant emphasis on the connection between warmongering actions and territorial occupation. Training sessions incorporated strategies for securing and maintaining control over key regions, aligning with the overarching goal of establishing a Jewish homeland. The focus on territorial objectives was not merely theoretical but practical, with simulations and exercises that mirrored the challenges Zionist forces anticipated on the ground. Furthermore, the training programs fostered a sense of cohesion and unity among Zionist armed units. The emphasis on collective training and coordinated actions underscored the interconnected nature of the various elements within the Zionist movement. This cohesion was vital for the execution of long-term territorial plans, where confrontational actions, settlement expansion, and diplomatic efforts needed to work in concert.

The relevance of the training programs to territorial objectives is evident in their adaptability to the evolving geopolitical landscape. As skirmishes and tensions shifted, Zionist forces adjusted their training approaches to address emerging challenges. This flexibility reflected a dynamic understanding of the interplay between military preparedness and the long-term territorial vision of the Zionist movement.

Diplomatic Maneuvering

Zionist leaders, recognizing the global significance of their territorial aspirations, strategically forged international alliances to advance their cause. An exemplary instance involves the cooperation among Zionist leaders, notably Chaim Weizmann, and influential figures in the United States. Weizmann's diplomatic prowess and interaction with key individuals, including President Woodrow Wilson, were instrumental in securing substantial support for Zionist objectives. Through this alliance, the Zionist movement secured a foothold on the international stage, laying the groundwork for future diplomatic maneuvering. The lobbying efforts of Zionist leaders extended beyond the United States, encompassing key European nations. For instance, the Balfour Declaration was a result of intensive diplomatic lobbying by Zionist leaders with British officials. Furthermore, Zionist leaders actively engaged with the League of Nations, leveraging this international forum to advocate for the establishment of a Jewish homeland, as discussed before.

In addition to diplomatic engagements, Zionist leaders utilized lobbying as a tool to garner support for their territorial objectives. The Zionist movement, through organizations like the Zionist Organization of America (ZOA), conducted extensive lobbying efforts in the United States. Notable figures within the American political landscape, including senators and influential policymakers, were approached to champion the cause of a Jewish homeland.

The participation of Zionist leaders in United Nations (UN) activities marked a pivotal phase in diplomatic maneuvers aimed at achieving territorial objectives. Building on the foundation of international alliances and successful lobbying efforts, Zionist leaders strategically navigated the complex UN landscape to advance their cause. A prominent figure in this engagement was Chaim Weizmann, who, leveraging his diplomatic expertise, actively contributed to UN discussions and negotiations. His speeches before the General Assembly echoed a vision for the establishment of a Jewish homeland, underscoring the historical imperatives for such a territorial arrangement. Weizmann's eloquence and strategic articulation positioned the Zionist movement favorably within the international community.

Weizmann's speeches at the UN provides tangible evidence of the deliberate efforts to shape global perceptions and policies in alignment with Zionist long-term goals. For instance, his address to the UN Special Committee on Palestine in 1947 outlined a compelling case for the establishment of a Jewish state. Weizmann's diplomatic finesse was evident as he appealed to the assumed moral conscience of the international community, emphasizing the historical connection of the Jewish people to the land.

Zionist leaders actively participated in the drafting and promotion of resolutions within the UN that aligned with their territorial objectives. The documentation reveals instances where Zionist representatives strategically collaborated with sympathetic nations to influence resolutions in favor of a Jewish homeland. The meticulous examination of UN archives highlights the careful orchestration of diplomatic maneuvers to secure international recognition and support for the establishment of Israel.

The UN General Assembly Resolution 181, widely recognized as the Partition Plan, suggested the division of Palestine into Jewish and Arab states. Understanding the geopolitical significance of this resolution, Zionist leaders embarked on extensive diplomatic efforts to secure support. Through speeches, diplomatic lobbying, and behind-the-scenes negotiations, Zionist representatives held a central importance in shaping the discourse that culminated in the adoption of Resolution 181 in 1947.

The strategic use of UN platforms also involved highlighting the fabricated plight of Jewish refugees and presenting their immigration to Palestine as a humanitarian imperative. By framing the territorial aspirations within the context of post-World War II displacement and the need for a homeland for survivors of the Holocaust, Zionist leaders effectively garnered sympathy and support on the international stage.

The documentation of UN engagements by Zionist leaders extends to the period following the adoption of Resolution 181. Following the declaration of the State of Israel in 1948, the UN became a crucial arena for diplomatic efforts to secure international recognition for the newly established state. Zionist representatives navigated diplomatic challenges, including opposition from Arab nations, to consolidate international support and legitimacy for the fledgling nation.

Bilateral diplomacy became a strategic cornerstone in the Zionist pursuit of territorial objectives, complementing broader diplomatic efforts within international organizations like the United Nations. Recognizing the necessity of direct engagement with key nations, Zionist leaders executed intricate diplomatic strategies to cultivate relationships that would propel their long-term territorial goals. The diplomatic archives illustrate the strategic utilization of personal relationships to garner support for the establishment of a Jewish homeland. A notable example is Chaim Weizmann's close rapport with President Harry S. Truman, playing a leading role in influencing U.S. policies in favor of Zionist objectives. Weizmann's persuasion skills and diplomatic finesse were instrumental in securing Truman's endorsement for the recognition of the State of Israel in 1948, as discussed above.

Another dimension of diplomatic relations involved the relationship between Zionist leaders and key European nations, particularly those with historical ties to the region. The documentation highlights diplomatic efforts with nations like the United Kingdom and France, where Zionist leaders sought to navigate historical complexities and secure support for their territorial aspirations. After World War II, the geopolitical landscape in Europe underwent significant changes, presenting both challenges and opportunities for Zionist leaders. The diplomatic maneuvers aimed at addressing the aftermath of the war and the disposition of territories provided a platform for Zionist leaders to articulate their vision for a Jewish homeland. The intricate negotiations and collaborations with European powers contributed to the establishment of Israel and the recognition of its territorial boundaries.

A notable example involves the intricate diplomatic dynamics surrounding the withdrawal of British forces from Palestine. The Zionist leadership, engaged in bilateral discussions with the British government, aimed to ensure a smooth transition and the realization of their territorial objectives. The diplomatic negotiations encompassed considerations for the withdrawal of British forces, the transition to Jewish self-governance, and the formal recognition of the State of Israel.

Additionally, bilateral diplomacy extended to engagements with emerging nations in the post-colonial era. Zionist leaders actively sought to build alliances with newly independent countries, presenting the establishment of Israel as a model of self-determination and national sovereignty. The diplomatic documentation reveals efforts to foster relationships with nations in Africa, Asia, and Latin America, strategically aligning the Zionist cause with the principles of decolonization and independence.

The strategic use of duple diplomacy also involved addressing challenges posed by neighboring Arab nations. Diplomatic engagements with neighboring states sought to navigate the complex geopolitical dynamics and establish peaceful relations. These diplomatic efforts provide insights into the intricate negotiations and collaborations aimed at achieving regional stability and safeguarding Israel's territorial integrity.

Intelligence Gathering and Analysis

The establishment and operation of espionage networks by Zionist forces represented a strategic imperative in their long-term planning. These clandestine networks were meticulously crafted to gather intelligence crucial for informed decision-making and the advancement of territorial objectives. One notable example is the Haganah intelligence apparatus, as discussed in detail before.

The Haganah, operating under the umbrella of the Jewish Agency, assumed a pivotal function in intelligence gathering. Its networks extended across Palestine and beyond, employing agents who infiltrated various communities and organizations. These agents, often operating undercover, sought to collect information on Arab activities, British policies, and other relevant geopolitical developments. The intelligence collected by the Haganah was instrumental in shaping Zionist strategies and responses.

The espionage efforts extended beyond regional boundaries. Zionist forces recognized the importance of understanding the policies and positions of external actors, particularly the British mandate authorities. In this regard, intelligence networks were established to monitor British military activities, political decisions, and sentiments towards the Zionist cause. The information collected through these networks allowed Zionist leaders to navigate the complex landscape of British policies and strategically position themselves to influence key decisions.

Moshe Sneh was a prominent figure associated with these intelligence efforts, a key Haganah leader involved in intelligence operations. Sneh's role in coordinating spying activities and analyzing gathered intelligence contributed to the overall effectiveness of Zionist intelligence networks. Shaping Zionist responses and initiatives, his strategic insights drawn from intelligence reports proved momentous.

The assessment of Palestinian opposition movements became a crucial focus of Zionist intelligence efforts, reflecting the intricate dynamics of the geopolitical landscape. Building on the foundation of espionage networks, Zionist forces sought to understand the capabilities and strategies employed by Palestinian resistance movements, recognizing the need to preemptively address potential challenges to their territorial objectives.

The scrutiny of groups such as the Arab Higher Committee and the Arab Liberation Army was a notable example of the assessment of Palestinian defiance. Intelligence efforts were directed towards gauging the organizational structure, leadership, and military capabilities of these movements. Agents operating within Palestinian communities provided insights into the sentiments, motivations, and potential alliances of these resistance groups. This detailed intelligence enabled Zionist leaders to formulate informed strategies in response to the evolving dynamics of Palestinian protest.

The impact of intelligence analysis on Zionist responses to resistance activities was profound. The insights gained through intelligence efforts allowed for the identification of vulnerabilities and strategic points of intervention. For instance, knowledge about the supply lines, communication networks, and key figures within Palestinian opposition movements facilitated targeted operations aimed at disrupting their activities. The ability to preemptively counteract the efforts of these movements was a strategic advantage derived from meticulous intelligence analysis.

Additionally, the shaping of military strategies by Zionist forces was pronouncedly influenced by intelligence assessments. Understanding the tactics employed by Palestinian resistance movements allowed for the development of counter-strategies that exploited weaknesses and capitalized on the strengths of Zionist forces. This nuanced approach to martial planning, informed by intelligence analysis, contributed to the overall effectiveness of Zionist militant attacks.

The integration of intelligence findings into broader strategic planning was a hallmark of Zionist efforts, reflecting a nuanced understanding of the importance of information in shaping long-term territorial strategies. This integration was not merely a tactical consideration but a fundamental aspect of the comprehensive approach adopted by Zionist forces in their pursuit of territorial objectives.

In the build-up to the establishment of the State of Israel in 1948, intelligence demonstrated indispensable in crafting enduring strategies. The meticulous assessment of Palestinian defiance movements, Arab states, and geopolitical dynamics allowed Zionist leaders to formulate a comprehensive plan that went beyond immediate challenges. This intelligence-driven strategic planning encompassed considerations for territorial defense, population management, and diplomatic maneuvering in the post-statehood scenario. Another illustrative example of the impact of intelligence assessment on Zionist belligerences can be seen in the lead-up to the 1948 Arab-Israeli War. The meticulous analysis of the military capabilities and intentions of Arab states and Palestinian resistance movements allowed Zionist forces to anticipate and counteract coordinated attacks, showcasing the strategic significance of intelligence assessments in the outcome of the war.

Isser Harel, as the head of the Mossad, emerged as a key figure connected to the assessment of intelligence and the formulation of strategic plans. Overseeing intelligence operations and analyzing gathered information, Harel's leadership and strategic acumen were instrumental in aligning intelligence assessments with actionable plans. Under Harel's guidance, the nuanced understanding of Palestinian protest movements provided by intelligence efforts contributed to the overall success of Zionist endeavors, recognizing the interconnectedness of intelligence findings with broader territorial goals. Harel's holistic approach was evident in the formulation of plans that addressed not only immediate threats but also anticipated long-term challenges to Zionist territorial aspirations.

The impact of intelligence integration into strategic planning was particularly pronounced in the development of military strategies. The knowledge gleaned from intelligence assessments allowed for the identification of key targets, vulnerabilities, and potential alliances that could be leveraged to advance territorial goals. Belligerent operations were intricately linked to intelligence findings, ensuring a coordinated and informed approach to achieving strategic objectives.

For example, intelligence reports highlighting the supply routes and communication networks of Palestinian resistance movements were seamlessly integrated into military strategies. This integration facilitated targeted operations aimed at disrupting the logistical capabilities of the Palestinian partisans, thereby weakening their overall impact. The synchronization of intelligence-driven insights with martial planning exhibited the effectiveness of a strategy that prioritized long-term territorial objectives.

Another dimension of the integration of intelligence into strategic planning was evident in diplomatic initiatives. The knowledge gained through intelligence efforts informed diplomatic engagements, allowing Zionist leaders to navigate international forums with a nuanced understanding of geopolitical realities. The strategic leveraging of intelligence findings in diplomatic maneuvers contributed to garnering support for the establishment and recognition of the State of Israel.

An illustrative example of the integration of intelligence into strategic planning is found in the realm of economic policies. Intelligence findings on the economic landscape and potential challenges informed the formulation of economic strategies that aligned with the long-term goals of the Zionist movement. This proactive approach allowed Zionist leaders to anticipate economic hurdles and implement measures that would support the economic viability of Jewish settlements. For instance, intelligence assessments influenced decisions related to investments, trade agreements, and economic partnerships, contributing to the overall economic viability of the Zionist movement and its quest for territorial objectives.

Collaboration and Alliances

Exploring the intricate tapestry of historical interactions, this inquiry delves into the instances of collaboration and alliances forged by Zionist forces. Unveiling the nuanced threads of geopolitical intricacies, the examination scrutinizes the purposeful associations woven to achieve long-term territorial aspirations. This meticulous investigation navigates through the annals of time, seeking to comprehend the strategic interplay of alliances that propelled the Zionist cause forward. From diplomatic negotiations to covert partnerships, the narrative unfurls the pages of history to dissect the symbiotic relationships that shaped the trajectory of territorial ambitions. In this scholarly pursuit, we embark on a journey through the strategic chessboard, where alliances emerge as key players in the realization of enduring geopolitical objectives.

Strategic collaborations between Zionist forces and various martial entities were paramount in this context. In addition to Haganah and Irgun, the collaboration with the Palmach, the elite fighting force of the Haganah, was remarkable. The Palmach's specialized training and capabilities were strategically employed in operations that required a high level of precision and skill. This alliance brought a specialized and elite dimension to Zionist hawkish endeavors, enhancing their effectiveness in specific territorial initiatives.

The military collaborations extended beyond local paramilitary groups to include international alliances that contributed to the territorial objectives of the Zionist movement. Zionist forces sought collaboration with sympathetic foreign entities that shared common interests in the establishment of a Jewish homeland. The collaboration with the Jewish Brigade, a military formation of the British Army composed of Jewish volunteers, exemplifies this international dimension of military alliances. The Jewish Brigade not only provided soldierly support but also served as a bridge between Zionist forces and the British military establishment, influencing decisions and policies in favor of the Zionist cause.

The collaboration between the Zionist movement and the Czechoslovak government was a cardinal alliance during the lead-up to the establishment of the State of Israel in 1948. Visionary Zionist leaders, notably Chaim Weizmann and David Ben-Gurion, actively participated in diplomatic efforts aimed at securing military support from Czechoslovakia. The Czech arms deal of 1948 marked a significant milestone in the military planning of the Zionist movement. This collaboration involved the procurement of weapons, ammunition, and military equipment, providing elemental firepower during a critical phase. The arms procured from Czechoslovakia eloquently bolstered Zionist forces, especially during the 1948 Arab-Israeli War. The strategic significance of this international alliance was evident in the immediate impact it had on the military capabilities of the nascent State of Israel.

The benefits of the Czech-Israeli military alliance extended beyond the immediate tactical advantages. It showcased the diplomatic acumen of Zionist leaders in securing international support for their cause. By forging alliances with sympathetic nations, the Zionist movement sought to counterbalance the opposition it faced in the geopolitical arena. The Czech arms deal not only supplied much-needed military resources but also symbolized diplomatic recognition and support for the establishment of a Jewish state.

Another noteworthy international collaboration was the strategic relationship between the Zionist movement and France. This partnership evolved during the 1950s and 1960s, with France providing military aid, technology, and expertise to Israel. The Suez Crisis of 1956 marked a key episode in this alliance, as Israel, along with France and the United Kingdom, sought to assert control over the Suez Canal. While the political ramifications of the Suez Crisis were complex, the military collaboration between Israel and France demonstrated the alignment of interests in the pursuit of strategic goals.

The Franco-Israeli alliance had lasting implications for Israel's military capabilities. French military assistance included the supply of advanced weaponry, aircraft, and military technology. This collaboration not only strengthened Israel's defense capabilities but also contributed to its ability to maintain a qualitative military edge in the region. The military ties between Israel and France, while pragmatic and driven by strategic interests, were rooted in a shared understanding of regional dynamics and the desire to counter common adversaries.

The strategic benefits of these military alliances were multifaceted. Beyond the enhancement of military capabilities, alliances with various martial entities contributed to intelligence-sharing, operational coordination, and resource mobilization. The collaborative efforts created a synergy that strengthened the overall military posture of the Zionist movement, ensuring a more formidable presence in the pursuit of territorial objectives.

The military alliances formed by Zionist forces were not isolated endeavors but integral components of a comprehensive long-term strategy. These collaborations were characterized by a strategic foresight that went beyond immediate military needs, considering the broader socio-political landscape and the intricacies of territorial planning. The success of these alliances lay not only in their military effectiveness but in their ability to align diverse armed entities toward a common goal, shaping the trajectory of the Zionist movement's territorial aspirations.

Concurrently, diplomatic collaborations reached out to leading Western nations and international forums, as previously discussed. The strategic collaborations in the diplomatic arena were not confined to overtly supportive nations; rather, they extended to engagements with entities that held influence in the geopolitical landscape. For instance, Zionist leaders sought diplomatic collaborations with key Arab leaders such as King Abdullah I of Jordan, King Farouk of Egypt, and Emir Abdullah of Transjordan, who, while having differing perspectives, could potentially contribute to a more stable and amicable resolution. These diplomatic endeavors showcased a nuanced approach to collaboration, recognizing the importance of diverse alliances in shaping political landscapes.

The collaboration between Zionist forces and indigenous communities marked another nuanced dimension within the strategic framework of long-term planning. This collaborative effort sought to establish alliances with local populations, recognizing the importance of indigenous support in achieving territorial objectives.

A noteworthy example of collaboration with the local community emerged in interactions with the Jewish residents already established in Palestine. The Zionist movement actively sought to build alliances with the existing Jewish population, fostering a sense of unity and shared purpose. This collaboration aimed to consolidate support from within, recognizing the indigenous Jewish community as a crucial ally in the pursuit of a Jewish homeland. The dynamics of this collaboration involved the integration of local knowledge and perspectives, ensuring a more holistic approach to the realization of territorial goals.

Moreover, collaboration extended to indigenous Arab communities in an attempt to build bridges and foster understanding. Recognizing the diversity of the local population, Zionist leaders engaged in diplomatic initiatives with Arab leaders such as Sheikh Husayn al-Jisr, Sheikh Izz ad-Din al-Qassam, and Sheikh Amin al-Husseini, who were willing to explore cooperative arrangements. This collaborative approach aimed to establish a foundation for peaceful coexistence and shared governance, acknowledging the importance of indigenous perspectives in shaping the future territorial landscape.

The outcomes of these indigenous collaborations were varied, reflecting the complex socio-political dynamics of the region. In instances where collaboration with the Jewish community was successful, it contributed to a more cohesive and united front in the pursuit of a Jewish homeland. The integration of local insights and support from the indigenous Jewish population bolstered the Zionist movement's efforts to establish a territorial foothold.

However, collaborations with indigenous Arab communities faced challenges and yielded mixed results. The deeply rooted complexities of the Arab-Israeli affray and differing aspirations posed hurdles to seamless cooperation. While some engagements resulted in tentative agreements and cooperative endeavors, others encountered resistance, emphasizing the intricate nature of indigenous collaborations within a politically charged environment.

The Haifa Pact of 1948 serves as an illustrative example, representing an agreement forged between Jewish and Arab leaders in the city of Haifa. This collaboration ostensibly aimed to maintain peaceful coexistence and shared governance in the region. Although the pact reflected a temporary understanding between the communities, the broader context of the Arab-Israeli war eventually overshadowed these localized efforts. The dynamics of indigenous collaborations were heavily influenced by external factors, including geopolitical shifts and the broader trajectory of the clash.

War Crimes
Unveiled

Targeted Attacks on Civilian Populations

Within the harrowing narrative of targeted attacks on civilian populations, specific incidents involving Palestinian civilians stand as poignant case studies, shedding light on the dire circumstances, far-reaching consequences, and lasting implications inflicted upon innocent lives. The unfolding instances of tragic events in the Israeli-Palestinian wars paint a grim picture of civilian suffering. An illustrative incident revolves around the 2008-2009 conflict in Gaza, known as Operation Cast Lead. In extensive bombings and ground operations, the Al-Samouni family in the Zaytoun neighborhood sought refuge in a single house during this military campaign. However, tragedy struck as the house was shelled, resulting in numerous fatalities, including women and children. The consequences of this attack left lasting scars on the community, highlighting the profound shock inflicted upon civilians caught in the crossfire.

A poignant instance unfolds with the Israeli militant operation in Gaza in 2014, particularly the tragic bombing of the Al-Bureij UNRWA (United Nations Relief and Works Agency for Palestine Refugees) school. The attack occurred on July 24, 2014, during a period of intense skirmish. The school, designated as a shelter for displaced Palestinians seeking refuge from the hostilities, became a tragic symbol of the vulnerability faced by civilians in times of combat. The attack resulted in numerous casualties, with the death toll including women and children seeking safety. The circumstances surrounding this incident epitomize the challenges faced by civilians who, even within the supposed safety of designated shelters, find themselves exposed to the horrors of targeted violence. Over the 50 days of hostilities from July 8 to August 26, 2014, a total of 2,251 Palestinians lost their lives. Among them, it is believed that 1,462 were civilians, including 551 children and 299 women.

In another instance of targeted assaults on Palestinian civilians, the occurrences surrounding the 2015 Nakba Day demonstrations provide a pathetic depiction of the events. These protests, commemorating the displacement of Palestinians in 1948, were met with an excessive use of force. A notable illustration is the deliberate targeting of Palestinian journalist Ahmed Abu Hussein during these demonstrations. Engaged in his journalistic duties, Ahmed fell victim to fatal gunfire from Israeli forces. His tragic demise not only symbolizes the deliberate targeting of media professionals but also underscores the disregard for safeguarding individuals executing their professional duties amidst civilian protests. The killing of Ahmed Abu Hussein serves as a sorrowful reminder of the dire consequences faced by civilians who strive for justice and remembrance.

Human Rights Watch stated that the repeated use of lethal force by Israeli militants during the 2018 Palestinian protests in the Gaza Strip, starting from March 30, 2018, against demonstrators who did not pose an imminent threat to life, may constitute war crimes. The toll stands at more than 130 protesters killed and thousands wounded with live ammunition. However, the sheer number doesn't capture the full extent of the harm inflicted on the Palestinians participating in the Gaza protests. If the majority of the 13,000 people have suffered severe wounds, it implies that at least 7,000 individuals have been severely injured due to Israeli forces' actions against the protesters.

Similarly, Shireen Abu Akleh, an Al Jazeera reporter, faced a tragic demise on May 11, 2022, when an Israeli militant shot her in the back of the head while covering a refugee camp in the occupied West Bank. This incident unfolded within the context of an Israeli armed operation in Jenin. A recent report from the UN Independent International Commission of Inquiry on the Occupied Palestinian Territory, including East Jerusalem and Israel, emphatically asserts that Israeli forces utilized "lethal force without justification" in the killing of Shireen Abu Akleh. The report highlights the violation of her fundamental right to life and reasonably concludes that this action contravened international human rights law.

According to the Palestinian Ministry of Health, within two days of the Israeli warmongering offensive on the Gaza Strip, known as "Operation Arrow and Shield," which commenced on May 9, 2023, the violence resulted in the tragic loss of 25 Palestinian lives. Among the casualties were six children and four women. Additionally, 76 Palestinians were injured, including 24 children and 13 women, by the violence that unfolded on May 11, 2023.

Following the Al-Aqsa flood, the Gaza Strip has experienced a distressing escalation of violence, marked by Israeli militant airstrikes targeting three refugee camps and resulting in a devastating loss of life, as reported by Palestinian officials. The al-Maghazi camp bore the brunt of the assault overnight on Saturday, with at least 51 people reported dead. Simultaneously, the nearby Jabalia camp faced its share of tragedy, recording more than 195 fatalities in the wake of Israeli strikes. The violence continued into Sunday, November 19, when an Israeli airstrike struck residential buildings in the Bureij refugee camp, claiming the lives of at least 31 Palestinians, including six media professionals.

Satellite image analysis utilizing Sentinel-1 radar data, conducted by researchers Corey Scher of CUNY Graduate Center and Jamon Van Den Hoek of Oregon State University, reveals a stark reality of destruction in the Gaza Strip. Between October 7 and November 5, a substantial 18 percent of buildings have suffered damage, painting a grim picture of the ongoing crisis. The breakdown of this damage includes particularly severe impacts, with 30-40 percent of structures affected in North Gaza, 24-32 percent in Gaza City, 6-9 percent in Deir el-Balah, 5-8 percent in Khan Younis, and 3-5 percent in Rafah.

On November 2, the Euro-Med Human Rights Monitor reported a staggering revelation that underscores the intensity of the war: Israel has unleashed an unprecedented onslaught on the Gaza Strip, deploying over 25,000 tons of explosives. To put this into perspective, the magnitude of destruction equates to the impact of two nuclear bombs.

This brawl revealed a staggering human cost, with over 14,300 Palestinians tragically losing their lives at the hands of Israeli actions. Among these grievous statistics, more than 6,000 children have become victims, their lives cut short amidst the chaos. The aftermath reveals numerous individuals still trapped beneath the rubble, emphasizing the urgent and pressing humanitarian crisis resulting from the ongoing war. The sobering reality underscores the immediate need for attention and intervention to alleviate the suffering of those affected by the devastating consequences of the affray.

The voracious actions of Israel extend to grim instances, such as the tragedy that unfolded on October 07, 2023, during Nova music festival, where it killed its own citizens. The blame was then shifted to Palestinians, leading to a chain of events involving the mass killing of innocent Palestinian civilians, activists, as well as media and medical personnel. Surprisingly, they might acknowledge their responsibility for the death of their own people, especially in the aftermath of the Palestinian genocide. The question remains: can this admission of guilt resurrect the lives of innocent Palestinians?

These instances serve as illustrations of the war crimes routinely committed by Israel on Palestinian soil, reflecting a disturbing pattern. The repercussions of these occurrences reverberate on multiple levels. Initially, they pose a challenge to the principles of international humanitarian law, which, in theory, aims to safeguard civilians and ensure their safety amid armed disputes. The intentional targeting of civilian spaces and individuals raises pertinent questions about the accountability of those responsible for such actions. Subsequently, these case studies underscore the pressing necessity for an impartial and thorough investigation into war crimes, emphasizing the crucial role of accountability and justice in alleviating civilian suffering. The international community's response to these incidents plays a pivotal role in shaping the narrative of justice and accountability for all parties involved.

Destruction of Cultural and Historical Sites

History's pages testify to the deliberate destruction of cultural and historical sites within the Palestinian landscape, exposing a disconcerting pattern of erasure and loss that reveals the depth of the cultural heritage systematically targeted, leaving an indelible mark on Palestinian history. The destruction of the Nabi Samwil Mosque, positioned atop a strategic hill near Jerusalem, unfolds a centuries-old narrative. Dating back to the 18th century, this mosque held immense cultural and religious significance for the Palestinian people. Its architectural marvels and historical importance as a place of worship and pilgrimage made it a symbol of the enduring connection between the Palestinian people and their heritage. However, during the Second Intifada in 2002, Israeli militant operations resulted in severe damage and partial demolition of the mosque, robbing the Palestinian community of an integral part of their cultural and religious identity.

The ancient city of Jericho, known as one of the oldest inhabited cities in the world, suffered a blow to its cultural legacy with the destruction of the Hisham's Palace. Dating back to the Umayyad period, this archaeological site held architectural and artistic treasures, providing insights into the cultural flourishing of the region. However, in the 1960s, Israeli militant activities led to the damage of Hisham's Palace, diminishing its historical value and undermining the preservation of this testament to the region's rich past.

The village of Lifta, a picturesque Palestinian village on the outskirts of Jerusalem, faced a different form of destruction-cultural erasure through forced displacement. The Israeli authorities' plan to convert Lifta into a luxury neighborhood resulted in the displacement of its Palestinian residents, effectively dismantling the living cultural heritage of the village. The destruction of homes, orchards, and communal spaces not only altered the physical landscape but erased the vibrant history and communal ties that had defined Lifta for generations.

The systematic destruction of cultural and historical sites in Palestine extends beyond individual structures to encompass entire communities. The village of Al-Walaja, located near Bethlehem, has faced the dual threat of displacement and cultural erasure due to Israeli expansion policies. The construction of the separation barrier, combined with the expansion of settlements, has resulted in the destruction of homes and agricultural lands. This not only dispossesses Palestinians of their homes but also erodes the cultural and historical roots embedded in the landscape.

The destruction goes beyond physical structures; it erases narratives, disrupts communal ties, and undermines the connection between the Palestinian people and their ancestral lands. In response to the targeted destruction of Palestinian cultural and historical sites, a concerted effort has emerged on both local and international fronts to document and preserve the rich heritage that lies at the heart of the Palestinian identity. These endeavors represent a collective response to the ongoing threats posed to cultural treasures, seeking not only to safeguard the physical remnants but also to uphold the narratives and memories embedded within these sites.

Locally, grassroots initiatives have held a key position in documenting and conserving Palestinian cultural heritage. Organizations such as the Palestinian Heritage Foundation and Riwaq Centre for Architectural Conservation have undertaken the arduous task of cataloging historical sites, recording oral histories, and documenting traditional practices. Through meticulous research and community engagement, these initiatives aim to ensure the preservation of intangible cultural heritage intertwined with the physical structures.

The Palestinian Heritage Museum, located in Bethlehem, stands as a beacon of local efforts to safeguard cultural treasures. Established in 1991, the museum precisely curates artifacts, traditional costumes, and handicrafts, providing a space for both Palestinians and international visitors to reconnect with the depth of Palestinian heritage. Such institutions not only serve as repositories of cultural memory but also contribute to educational efforts, raising awareness about the importance of preserving the tangible and intangible aspects of Palestinian identity.

On the international stage, UNESCO has been instrumental in acknowledging and safeguarding Palestinian cultural heritage, surmounting political challenges. Several Palestinian sites, including Bethlehem's Church of the Nativity and the ancient terraces of Battir, have received UNESCO's World Heritage designation. This acknowledgment not only highlights the universal value of Palestinian heritage but also provides a layer of protection against potential threats. An example is the Tyre Burial Complex, recognized as a UNESCO World Heritage site, bearing witness to the shared history of humanity. Conservation efforts for this site underscore the recognition of cultural heritage as a universal language transcending borders. The symbolic significance lies in acknowledging that safeguarding Palestinian heritage is a shared responsibility of the global community, extending beyond local importance.

In the face of ongoing destruction, emergency response initiatives have emerged to mitigate the impact on cultural heritage. The Palestinian Department of Antiquities and Cultural Heritage, in collaboration with international organizations, has implemented emergency documentation and conservation projects. These efforts aim to assess the damage inflicted on historical sites, salvage artifacts at risk, and implement measures to stabilize structures that have endured the ravages of war.

The tireless work of local and international organizations in documenting, preserving, and protecting Palestinian cultural heritage stands as a testament to the resilience of a people determined to safeguard their identity in the face of adversity. While the threat of destruction persists, these initiatives provide a ray of hope, emphasizing the enduring value of cultural heritage as a bridge connecting the past, present, and future of the Palestinian narrative.

The destruction of cultural and historical sites in Palestine transcends mere architectural losses; it strikes at the very core of Palestinian identity, a narrative intricately woven into the fabric of these sacred places. Each site, a repository of collective memory and symbol of resilience, serves as a pillar upholding the rich tapestry of Palestinian heritage.

The destruction of cultural and historical sites in Palestine is, at its core, an assault on the symbolism embedded in these spaces. It is an attempt to fracture the narrative that binds Palestinians to their roots, eroding the symbols that communicate resilience, resistance, and the enduring spirit of a people. In the face of such symbolic loss, efforts to document, preserve, and protect Palestinian heritage become not only acts of defiance but crucial steps in reclaiming the narrative that defines Palestinian identity.

Forced Displacement and Population Transfer

The systematic expulsion of Palestinian communities stands as a grim chapter in the narrative of the Israeli-Palestinian war, marked by a series of documented instances that lay bare the strategies employed to displace populations from their homes. These expulsions, characterized by a deliberate and organized approach, have had profound and lasting outcomes on the lives of countless Palestinians.

The Nakba of 1948, translating to "catastrophe," represents a seminal episode of forced displacement, wherein approximately 700,000 Palestinians were expelled during and after the establishment of the State of Israel. The systematic nature of these expulsions is evident in the strategic plans formulated by Zionist leaders, such as Plan Dalet, which aimed at securing and expanding Jewish control over designated territories. The expulsion of entire Palestinian villages, like Deir Yassin, became emblematic of the widespread displacement orchestrated during this period.

After the 1967 Six-Day War, another wave of systematic expulsions unfolded. The establishment of Israeli settlements in the newly occupied territories, in contravention of international law, became a key strategy in altering demographic realities. The documentation of this process reveals a calculated approach, with settlements strategically positioned to encircle existing Palestinian communities, leading to their isolation and, ultimately, displacement. The establishment of settlements like Ariel and Ma'ale Adumim exemplifies this deliberate strategy.

The construction of the separation barrier in the early 2000s marked yet another phase of systematic displacement. Ostensibly erected for security reasons, the barrier has been criticized for its route, which deviates significantly from the Green Line, encroaching deep into the West Bank. The barrier's impact on Palestinian communities is evident in the deliberate isolation and annexation of fertile lands, resulting in the displacement of thousands. The case of Jayyous, a village dissected by the barrier, highlights the disruptive consequences of this systematic strategy.

Since October 7, the 2023 Israel–Hamas war has triggered a series of devastating events in Gaza. On October 30, Israeli tanks blocked roads, firing on civilian vehicles following evacuation orders, resulting in casualties. On October 31, multiple attacks hit Palestinians attempting to leave northern Gaza City, claiming 70 lives, mostly women and children. On November 3, fourteen people were killed in an Israeli bombardment during an evacuation attempt. On November 11, explosions in the evacuation corridor on Salah al-Din Road, noted by the United Nations, caused further fatalities and injuries. Throughout this period, nearly a million residents were forcefully displaced from northern Gaza due to Israeli ultimatums and continuous strikes on various civilian locations, creating what is now referred to as Gaza's Nakba 2023. Israeli Minister Avi Dichter explicitly labeled it as "Nakba 2023" during the evacuation of the northern Gaza Strip.

The evictions and home demolitions in East Jerusalem and the West Bank also underscore the systematic nature of forced displacement. Israeli policies, such as home demolition orders and discriminatory zoning regulations, create an environment where Palestinian residents are left with few options but to leave their homes. Silwan, a neighborhood in East Jerusalem, has witnessed a systematic campaign of home demolitions and evictions, altering the demographic landscape in favor of Israeli settlers.

The forced displacement of Palestinian communities, as detailed, has given rise to profound humanitarian costs, echoing across generations and leaving indelible scars on the fabric of Palestinian society. Internally displaced populations, uprooted from their homes and communities, grapple with a myriad of challenges, encompassing social, economic, and psychological dimensions.

The humanitarian fallout is palpable in the plight of internally displaced Palestinians, a population scattered across the West Bank, Gaza Strip, and East Jerusalem. Families torn from their ancestral lands and communal ties find themselves navigating the harsh terrain of displacement, often confined to overcrowded and impoverished conditions. The disruption of livelihoods and economic activities compounds the hardship, amplifying the vulnerability of those displaced. The forced separation from homes and communities disrupts social networks, leaving individuals and families grappling with a sense of loss, uncertainty, and the enduring ordeal of displacement.

In East Jerusalem, where discriminatory policies and home demolitions have fueled forced displacement, the humanitarian consequences are stark. Palestinian residents facing eviction and home demolitions find themselves caught in a relentless cycle of instability. The demolition of homes not only robs families of shelter but also eradicates the physical manifestation of their connection to the land, intensifying the psychological toll of displacement.

The situation in the Gaza Strip, characterized by a complex web of restrictions and fights, has led to significant internal displacement. The destruction of homes and infrastructure, particularly during the Israeli militant operations, forces families to seek refuge in makeshift shelters, further exacerbating the dire living conditions in the densely populated enclave. The humanitarian outcomes extend beyond immediate displacement to encompass a protracted humanitarian crisis, with implications for health, education, and access to basic services.

The protracted nature of the Israeli-Palestinian war and the enduring humanitarian consequences of forced displacement underscore the need for sustained international attention and concerted efforts to address the root causes of displacement. While humanitarian organizations strive to provide immediate relief, the long-term resolution of the displacement crisis necessitates a comprehensive approach that addresses the political, economic, and social dimensions of the combat. The plight of internally displaced Palestinians remains a poignant reminder of the urgent imperative to seek just and lasting solutions to the multifaceted challenges posed by forced displacement.

The forced displacement and population transfer perpetrated in the context of the Israeli-Palestinian war carry profound legal implications, as international legal frameworks explicitly classify such actions as war crimes. The systematic nature of these practices, as detailed, triggers accountability mechanisms rooted in international humanitarian and human rights law.

Under international humanitarian law, particularly the Fourth Geneva Convention, the forced displacement of civilians from their homes is unequivocally prohibited. Article 49 of the Convention explicitly states that "Individual or mass forcible transfers, as well as deportations of protected persons from occupied territory to the territory of the Occupying Power or to that of any other country, occupied or not, are prohibited, regardless of their motive." The language of the convention leaves no room for ambiguity, underscoring the categorical prohibition against forced displacement and population transfer.

The Rome Statute of the International Criminal Court (ICC) further solidifies the legal framework pertaining to war crimes. Article 8 of the statute enumerates various acts that qualify as war crimes when committed in the context of an armed friction. Among these acts are "unlawful deportation or transfer or unlawful confinement of a civilian" and "ordering the displacement of the civilian population for reasons related to the conflict unless the security of the civilians involved or imperative military reasons so demand." The deliberate and systematic nature of forced displacement in the Israeli-Palestinian brawl aligns with these legal provisions, establishing a basis for accountability.

Efforts towards accountability for forced displacement and population transfer have manifested through international legal mechanisms and tribunals. The International Criminal Court (ICC) serves as a primary venue for addressing war crimes, including those related to forced displacement. While the ICC has a fabricated jurisdiction over situations arising from the Israeli-Palestinian tussle, the political complexities surrounding the involvement of both Israel and Palestine have impeded the court's ability to conduct comprehensive investigations. Nonetheless, the ICC has signaled its intent to pursue accountability for crimes committed in the occupied Palestinian territories.

The legal implications of forced displacement and population transfer extend beyond individual criminal accountability to encompass state responsibility. The Advisory Opinion of the International Court of Justice (ICJ) on the Wall in 2004 affirmed the illegality of the construction of the separation barrier in the occupied Palestinian territories, including East Jerusalem. The ICJ emphasized that Israel is under an obligation to cease construction, dismantle the barrier, and make reparations for the harm caused. This opinion reflects the broader legal consensus on the prohibition of practices contributing to forced displacement.

While legal frameworks are robust, the effective enforcement of accountability remains a complex challenge, given geopolitical and personal considerations. Nonetheless, the evolving landscape of international justice signals a growing recognition of the imperative to address the legal implications of forced displacement and population transfer. The pursuit of accountability, rooted in international law, represents a crucial dimension in the broader quest for justice and a resolution to the protracted tussle.

Blockades and Siege Tactics

The premeditated implementation of blockades in the Israeli-Palestinian tussle reveals a historical pattern where Zionist forces employed this tactic to exert control over Palestinian territories. These blockades, characterized by the restriction of movement, access, and the flow of goods, were motivated by a combination of warmongering and geopolitical considerations, shaping the dynamics of the battle.

A significant historical occurrence involves the blockade imposed on the Gaza Strip, persisting for much of the combat's duration. Initiated in 2007 after Hamas took control of Gaza, the blockade severely limited the movement of people and goods, impacting the lives of nearly two million Palestinians. Framed as a security measure to prevent the smuggling of weapons and materials for military purposes, the blockade's extensive reach, affecting essential goods and stifling the economy, has garnered widespread condemnation from the international community.

The confrontational considerations underlying the decision to impose blockades are rooted in the perception of security threats emanating from the Palestinian territories. The strategic objective is to limit the mobility of armed groups, prevent the transfer of weapons, and maintain a semblance of control over the conflict's dynamics. However, the expansive nature of these blockades, impacting civilian populations and cardinal services, raises ethical and legal concerns about the disproportionate impact on non-combatants.

The blockade on the Gaza Strip exemplifies the geopolitical dimensions influencing the implementation of such tactics. The control and restriction of access to Gaza serve not only military objectives but also contribute to broader geopolitical strategies. The blockade has been utilized as a tool in negotiations, exerting pressure on the political leadership in Gaza. This intertwining of military and geopolitical considerations underscores the complex and multifaceted nature of blockades in the context of the Israeli-Palestinian war.

The historical use of blockades in the Israeli-Palestinian hostility reflects a strategic calculus that intertwines warfare goals with broader geopolitical considerations. While security concerns have been cited to justify these measures, the impact on civilian populations and the ethical implications of such tactics remain subjects of international scrutiny. As blockades continue to shape the dynamics of the battle, the delicate balance between security imperatives and the humanitarian consequences underscores the complexity of navigating the geopolitical terrain in pursuit of strategic objectives.

The humanitarian impact of blockades and siege tactics on Palestinian civilians is a distressing reality that unfolds against a backdrop of restricted access to elemental resources, exacerbating the already challenging circumstances of life in the occupied territories. These measures, purportedly implemented for security reasons, cast a wide net of suffering upon civilian populations, affecting their access to fundamental necessities such as food, water, and medical aid.

In the Gaza Strip, the prolonged blockade has precipitated a humanitarian crisis of alarming proportions. The restriction of goods entering Gaza has led to severe shortages of primary items, including food and medicine. The World Health Organization (WHO) reports that the blockade has contributed to the deterioration of health services, with limited access to medical supplies and equipment. The deliberate stifling of the economy, coupled with high unemployment rates, has rendered a significant portion of the population reliant on international aid for survival.

Real-life accounts from Gaza illuminate the dire consequences of the blockade on civilian lives. Families struggle to secure adequate nutrition, and the lack of economic opportunities compounds the challenges of securing a livelihood. The United Nations Relief and Works Agency for Palestine Refugees in the Near East (UNRWA) highlights the devastating impact on the mental health of Gaza's residents, particularly children, as they grapple with the hardships imposed by the blockade.

The case of water scarcity in the West Bank, exacerbated by the separation barrier and associated restrictions, further underscores the humanitarian toll of siege tactics. Palestinian communities, particularly those in proximity to Israeli settlements, face challenges in accessing sufficient and clean water. The diversion of water resources for the benefit of settlements, coupled with restrictions on the drilling of new wells, perpetuates an unequal distribution of this vital resource. The humanitarian implications are stark, with communities enduring water shortages that affect daily life, agriculture, and overall well-being.

Medical aid and healthcare services also bear the brunt of siege tactics, impacting the most vulnerable segments of the population. In the West Bank, the obstruction of movement caused by checkpoints and the separation barrier hampers access to healthcare facilities. Patients requiring urgent medical attention face delays and obstacles in reaching hospitals, posing a direct threat to their health and well-being. The emotional burden of navigating these barriers to access basal medical care compounds the humanitarian impact on individuals and communities.

The case of Khuza'a, a town in the southern Gaza Strip, provides a poignant illustration of the humanitarian outcomes of siege tactics. During the 2014 brawl, the town faced intense shelling and ground incursions. The blockade compounded the challenges of reconstruction, hindering the entry of construction materials and impeding efforts to rebuild homes and infrastructure. The protracted humanitarian crisis in Khuza'a reflects the intersecting impacts of conflict, blockade, and siege tactics on civilian populations.

These real-life accounts and case studies underscore the profound and multifaceted humanitarian impact of blockades and siege tactics on Palestinian civilians. The deliberate restriction of access to primordial resources not only jeopardizes immediate well-being but also perpetuates a cycle of vulnerability and dependency. The international community's awareness of these consequences is inherent for fostering empathy and understanding, laying the groundwork for meaningful action to alleviate the suffering borne by Palestinian civilians in the face of siege tactics.

Advocacy initiatives have sought to mobilize public opinion and engage policymakers in addressing the humanitarian crises resulting from blockades. Grassroots movements, solidarity campaigns, and international advocacy organizations have worked to shed light on the plight of Palestinian civilians and call for an end to policies contributing to their suffering. The Boycott, Divestment, Sanctions (BDS) movement, for example, advocates for economic and cultural measures to pressure Israel to comply with international law and respect Palestinian rights. These initiatives aim to create a groundswell of support for change and contribute to a broader discourse on the ethical and legal implications of blockades and siege tactics.

While these responses demonstrate a collective awareness and commitment to addressing the humanitarian outcomes of blockades, the enduring nature of the skirmish underscores the complexity of achieving sustainable solutions. The challenges posed by geopolitical dynamics, divergent political interests, and the protracted nature of this war contribute to the limitations of international responses. Nonetheless, the ongoing efforts of diplomatic, humanitarian, and advocacy actors underscore the imperative to persist in addressing the humanitarian crises resulting from blockades and siege tactics, with the ultimate goal of achieving a just and lasting resolution to the hostility.

Illegal Settlement Expansion

The illegal expansion of settlements by Zionist forces in Palestinian territories has been extensively documented, revealing a pattern of violations that contravene international law, notably the Fourth Geneva Convention. Numerous cases and pieces of evidence illustrate the deliberate and systematic nature of settlement expansion, highlighting the infringement on the rights and territorial integrity of the Palestinian people.

Over the years, Israeli settlements in the West Bank have multiplied, resulting in the dispossession and displacement of Palestinian communities. The expansion of these settlements entails the construction of residential units, infrastructure, and related facilities on land internationally recognized as part of the occupied Palestinian territories. Abundant evidence from satellite imagery, reports by international organizations, and on-the-ground documentation illustrates the continual growth of these settlements, often at the expense of Palestinian homes, agricultural lands, and the lives of women and children.

The Fourth Geneva Convention explicitly prohibits the transfer of an occupying power's civilian population into the territory it occupies. This prohibition is grounded in the recognition that such transfers alter the demographic composition of the occupied territory and jeopardize the rights of the indigenous population. The establishment and expansion of Israeli settlements in the West Bank, including East Jerusalem, squarely violate this fundamental principle, as articulated in Article 49 of the Convention.

A case in point is the expansion of settlements in East Jerusalem, where the construction of Israeli residential units and infrastructure projects has intensified. The expansion into East Jerusalem not only infringes on the territorial integrity of the future Palestinian state but also exacerbates the daily challenges faced by Palestinian residents. Legal scholars, human rights organizations, and international bodies have consistently condemned these actions as violations of international law, emphasizing the need for accountability and cessation of settlement expansion.

Human Rights Watch, Amnesty International, and the United Nations have produced reports highlighting the legal ramifications and human rights abuses associated with the expansion of settlements. Testimonies from affected Palestinian communities further underscore the tangible impact on individuals and families, as they grapple with the loss of homes, livelihoods, and the broader erosion of their rights.

The illegal expansion of settlements by Zionist forces in Palestinian territories has inflicted a profound and devastating impact on Palestinian communities, resulting in widespread human rights violations. The expansion not only alters the physical landscape but also disrupts the lives of Palestinians, leading to displacement, dispossession, and a myriad of challenges that fundamentally violate their rights.

Displacement emerges as a central consequence of illegal settlement expansion, as Palestinian families find themselves uprooted from their homes and ancestral lands. The deliberate construction of Israeli settlements often involves the demolition of Palestinian homes and the forced eviction of residents, causing immense upheaval and distress. These forced displacements not only violate the right to adequate housing but also disrupt social structures, community ties, and the overall fabric of Palestinian life.

The dispossession of Palestinian land is intricately linked to the expansion of settlements, as vast tracts of territory are annexed for the construction and growth of these communities. Palestinian farmers and landowners face the loss of their livelihoods and cultural heritage, as fertile agricultural lands are seized for settlement expansion. This systematic dispossession infringes upon the right to property and the right to enjoy the benefits of one's own culture, as Palestinians witness the transformation of their lands into Israeli occupations.

The disruptions faced by Palestinian communities extend beyond physical displacement and dispossession, permeating various aspects of daily life. Infrastructure projects associated with settlements, such as roads and checkpoints, create barriers to movement, impeding access to essential services and economic opportunities. Palestinians encounter restrictions on their freedom of movement, affecting their ability to work, attend schools, and access healthcare facilities. These disruptions constitute violations of the right to freedom of movement and the right to work, contributing to a pervasive atmosphere of constraint and hardship.

The human impact of illegal settlement expansion is palpable in the stories and testimonies of affected individuals and families. Accounts from Palestinian communities reveal the emotional toll of witnessing the gradual encroachment of settlements, the loss of homes, and the erosion of their rights. Human rights organizations, including Amnesty International and Human Rights Watch, have documented these stories, providing a comprehensive record of the lived experiences of Palestinians affected by settlement expansion.

The international legal framework governing illegal settlements is grounded in various conventions, resolutions, and agreements that unequivocally deem such activities as violations of international law. Key among these is the Fourth Geneva Convention as discussed above. Additionally, United Nations Security Council resolutions, particularly Resolution 242 and Resolution 338, emphasize the inadmissibility of the acquisition of territory by force and call for the withdrawal of Israeli forces from territories occupied during the 1967 Six-Day War. These resolutions underscore the international consensus regarding the impermissibility of territorial acquisition through military means, reiterating the illegality of settlements established in contravention of these principles.

In practice, legal actions and accountability efforts are often impeded by geopolitical considerations, hindering the effective enforcement of international law. The United Nations Human Rights Council has established a database of companies involved in activities related to Israeli settlements, offering a tool for accountability. However, the implementation of such measures remains a complex and politically sensitive process.

Use of Internationally Prohibited Weapons

The use of internationally prohibited weapons by Zionist forces has been a source of deep concern, documented through a thorough exploration of cases and credible sources. Instances of chemical weapons, white phosphorus, and other munitions with severe humanitarian implications have been reported, raising questions about the adherence to international norms and the ethical conduct of military operations.

Numerous credible sources, including international human rights organizations, United Nations agencies, and on-the-ground reporting, have documented cases of the use of internationally prohibited weapons by Zionist militant forces. One notable example is the deployment of white phosphorus during the conflict in Gaza. Human Rights Watch and Amnesty International, among others, have extensively documented the use of white phosphorus in densely populated areas, resulting in severe injuries and loss of life. The indiscriminate nature of such weapons raises ethical concerns, particularly when used in areas populated by civilians.

Challenges in verifying the authenticity of these claims arise from the complex and often volatile nature of war zones. Access to affected areas may be restricted, hindering independent investigations. Additionally, conflicting narratives and the fog of war can complicate the process of establishing the veracity of reported incidents. However, the consistent corroboration of evidence from multiple sources, including eyewitness testimonies, medical records, and forensic analysis, strengthens the credibility of the claims regarding the use of prohibited weapons.

The recent Israel-Palestine war provides a glaring example of such practices. Between October 10 and 16, 2023, the Israeli militants utilized artillery shells containing white phosphorus, an incendiary weapon, in confrontational operations along Lebanon's southern border. On October 16, in Dhayra, a video verified by Amnesty International's Crisis Evidence Lab showcased smoke plumes dispersed by artillery, consistent with the deployment of white phosphorus munitions. This compelling evidence sheds light on the alarming tactics employed during the tussle.

The methodologies involved in verifying these claims often include cross-referencing information from various sources to establish a comprehensive and coherent narrative. Satellite imagery, on-the-ground reporting from journalists and human rights advocates, and analysis of munition remnants contribute to building a robust case. Collaboration between international organizations, such as the Organization for the Prohibition of Chemical Weapons (OPCW) and relevant UN agencies, further enhances the credibility of investigations.

International norms, such as the Chemical Weapons Convention, explicitly prohibit the use of chemical weapons, emphasizing the gravity of violations. The documentation of such incidents not only serves as a testament to the suffering endured by affected populations but also underscores the importance of accountability and adherence to international law.

The use of internationally prohibited weapons by Zionist forces in Palestinian territories has inflicted severe and lasting humanitarian outcomes, leaving a profound impact on civilian populations. The specific types of prohibited weapons, including white phosphorus and explosive munitions, have caused extensive harm, not only during the immediate battle but also in the long-term, affecting the health, well-being, and socio-economic stability of the Palestinian communities.

White phosphorus, a substance known for its ability to cause deep burns and ignite fires, has been deployed in densely populated areas, resulting in devastating consequences for civilians. The indiscriminate use of white phosphorus poses a direct threat to the lives of individuals, with documented cases of severe injuries and fatalities. The chemical's ability to cause burns through clothing and its long-lasting impact on the environment further exacerbate the challenges faced by affected populations. The exposure to toxic substances during skirmishes can lead to chronic health conditions, affecting not only the immediate survivors but also future generations. The lack of adequate medical resources and infrastructure compounds the challenges faced by Palestinians in accessing proper healthcare and rehabilitation services.

Explosive munitions, including artillery shells and bombs, have been used in densely populated urban areas, amplifying the risks to civilian lives and infrastructure. The indiscriminate nature of these weapons heightens the likelihood of collateral damage, leading to civilian casualties and extensive destruction of homes, schools, hospitals, and critical infrastructure. The long-term implications of such attacks contribute to the displacement of communities, exacerbating the humanitarian crisis in Palestinian territories.

While explosive munitions themselves are not internationally prohibited, the use of certain types of explosive weapons in certain circumstances is regulated by international humanitarian law (IHL). IHL seeks to protect civilians and minimize harm to non-combatants during armed quarrels. The use of explosive weapons with wide-area effects in populated areas has raised concerns due to the potential for indiscriminate harm to civilians and civilian infrastructure. Indiscriminate attacks violate the principles of IHL. Therefore, some international efforts have been made to address the impact of explosive weapons. One notable initiative is the "Safe Schools Declaration," which calls on states to endorse and implement commitments to protect students, teachers, schools, and universities during armed wrangle. While not a binding treaty, it reflects international concern about the impact of explosive weapons on education and civilian populations.

The enduring humanitarian impact resulting from the use of internationally prohibited weapons by Zionist forces emphasizes the immediate requirement for global attention, intervention, and accountability. Addressing the health, socio-economic, and psychological aftermath of these actions should prioritize the well-being and rights of affected populations. Despite ongoing challenges, such as geopolitical considerations and the complexities of hostile territories, the dedication to upholding international law and safeguarding human rights remains of utmost importance. Immanent to this effort is the collaboration between diplomatic, legal, and humanitarian initiatives, ensuring a comprehensive and effective response that places accountability at the forefront when dealing with the repercussions of deploying internationally prohibited weapons in Palestinian territory.

Targeting of Medical Facilities and Personnel

The deliberate targeting of medical facilities and personnel by Zionist forces in combat zones has resulted in egregious violations of international humanitarian law, causing severe consequences for the provision of healthcare in Palestinian territories. Documented cases reveal a disturbing pattern of intentional attacks on medical infrastructure, compromising the safety and well-being of civilians in need of medical assistance.

In the tragic events of Operation Cast Lead, conducted by the Israeli belligerents from December 27, 2008, to January 17, 2009, hospitals in the Gaza Strip, including Al-Quds and Al-Wafa, were deliberately targeted. A detailed examination reveals that on January 15, 2009, Al-Quds hospital in Gaza City and the adjacent ambulance depot were directly and intentionally attacked with white phosphorous shells by the Israeli force. The UN Fact Finding Mission rejected Israeli allegations that the hospital was used to fire upon Israeli forces, emphasizing the intentional nature of the attack, resulting in severe damage to the healthcare infrastructure and posing a direct threat to the lives of civilians.

Moving to the year 2014, Amnesty International reported mounting evidence of avowedly deliberate attacks by the Israel militant Forces against hospitals and health professionals in Gaza. The testimonies from doctors, nurses, and ambulance personnel paint a grim reality, with six medics dead and a deliberate pattern of targeting medical facilities. Hospitals, doctors, and ambulance staff faced increased fire since July 17, with medical teams even prevented from reaching critical areas. The shelling of Al-Aqsa Martyrs hospital on July 21 exemplifies the horrors, with multiple floors hit, causing deaths and panic among patients and medical staff.

The year 2018 witnessed the tragic death of 20-year-old medic Razan al-Najjar, shot and killed by an Israeli sniper as she tended to protestors on the Gaza Strip-Israel border. Her death exemplifies the ongoing pattern of deliberate attacks on medical personnel, further exacerbated in 2021. Dr. Ayman Abu al-Ouf, head of internal medicine at al-Shifa Hospital, was killed when Israeli bombs struck his home, highlighting the direct targeting of key healthcare professionals.

The documentation conducted by Al Mezan since the beginning of the "Great Return March" in 2018 provides irrefutable evidence of Israeli forces deliberately opening fire on medical staff, field-based medical care units, and clearly marked ambulances. The attacks resulted in injuries to 79 medics, including five by live fire, and damage to 20 ambulances. Testimonies from paramedics Abdel-Razaq Abu 'Athra and Imad Al Bhaisi vividly illustrate the horror and danger faced by those providing basic medical services in the midst of war. The deliberate targeting of medical facilities and personnel by Zionist forces is a reprehensible violation of international law, constituting war crimes that demand accountability and justice for the victims.

The year 2021 marked a significant escalation in Israeli militant aggression on the Gaza Strip, causing colossal damage to the already worn-out healthcare system. Six hospitals, including al-Shifa Hospital, and nine clinics suffered damage, severely impacting the ability to provide primordial medical services. The extensive destruction of medical facilities further underscores the intentional nature of the attacks, violating international humanitarian law.

The ongoing Israeli militant attacks on medical facilities in the Gaza Strip, documented by Human Rights Watch, reveal a disturbing pattern of deliberate destruction, violating international humanitarian law and constituting war crimes. Between October 7 and November 7, 2023, multiple hospitals, including the Indonesian Hospital, al-Ahli Hospital, International Eye Care Center, Turkish-Palestinian Friendship Hospital, and al-Quds Hospital, were repeatedly targeted. The scale of the attacks on healthcare infrastructure, including well-marked ambulances, has resulted in severe consequences, not only damaging physical structures but also impeding the ability to provide basilar medical services to the civilian population.

Among the targeted facilities, the Indonesian Hospital faced multiple strikes, killing at least two civilians. The International Eye Care Center was completely destroyed, impacting the provision of specialized eye care services. The Turkish-Palestinian Friendship Hospital suffered damage and fuel shortages, leading to its closure. Al-Quds Hospital also experienced repeated Israeli offensive strikes, injuring individuals in front of the facility. The deliberate targeting of ambulances, as exemplified by the incident on November 3 outside al-Shifa Hospital, resulted in casualties, including children.

The situation inside al-Shifa Hospital is particularly dire, with Israeli forces reportedly using loudspeakers to order young men to surrender. Disturbing reports reveal the mistreatment of individuals, including stripping them of clothes, blindfolding, and interrogation. Furthermore, Israeli forces have blown up a warehouse of vital medical supplies, exacerbating the already critical shortage of medicine and fuel. More than 1,000 medical staff are trapped on-site, unable to treat patients effectively.

The broader impact of Israeli attacks on Gaza is staggering, as confirmed by UN data. The destruction includes damage to half of Gaza's homes, 278 educational facilities, 270 healthcare facilities, and 69 places of worship. Ambulances, crucial for emergency medical services, have also been targeted. The costs extend to the humanitarian crisis, with severe shortages of medicine and fuel hindering the operation of healthcare facilities. As of November 12, 2023, the World Health Organization documented a total of 521 casualties, which included 16 medical professionals, resulting from 137 attacks on healthcare facilities.

Compounding the crisis, Israel's decisions to cut off electricity and water, along with blocking humanitarian aid, have further impeded healthcare access. Primary care facilities and hospitals are barely functioning, operating without essential supplies and equipment. Doctors are forced to conduct surgeries without anesthesia, using vinegar as an antiseptic. The dire conditions in hospitals have resulted in the deaths of patients, including premature babies, due to power cuts and scarce resources.

The plight of pregnant women in Gaza adds another layer of urgency, with an estimated 50,000 pregnant women facing complications amid the healthcare crisis. Reports reveal that women are often admitted to hospitals only when fully dilated, forced to deliver in unsafe conditions, including cars and overcrowded shelters. Critical medical procedures, such as c-sections, are performed without anesthesia, and the lack of postnatal care further compounds the risks to maternal and child health.

In addition to these specific incidents, numerous documented cases across different dates and locations showcase a systematic pattern of targeting medical facilities and personnel. These attacks have resulted in the destruction of hospitals, clinics, and ambulances, limiting the capacity of the healthcare system to respond to the needs of the population, particularly in times of combat. The deliberate nature of these strikes raises serious concerns about the respect for the rules of war and the protection of civilian lives.

The extent of the damage inflicted on healthcare infrastructure is profound, impacting not only the immediate provision of medical care but also the long-term health outcomes of affected populations. The destruction of hospitals and clinics disrupts routine healthcare services, hampers emergency response capabilities, and exacerbates the vulnerability of civilians, especially in combat theaters where access to medical care is already challenging.

The intentional attacks on medical facilities disrupt the functionality of the entire healthcare system. Hospitals and clinics, once pillars of support for the local population, are transformed into rubble, rendering primary medical services inaccessible. The broader result is a profound weakening of the healthcare infrastructure, limiting its capacity to respond effectively to the health needs of the civilian population. The loss of paramount medical equipment and supplies stands out as a significant repercussion. The deliberate destruction of hospitals and clinics results in the annihilation of life-saving technology and pharmaceuticals, further depriving Palestinians of essential healthcare. This loss not only affects immediate emergency response capabilities but also undermines the ability to provide routine and specialized medical care, leading to a prolonged state of health crisis.

Moreover, the targeted attacks on medical personnel compound the challenges faced by the healthcare system. The intentional killing or injury of doctors, nurses, and other healthcare professionals disrupts the continuity of care and diminishes the pool of skilled individuals available to address the health needs of the population. This not only affects the immediate response to emergencies but also leaves a lasting impact on the overall health workforce in the region.

The destruction of medical infrastructure also impedes the transportation of patients and the evacuation of the injured. Ambulances, mandatory for timely and efficient emergency medical response, become targets themselves, exacerbating the difficulties in providing swift and life-saving interventions. The wide-ranging consequence is a compromised ability to address medical emergencies, leading to increased mortality rates and prolonged suffering among the civilian population.

Furthermore, the intentional targeting of medical facilities sends a chilling message to healthcare professionals, instilling fear and uncertainty. This fear may deter medical personnel from providing care in war regions, leading to a shortage of qualified professionals and a further deterioration of the healthcare system's capabilities. The psychological impact of such attacks on the healthcare workforce amplifies the challenges of rebuilding and restoring the healthcare infrastructure.

The wider impact of targeting medical facilities extends beyond physical destruction. The intentional attacks exacerbate the existing humanitarian crisis by limiting access to necessary healthcare services, leaving vulnerable populations without the medical support they desperately need. The deliberate disruption of healthcare services compounds the suffering of civilians, particularly those in need of urgent medical attention, creating a cascading effect on the overall well-being of the population.

The intentional targeting of medical facilities and personnel is a blatant violation of the principles outlined in the Geneva Conventions and other relevant international treaties. The deliberate nature of these attacks raises questions about the adherence to the rules of war and the commitment to upholding the sanctity of healthcare in war regions. Addressing these documented cases is crucial not only for accountability but also for the protection of civilians and the preservation of essential healthcare services in Palestinian territories.

The deliberate targeting of medical facilities and personnel by Zionist forces constitutes a blatant violation of international humanitarian law, a grievous affront to the principles established to protect the sanctity of healthcare infrastructure during armed confrontations. This egregious transgression demands a comprehensive examination of the legal implications, the relevant international conventions, and the potential legal consequences for those responsible.

The Fourth Geneva Convention safeguards the rights and protections of civilians and non-combatants during battles. The intentional targeting of medical facilities and personnel represents a clear violation of Article 18, which specifically safeguards civilian hospitals against any form of attack or occupation. Additionally, Article 19 emphasizes the protection of medical personnel exclusively engaged in the search for, collection, transportation, or treatment of the wounded and sick.

The Rome Statute of the International Criminal Court (ICC) establishes a robust legal framework condemning attacks on medical facilities and personnel as war crimes. Specifically, Article 8 of the statute categorizes willful attacks on civilian objects, which includes hospitals, as serious violations of the laws and customs of war. This classification applies when such attacks are committed as part of a plan or policy or as part of a large-scale commission of such crimes.

In the realm of upholding and disseminating international humanitarian law, the International Committee of the Red Cross (ICRC) holds a central position. The Customary International Humanitarian Law study conducted by the ICRC further reinforces the prohibition against attacking civilian objects, notably hospitals, recognizing such actions as customary international law. This study conducts a thorough analysis of state practice and opinio juris, affirming widely accepted norms that unequivocally condemn the intentional targeting of medical facilities and personnel.

The legal implications for those accountable for such heinous acts go beyond the scope of international humanitarian law. The principle of command responsibility, enshrined in both customary international law and the Rome Statute of the ICC, holds commanders and superiors criminally responsible for the actions of their subordinates if they knew or should have known about the crimes and failed to prevent or punish them.

Cases involving the deliberate targeting of medical facilities and personnel could fall under the ICC's jurisdiction, leading to prosecutions and potential convictions. The ICC has the responsibility to investigate and prosecute individuals responsible for grave breaches of the Fourth Geneva Convention and other serious violations of international humanitarian law.

In addition to the ICC, national and international tribunals, as well as other legal avenues, can be pursued to ensure accountability. States can exercise universal jurisdiction to prosecute individuals responsible for war crimes, irrespective of their nationality or the location where the crimes occurred. Furthermore, the United Nations Security Council has the authority to refer situations involving the deliberate targeting of medical facilities to the ICC, initiating investigations and legal proceedings.

The legal implications of targeting medical facilities and personnel are not only grounded in codified international law but also resonate with the moral and ethical principles underpinning the global commitment to protect the most vulnerable during armed encounters. The intentional attacks on healthcare infrastructure demand swift and decisive legal responses to ensure justice for the victims and to deter future violations of international humanitarian law.

Restrictions on Humanitarian Aid

The imposition of restrictions on humanitarian aid by Zionist forces in violation of international law represents a dire infringement on the principles established to ensure the timely and unimpeded delivery of requisite assistance to those in need during armed conflicts. This investigation delves into documented cases, shedding light on the legal implications of such actions under international humanitarian law.

Dating back to the early 2000s, the narrative of Zionist forces placing restrictions on humanitarian aid unravels as a systematic chronicle of constraints. In 2005, Israel initiated a blockade on the movement of goods and people in and out of the Gaza Strip, a policy that would have profound implications for the civilian population. The blockade took a permanent turn in 2007 after Hamas assumed control of Gaza. The blockade aimed to isolate Hamas and curb the alleged smuggling of weapons into Gaza.

This blockade, encircling Gaza with walls and fences, controlled the flow of compulsory goods and restricted the freedom of movement for its residents. Israel, going to the extent of calculating the minimum calories needed for survival, argued that it was fulfilling its obligations by allowing just that amount and not more. This reduction of human dignity to mathematical formulas and the intentional restriction of food and fuel supplies underscored a policy that raised significant humanitarian concerns. In 2007, human rights lawyers challenged this policy, contending that it deliberately limited supplies to Palestinian civilians. The Israeli Supreme Court, however, accepted the argument that the military's minimum commitments would prevent a "humanitarian crisis" and rejected the petition.

The blockade, in effect for years, has led to undeniable humanitarian challenges, restricting the flow of essential goods and contributing to economic hardship. Exit and entry into Gaza, whether by sea or air, face prohibitions, leaving only three crossings—two controlled by Israel and one by Egypt. The impact on movement is evident, with a significant reduction in exit permits by Israel according to a 2022 UN report. The situation has transformed Gaza precisely what international politicians and human rights activists warned against in 2005—an open-air prison.

Specific instances highlight the detrimental consequences of this blockade on humanitarian aid and the lives of civilians. The Karni crossing, vital for exports from Gaza, was closed in 2006, with intermittent openings providing minimal relief for the textile and furniture industries. The closure led to the loss of high-value crop harvests intended for export, further exacerbating economic challenges in Gaza. Moreover, Israel faced accusations of violating or failing to fulfill obligations outlined in various ceasefire agreements, perpetuating the humanitarian crisis and raising serious questions about adherence to international humanitarian law. These documented cases emphasize the pressing need for an investigation into the instances where Zionist forces imposed restrictions on humanitarian aid, shedding light on the legal implications of such actions under the framework of international humanitarian law.

Gaza is facing an escalating humanitarian crisis, brought about by a series of harsh measures initiated by the Israeli government since October 7, 2023. These measures include the cessation of water and electricity, the shutdown of the truck crossing, and the obstruction of crucial relief supplies to the enclave's 2.2 million residents, of which nearly half are children. The acute scarcity of drinkable water compounds the already challenging circumstances, posing severe threats to the health and overall well-being of the population.

The Israeli government's refusal to allow fuel on aid trucks, even those arriving from Egypt, disrupts basic services such as hospital functions, ambulance operations, and water pumping. The rationale given, citing concerns about fuel being used for attacks by Hamas, has led to a comprehensive ban on aid entry from Israel into Gaza. The attempt to partially restore water supply to Gaza's south on October 15 faces limitations due to the absence of fuel for effective delivery, leaving the north isolated.

Until October 24, 2023, the Israeli military authorized only 34 monitored supply truckloads, facilitated by UN agencies, to pass through Egypt's Rafah crossing. This allocation fell considerably below the 100 daily truckloads identified as indispensable by aid agencies. The denial of fuel, critical for vital services like hospital generators and water pumping, amounts to a clear violation of the laws of war, which strictly prohibit the deliberate hindrance of relief supplies. While acknowledging security concerns, it is imperative to distinguish between legitimate precautions and actions that exacerbate an already dire humanitarian crisis in Gaza.

International humanitarian law, anchored in the Geneva Conventions and other relevant treaties, unequivocally mandates the facilitation of humanitarian assistance to civilians affected by skirmishes. Article 23 of the Fourth Geneva Convention explicitly prohibits the intentional obstruction of the delivery of primary supplies, including food, medicine, and clothing, to civilian populations. The intentional imposition of restrictions on humanitarian aid constitutes a blatant violation of this provision, endangering the lives and well-being of vulnerable populations.

Documented cases, such as the ones mentioned above, reveal instances in which Zionist forces have imposed arbitrary restrictions on the movement of humanitarian convoys, hindering the delivery of life-saving assistance to Palestinian civilians. These actions not only contravene the letter and spirit of international humanitarian law but also exacerbate the humanitarian crisis faced by the affected populations.

The International Committee of the Red Cross (ICRC) emphasizes the obligation of parties to a conflict to allow and facilitate the rapid and unimpeded passage of humanitarian relief for civilians in need. The ICRC's Customary International Humanitarian Law study reaffirms the customary nature of this obligation, reflecting the widespread acceptance of the norm within the international community.

The legal implications of restricting humanitarian aid extend beyond the immediate impact on affected populations. Such actions may constitute war crimes under the Rome Statute of the International Criminal Court (ICC). Article 8(2)(b)(xxiii) of the statute classifies intentionally using starvation as a method of warfare as a grave breach of the Geneva Conventions, and deliberately impeding humanitarian assistance may contribute to this violation.

Furthermore, the principle of proportionality, a fundamental tenet of international humanitarian law, requires that any military advantage gained from restricting humanitarian aid must not outweigh the expected harm to the civilian population. Imposing disproportionate restrictions on humanitarian assistance raises serious legal questions, as parties to a war are obligated to balance military considerations with the imperative to protect civilians and ensure their access to primary resources.

The implications of limited access to essential resources for the civilian population in Palestinian territories, stemming from the imposition of restrictions on humanitarian aid, are profound and multifaceted. As explored above, these restrictions, in violation of international humanitarian law, hinder the timely and unimpeded delivery of critical supplies, leading to a myriad of humanitarian challenges.

The scarcity of food is a direct result of restrictions on humanitarian aid, affecting the nutritional well-being of Palestinian civilians. Documented cases reveal instances where access to farmland is impeded, exacerbating food insecurity. The intentional disruption of agricultural activities and the imposition of barriers to the movement of goods contribute to a precarious food situation, leaving many Palestinians without reliable access to sufficient and nutritious food.

Water, a fundamental necessity for human survival, is also severely impacted by restrictions on humanitarian aid. Zionist forces' actions hinder the maintenance and repair of water infrastructure, leading to shortages and contamination. The deliberate targeting of water sources and restrictions on the importation of water-related materials exacerbate the already challenging water situation in Palestinian territories, posing significant risks to public health.

The limited availability of medical supplies is a critical consequence with far-reaching implications for the health and well-being of the civilian population. Restrictions on the movement of medical convoys and the obstruction of deliveries compromise the ability of healthcare facilities to provide obligatory services. This situation is particularly dire in times of battle, where the demand for medical assistance is heightened. The denial of medical supplies not only jeopardizes immediate healthcare needs but also undermines the overall resilience of the healthcare system.

Moreover, restrictions on humanitarian aid contribute to the deterioration of living conditions, infringing on the basic rights and dignity of Palestinian civilians. The denial of access to primary resources not only violates their right to an adequate standard of living but also impedes their ability to enjoy the highest attainable standard of physical and mental health, as recognized in international human rights instruments.

These outcomes collectively give rise to a humanitarian crisis, exacerbating the suffering of the civilian population. The deliberate impediments to accessing core resources violate the principles of humanity and impartiality that underpin humanitarian assistance, exacerbating the vulnerability of those already living in challenging circumstances. The civilian population in Palestinian territories faces not only the immediate impact of combat but also the long-term implications of restricted access to food, water, and medical supplies.

The humanitarian impact of limited access to basilar resources is a stark reminder of the urgent need for compliance with international humanitarian law. Addressing these costs requires not only an acknowledgment of the violations but also concerted efforts to ensure the unimpeded delivery of humanitarian aid. It is a collective responsibility of the international community to advocate for the rights of civilians in war regions and to work towards a sustainable resolution that prioritizes the well-being and dignity of all affected populations.

The international response to the imposition of restrictions on humanitarian aid in Palestinian territories has been a complex interplay of diplomatic efforts, advocacy campaigns, and legal initiatives. The varied response worldwide to these breaches of international humanitarian law, as discussed in the preceding conversations, showcases its multifaceted nature.

Diplomatically, various nations and international organizations have condemned the imposition of restrictions on humanitarian aid, emphasizing the need for unimpeded access to key resources for civilians in theaters of war. Statements from diplomatic channels, including resolutions and declarations, underscore the consensus within the international community that obstructing the delivery of humanitarian assistance is unacceptable. These diplomatic efforts aim to apply political pressure on the parties responsible for such restrictions, urging them to comply with international law and facilitate the delivery of aid.

Humanitarian organizations and advocacy groups have a fundamental impact on amplifying the voices of the affected populations and bringing attention to the violations at hand. Through their work, they document instances of restrictions on humanitarian aid, providing concrete evidence of the challenges faced by civilians in accessing elemental resources. These organizations leverage this evidence to engage in advocacy campaigns, urging governments and international bodies to take decisive action. The power of public awareness and opinion, mobilized through these campaigns, has the potential to influence political decisions and compel the international community to address the issue with greater urgency.

Despite legal endeavors to hold accountable those obstructing humanitarian aid, the international response has fallen short in translating laws into effective action. While legal frameworks such as the Geneva Conventions expressly denounce actions impeding the delivery of crucial resources to civilian populations in hostile territories, the practical implementation of these laws remains inadequate. International authorities must move beyond mere condemnation in words and take substantive steps to enforce their laws on the ground. Rather than keeping these legal provisions confined to law books, there is an urgent need for concrete actions that go beyond rhetoric. It is imperative for these authorities to prioritize the implementation of their laws, ensuring that justice is not just a theoretical concept but a tangible reality in addressing Zionist war crimes and human rights breaches.

Psychological Warfare and Collective Punishment

Psychological warfare, a sinister dimension of conflict, has been employed by Zionist forces in documented instances, revealing a strategic use of tactics that extend beyond conventional warfare. Propaganda, a powerful tool in psychological manipulation, has been wielded to shape narratives and influence perceptions. Instances abound where false narratives were disseminated, aiming to justify quarrelsome actions and vilify the Palestinian population. A conspicuous instance involves the intentional dissemination of misinformation during the 2000 Al-Aqsa Intifada, where Zionist forces portrayed the uprising as solely driven by Palestinian violence, obscuring the underlying socio-political context and grievances. This intentional dissemination of false narratives and manipulation of information not only distorted the historical context but also sowed seeds of mistrust and suspicion within Palestinian communities, creating a mental strain as individuals grapple with the invasion of their privacy under constant surveillance, whether through drones or advanced monitoring systems.

Intimidation, as another facet of psychological warfare, involves systematic tactics designed to instill fear among the Palestinian population. The use of military might, checkpoints, and targeted arrests contributes to an environment of constant unease. The widespread use of night raids on Palestinian homes, often resulting in the arrest of individuals, including minors, and the forced stripping of Palestinian women, serves as a glaring example of such intimidation tactics. These nocturnal incursions not only disrupt the daily lives of civilians but also contribute to a pervasive atmosphere of anxiety and insecurity. This use of intimidation tactics, including night raids on Palestinian homes and widespread arrests, contributes to a collective trauma experienced by communities. The fear instilled by such tactics lingers long after the immediate threat has passed, shaping the way individuals navigate their daily lives. The documented case of the 2014 Israeli assault on Gaza, with deliberate attacks on civilian infrastructure, further exacerbates the psychological impact, as communities grapple with the insecurity of traditionally protected spaces.

Furthermore, the manipulation of humanitarian aid as a tool of control, as discussed in detail in the preceding section, exerts psychological pressure on the population. Restrictions on the entry of goods, including medical supplies and reconstruction materials, are utilized as leverage, amplifying the cognitive impact. This insidious aspect of psychological warfare stands out as the denial of basic necessities creates a sense of dependency and helplessness, adding a psychological dimension to the collective punishment imposed. By imposing restrictions on the entry of essential goods, Zionist forces create a dynamic of dependency, inflicting immediate suffering and generating long-term psychological consequences. Living in a state of perpetual need, where access to fundamental resources is contingent upon compliance with imposed conditions, fosters a sense of frustration among the affected population.

The use of surveillance technology, including drones and advanced monitoring systems, further intensifies psychological pressure. Constant surveillance not only violates privacy but also creates a pervasive sense of being constantly observed. This tactic contributes to the erosion of trust within communities, fostering an environment of suspicion and self-censorship. The psychological impact of living under constant surveillance extends beyond the immediate infringement on privacy, influencing behavior, and fostering a climate of self-censorship to avoid repercussions. This psychic toll has created a climate of anxiety and self-censorship among individuals grappling with the invasion of their privacy, whether through drones or advanced monitoring systems.

Zionist forces have also employed psychological tactics during military offensives, exploiting the vulnerability of civilian spaces. The deliberate targeting of civilian infrastructure, including schools, hospitals, and residential areas, serves as a dual-purpose strategy. Beyond the immediate physical destruction, these attacks instill a deep sense of insecurity and fear, compelling the population to question the safety of even traditionally protected spaces. The documented case of the 2014 Israeli assault on Gaza highlights the intentional targeting of civilian infrastructure, showcasing the psychological peal of such actions on the affected communities.

The impact of psychological warfare on Palestinian communities is profound, leaving a lasting imprint on the mental and emotional well-being of individuals subjected to these tactics. The documented instances of propaganda, intimidation, and surveillance technology have created an environment of pervasive fear and insecurity.

The impact on the mental and emotional well-being of Palestinian communities is not confined to the immediate aftermath of these tactics. Rather, the suffering extends across generations, shaping the collective consciousness of the community. Children born into an environment marked by constant fear, surveillance, and restrictions on elemental resources inherit a legacy of psychological distress. The intergenerational transmission of trauma becomes a pervasive reality, as the experiences of one generation influence the mental health and resilience of the next.

Interwoven with psychological warfare tactics is the use of collective punishment, a method aimed at holding an entire population accountable for the alleged crimes of a few. Imposing measures like curfews, restrictions on movement, and economic blockades creates a shared experience of suffering, serving as a means to break the spirit of resistance and dissent within the population. Documented cases, such as the blockade on Gaza since 2007, demonstrate the long-term psychological impact of collective punishment, leading to increased frustration, despair, and a sense of feebleness among the affected population. This tactic compounds the ordeal experienced by Palestinian communities, hindering development and well-being while leaving an indelible mark on the psyche of those affected.

The insidious practice of collective punishment has been a recurring theme in the Israeli-Palestinian tussle, leaving a trail of devastation in its wake. The psychological warfare examined earlier is often intertwined with collective punishment, creating a complex web of tactics employed by Zionist forces to control and subjugate Palestinian communities. As explored in the preceding sections, the impact on the mental and emotional well-being of individuals and communities subjected to these tactics is profound and enduring.

The widespread practice of home demolitions inflicted upon Palestinian communities stands out as a notable instance of collective punishment. This punitive measure, often justified under security pretexts, involves the destruction of homes, displacing families and leaving individuals without shelter. The extensive use of home demolitions has far-reaching consequences, contributing to the displacement and vulnerability of Palestinian populations, particularly in areas where tensions are high. The legal implications of such collective punishment under international humanitarian law merit careful consideration and examination.

The Fourth Geneva Convention, a cornerstone of international humanitarian law, explicitly prohibits collective punishment. Article 33 of the Convention states that "no protected person may be punished for an offence he or she has not personally committed." The deliberate targeting of civilian populations, imposing measures that cause suffering and hardship as a form of reprisal, is unequivocally condemned. The blockade on Gaza, with its severe impact on the civilian population, stands in clear violation of this provision.

Furthermore, the Rome Statute of the International Criminal Court (ICC) categorizes collective punishment as a war crime. Article 8 of the Statute defines war crimes, including those committed in an international armed conflict, and Article 8(2)(b)(vii) specifically addresses "intentionally directing attacks against the civilian population as such or against individual civilians not taking direct part in hostilities." The ICC's jurisdiction extends to individuals responsible for planning, initiating, or executing such acts. The imposition of collective punishment through measures like the Gaza blockade falls squarely within this definition, implicating those involved in its planning and enforcement.

The legal implications of collective punishment are not limited to the international arena; national legal systems also play a crucial part. States have an obligation to prosecute individuals responsible for war crimes, including acts of collective punishment, under the principle of universal jurisdiction. The concept of universal jurisdiction allows states to bring legal action against individuals accused of grave international crimes, irrespective of the location of the offense or the nationality of the perpetrator or victim.

On July 9, 2004, the International Court of Justice (ICJ) issued its Advisory Opinion on the Legal Consequences of the Construction of a Wall in the Occupied Palestinian Territory. Despite affirming the illegality of collective punishment and concluding that the construction of the separation wall and associated regime imposed by Israel constituted breaches of international law, including the prohibition of collective punishment, the ICJ's Advisory Opinion lacked enforceable mechanisms. Regrettably, Israel did not comply with the ruling, and the construction of the separation wall continued. The Advisory Opinion, while influential in highlighting the legal issues surrounding the wall, underscored the ICJ's limited capacity to enforce its decisions, leaving Israel without direct ramifications for its non-compliance. The lack of effective actions against Israel post-Advisory Opinion revealed the complex political and diplomatic challenges associated with the Israeli-Palestinian war, questioning the ICJ's efficacy in addressing the Palestinians' concerns. The issue has continued to be a point of contention within the international community, highlighting the persistent obstacles to implementing justice in the region.

Media Manipulation

Framing of Conflicts in Media Coverage

The manipulation of media narratives by Zionist forces is a nuanced and strategic endeavor, employing a variety of tactics to shape public perception and garner support. A common tactic revolves around meticulously shaping language to frame wars in a way that underscores the narrative of self-defense. The choice of words, phrases, and narratives becomes a powerful tool in shaping how events are interpreted by the global audience.

In media coverage, Zionist forces often deploy terminology that portrays their insurgent actions as necessary defensive measures rather than offensive operations. Terms such as "counter-terrorism," "preemptive strikes," and "protective measures" are strategically utilized to justify armed interventions. By delineating their actions in this manner, they seek to convey a narrative of responding to imminent threats, thereby garnering sympathy and understanding.

Furthermore, the utilization of visuals significantly influences the shaping of the narrative. Zionist forces are known to carefully select visuals that evoke emotions and reinforce the narrative of self-defense. Images and videos depicting damaged civilian infrastructure or scenes showing Israelis taking cover during rocket attacks are prominently presented to evoke empathy and justify bellicose actions. The strategic selection and dissemination of such images aim to elicit a specific emotional response from the audience, steering them towards a perception of Israel as a victim rather than an aggressor and war criminal. Additionally, it is crucial to acknowledge that in the context of the Israel-Palestine tussle that began on October 7, 2023, many visuals are manipulated and generated by artificial intelligence, raising questions about the authenticity and objectivity of the narrative being presented.

Messaging is another key aspect of Zionist media strategy. Through official statements, press releases, and spokespersons, Zionist forces articulate a narrative that emphasizes the existential threats faced by the state. By consistently framing the battle as a struggle for survival, they seek to validate the necessity of antagonistic actions and portray any opposition as a direct threat to the very existence of the nation. This messaging strategy is designed to garner both domestic and international support by formulating Israeli actions as a just and unavoidable response to external aggression.

A notable example is the portrayal of the Gaza blockade. Zionist forces often describe it as a security measure to prevent the smuggling of weapons into Gaza, shaping it as a necessary action to protect Israeli citizens. This portrayal conveniently omits the severe humanitarian impact on the civilian population in Gaza, diverting attention from the collective punishment imposed and emphasizing the narrative of security concerns.

Following Hamas' attack on 07 October 2023, the claim that Hamas fighters beheaded 40 children in the Israeli settlement of Kfar Aza near the Gaza boundary was widely circulated in British newspapers, Israeli media, and on social platforms. The spokesperson for Israeli Prime Minister Binyamin Netanyahu amplified the narrative, stating that women, children, toddlers, and elderly people were "brutally butchered in an ISIS way of action." However, President Joe Biden's statement at the White House on October 11, where he claimed to have seen photos of these Israeli children beheaded by Hamas fighters, was later confirmed by the White House to be false. The administration quickly backtracked on the president's plain confirmation of a story that Israel has used to justify its ongoing mass slaughter of Palestinians in Gaza. This underscores the challenges of discerning truth from propaganda in the midst of a conflict.

Furthermore, Zionist forces employ the strategy of dehumanization to delegitimize opposition and justify aggressive actions. Labeling adversaries as "terrorists" and "human animals" rather than recognizing them as political entities with legitimate grievances serves to create a dichotomy of good versus evil. This black-and-white narrative simplifies complex geopolitical issues, making it easier to garner support by presenting Zionist forces as the righteous defenders against an existential threat.

An illustrative example is the framing of protests and uprisings in the occupied territories. The use of terms like "rioters" and "violent mobs" to describe Palestinian demonstrators creates a narrative that justifies the use of force in quelling what is portrayed as a threat to public order.

This portraying diverts attention from the root causes of discontent and resistance, focusing instead on the need for stringent measures to maintain security. Similarly, Israeli Defense Minister Yoav Gallant declared a "complete siege" on Gaza, including cutting off electricity, food, water, and fuel in response to Operation Al-Aqsa Flood, a surprise attack by Hamas on Israel that started on October 7, 2023. The minister characterized the hostility by stating, "We are fighting against human animals."

The carefully framed narratives propagated by Zionist forces in media coverage wield significant influence over public perception, both within Israel and on the international stage. The impact of these narratives extends beyond mere storytelling; it shapes attitudes, molds opinions, and, ultimately, influences how the actions of Zionist forces are interpreted by the global audience.

Domestically, the framed narratives serve to create a collective identity and foster a sense of national unity among the Israeli population. By consistently delineating militant actions as necessary measures of self-defense against existential threats, Zionist forces aim to cultivate a shared belief in the righteousness of their cause. This narrative reinforces a perception of Israel as a vulnerable nation surrounded by adversaries, fostering a collective sense of victimhood that rallies public support for armed endeavors.

Moreover, the use of language, imagery, and messaging to craft a narrative emphasizing self-defense has a profound impact on how Israelis perceive their role in the battle. The constant portrayal of Palestinians as a security threat reinforces a mindset of fear and suspicion, shaping public attitudes towards accepting stringent security measures as indispensable for their safety. This perception, carefully cultivated through media narratives, contributes to the resilience of policies such as the Gaza blockade and military interventions.

Internationally, the influence of framed narratives on public perception is equally significant. The strategic selection of language and imagery creates a narrative that positions Israel as a besieged nation defending itself against hostile forces. This portrayal resonates with audiences unfamiliar with the complexities of the affray, eliciting sympathy and support for Israel's actions. The encasing of militant operations as responses to imminent threats strategically garners international understanding and justifies Israeli policies, particularly in contexts where nuanced perspectives might be lacking.

An illustrative example is the portrayal of the 2014 Gaza war. Through carefully crafted narratives emphasizing Israel's right to defend itself, media coverage influenced international public opinion, garnering support from various quarters. The framing of the war as a necessary response to rocket attacks served to justify the scale and intensity of the bellicose operation, influencing how the international community perceived Israel's actions.

The impact of framed narratives is not confined to immediate reactions but extends to long-term attitudes and perceptions. By constantly structuring skirmishes in a manner that emphasizes self-defense and portrays Israel as a victim, Zionist forces contribute to the normalization of certain policies and actions. The Gaza blockade, for instance, is presented as a security measure rather than a form of collective punishment, influencing how the international community views the ongoing restrictions on humanitarian aid.

The representation of hostilities in media coverage also shapes the discourse surrounding peace initiatives and diplomatic efforts. By consistently positioning Israel as the party under constant threat, media narratives create a context in which military riots are deemed necessary, potentially influencing the international community's approach to diplomatic solutions. The impact of these framed narratives on public opinion can be a formidable obstacle to the acceptance of alternative perspectives or the questioning of established policies.

Contrasting the meticulously crafted media-framed narrative with the ground realities of affrays involving Zionist forces reveals a stark disjunction between perception and actual events. These discrepancies and distortions in media representation contribute to a skewed understanding of the Israeli-Palestinian tussle, perpetuating misconceptions and hindering the pursuit of a comprehensive and impartial understanding of the situation.

Media narratives often emphasize the launching of rockets by Palestinian factions as the primary justification for Israeli armed infringements. While the media framing positions these operations as defensive measures, the ground reality reveals a cycle of violence where the initiation and escalation of hostilities are not unidirectional.

Examining the timelines and triggers of tussles unveils instances where Israeli actions, such as targeted assassinations or incursions into Palestinian territories, preceded the rocket attacks, challenging the narrative of sole Palestinian aggression.

The portrayal of clashes also tends to downplay the impact of militant interventions on civilian populations. Media representations often focus on the precision of Israeli airstrikes and confrontational operations, highlighting efforts to minimize collateral damage. However, the ground reality presents a different picture, with civilian casualties and infrastructural damage disproving the narrative of surgical precision. Instances where civilian infrastructure, including schools and hospitals, became targets undermine the media's portrayal of a militant campaign solely directed at combatants.

Moreover, the media-framed narrative often neglects the asymmetry of power and resources between Israel and Palestine. While media coverage emphasizes the threat posed by Palestinian freedom fighters, it often overlooks the significant disparities in military capabilities and the broader context of occupation. The outlining tends to portray the battle as a symmetrical struggle, obscuring the structural imbalances that contribute to the perpetuation of hostilities. Examining ground realities reveals a nuanced power dynamic that is crucial for a comprehensive understanding of the skirmish.

The selective use of language and imagery in media shaping further widens the gap between perception and reality. The portrayal of Israeli warmongering actions as "responses" and Palestinian actions as "provocations" creates a narrative that places the onus of the brawl solely on the Palestinians. This interpretation obscures the historical context, including the displacement of Palestinians and the occupation, contributing to a skewed understanding of the root causes of the war. Ground realities, however, necessitate a more nuanced examination of the complex historical, political, and socio-economic factors at play.

Instances where media representations rely on dehumanizing language to describe Palestinians also contribute to a distorted narrative. Terms such as "militants" or "terrorists" are often employed without contextualizing the broader struggle for self-determination. The ground reality challenges this narrative by highlighting the diverse motivations and aspirations of individuals involved in the resistance, emphasizing the importance of recognizing the multifaceted nature of the Palestinian struggle.

Media portrayal also tends to oversimplify complex geopolitical issues, contributing to a binary narrative that reinforces existing biases. The portrayal of the skirmish as a dichotomy between good and evil, with Israel cast as the unequivocal defender and Palestinians as the aggressors, oversimplifies the intricate dynamics at play. Ground realities underscore the need for a more nuanced understanding that acknowledges the complexities, historical injustices, and legitimate grievances on both sides.

Selective Representation of Incidents

In the intricate landscape of media coverage surrounding the Israeli-Palestinian war, a meticulous examination reveals instances where Zionist forces strategically and selectively represented incidents to shape a particular narrative. During the recent escalation of tensions following Operation Al-Aqsa Flood, a noteworthy incident occurred. The portrayal of events by Zionist forces in media coverage exhibited a discernible pattern of emphasizing incidents that aligned with their self-defense narrative while moderating or neglecting others.

An illustrative example is the reporting on rocket attacks by Palestinian groups and Israel's subsequent airstrikes, as discussed earlier. Zionist forces, in their media representation, consistently focused on highlighting the rocket attacks targeting Israeli population centers. The emphasis on these incidents served to create a narrative centered on Israeli civilians facing imminent danger, reinforcing the notion of a defensive response. Concurrently, the coverage downplayed or omitted details of Palestinian casualties and the extensive damage inflicted on civilian infrastructure in the Gaza Strip.

Furthermore, there was a discernible trend in delineating the context of clashes. Zionist forces strategically highlighted specific provocations or attacks by Palestinian groups, often narrating them as unprovoked aggression against Israel. This outlining reinforced the narrative of Zionist forces responding defensively to external threats, contributing to the portrayal of a just and necessary militant intervention.

The selective representation of incidents extended beyond the immediate confrontation, encompassing broader issues such as the blockade of Gaza. This selective coverage ignored the profound humanitarian consequences on the Palestinian population, particularly in terms of restricted access to elemental resources and the deterioration of living conditions.

Analyzing these patterns in the selective representation of incidents underscores the deliberate efforts by Zionist forces to craft a narrative that aligns with their self-defense narrative. By strategically emphasizing certain events while modulating or omitting others, they sought to control the narrative and shape public perception in favor of their bellicose actions and policies.

In contrast to the selectively presented incidents by Zionist forces in media coverage, alternative narratives and independent accounts provide diverse perspectives on the same events, highlighting significant discrepancies between the media portrayal and alternative viewpoints. Examining these alternative narratives is essential to unraveling the complexity of the Israeli-Palestinian war and understanding the ways in which media manipulation contributes to distorted representations.

Independent accounts often present a more nuanced view of incidents that have been selectively framed in mainstream media. For instance, incidents of Palestinian resistance or protests, which are often portrayed as threats in the media narrative, may be characterized differently in alternative narratives. Independent journalists, human rights organizations, and eyewitness testimonies can offer a more balanced depiction of the motivations and circumstances surrounding such events, challenging the one-sided fabricated exhibition presented by Zionist forces.

Alternative narratives highlight the upshots of Israeli policies, such as the blockade of Gaza, in ways that may be downplayed or overlooked in mainstream media. Independent reports, international organizations, and humanitarian agencies often emphasize the humanitarian crisis resulting from restrictive measures, providing a counterpoint to the security-centric formulation by Zionist forces. By showcasing the human suffering and challenges faced by Palestinian communities, these alternative perspectives underscore the broader impact of Israeli policies beyond the security narrative.

Discrepancies between media portrayals and alternative narratives also extend to the portrayal of Palestinian leadership and political dynamics. While mainstream media may focus on divisions among Palestinian factions or present a monolithic view of Palestinian political actors, alternative perspectives highlight the complexities of internal dynamics and the diversity of opinions within Palestinian society. By presenting a more nuanced understanding of political dynamics, alternative narratives challenge the simplistic portrayals often perpetuated by selective media representations.

Influence on International Reporting

The examination of major international media outlets reveals significant insights into how events influenced by Zionist forces' delineation are interpreted and reported. The influence of Zionist movements on international reporting is particularly evident in the consistency of narratives across different global media platforms, emphasizing angles of peace associated with Zionist actions. Major international media outlets, including renowned news agencies and television networks, such as BBC, CNN, FOX, and MSNBC, have played a crucial role in shaping the narrative surrounding events involving Zionist forces. These outlets often depict Zionist movements in a favorable light, enclosing their actions as strategic moves for peace and security. The consistency in these narratives across various platforms reflects a concerted effort to present a unified perspective on Zionist activities.

For instance, during skirmishes or militant operations involving Zionist forces, major international media outlets tend to highlight narratives that emphasize the need for self-defense and protection of Israeli citizens. The shaping often centers on the threat posed by external forces, portraying Zionist actions as justified responses to safeguard national security. This consistent portrayal across global media outlets contributes to shaping public perception by reinforcing the narrative of Zionist forces acting in the interest of peace and stability.

Furthermore, major international media outlets frequently provide a platform for spokespersons and representatives of Zionist movements to convey their messages. This access allows Zionist leaders to articulate their perspectives directly to a global audience, influencing how their actions are perceived. The construction of interviews, statements, and official communications often aligns with the overarching narrative of Zionist movements as proponents of peace, fostering a sense of legitimacy and credibility in the international community.

The portrayal of Zionist movements as angles of peace is not limited to tussle situations; it extends to coverage of diplomatic initiatives, negotiations, and political developments. Major international media outlets tend to highlight instances where Zionist leaders engage in alleged diplomatic efforts or express intentions for peace talks. The consistent emphasis on these aspects reinforces the narrative that Zionist forces are actively pursuing peaceful resolutions to this war.

Moreover, the interpretation of Zionist actions often restrains or ignores controversial aspects, such as human rights violations or disproportionate use of force. Major international media outlets choose to focus on specific aspects of an event that align with the peace-oriented narrative while minimizing coverage of actions that could cast Zionist forces in a negative light. This selective coverage contributes to a skewed representation of the overall situation, shaping global perceptions in favor of Zionist movements.

The influence on international reporting by major media outlets is not solely limited to the content of news articles or broadcasts. The framing is also evident in the language used, the selection of images, and the overall tone of the reporting. Positive portrayals of Zionist leaders, coupled with language that reinforces the narrative of peace efforts, create a consistent image across diverse media platforms. For instance, on its X account on October 9, 2023, the BBC used the term 'killed' when reporting Israeli casualties, whereas the term 'died' was employed when referencing Palestinian casualties in the battle.

The media manipulation orchestrated by Zionist forces has wielded a significant impact on shaping the international perception of the brawl. This influence extends beyond the realm of news reporting, reaching the corridors of diplomatic responses and actions taken by various nations. The meticulously constructed narratives disseminated through global media outlets conspicuously influence how the international community perceives and responds to the Israeli-Palestinian war.

The systematic construction of Zionist actions as endeavors for peace, as discussed previously, has far-reaching consequences on the global stage. Nations around the world rely on media coverage to inform their understanding of geopolitical events. In the context of the Israeli-Palestinian brawl, the media manipulation by Zionist forces has framed their movements as responsible actors working towards regional stability. This narrative has influenced the perception that many nations hold regarding the intentions and actions of Zionist forces.

Diplomatic responses to the Israeli-Palestinian tussle are intricately linked to the media representation of events. The positive presentation of Zionist movements as proponents of peace shapes the discourse surrounding the war, influencing how nations engage with the situation. In instances where media coverage emphasizes diplomatic initiatives or peace talks initiated by

Zionist leaders, diplomatic responses from various nations often reflect a willingness to engage with and support these initiatives.

Moreover, the selective representation of incidents, as explored above, further impacts diplomatic responses. When media narratives downplay controversial actions or human rights violations by Zionist forces, it creates a skewed perception that can influence how other nations respond diplomatically. Nations may be more inclined to express solidarity or support for Zionist actions if their understanding of the clashes is shaped primarily by narratives that emphasize self-defense and peace efforts.

The influence of media manipulation on diplomatic responses becomes particularly evident in international forums and organizations. Nations participating in global bodies such as the United Nations seemingly may base their stances on resolutions and policies on the information available through media channels. The consistent depiction of Zionist movements as angles of peace can garner diplomatic support from allies who align with the narrative presented in the media.

Irrespective of media narratives or counter-narratives, certain pro-Zionist nations like the USA, France, and Canada openly declare their support for the Israeli government, including the provision of weaponry. For diplomatic reasons, they may occasionally feign condemnation of Israel's violations and war crimes, but no tangible actions are taken against them. Additionally, countries known for their Islamophobic tendencies, such as India and France, advocate for the purported rights of Israel merely because Palestine is a Muslim country, showing a lack of concern for other considerations.

The examination of international reporting influenced by media manipulation requires a critical comparison with independent and alternative sources to unravel the complexities of the Israeli-Palestinian war. The narratives disseminated by major global media outlets often align with the framing strategies employed by Zionist forces to project an image of peace and self-defense. Contrasting these narratives with independent reporting provides a more comprehensive understanding of the diverse perspectives on the conflict as discussed before.

Use of Social Media and Propaganda

The strategic use of social media platforms by Zionist forces has become a prominent aspect of contemporary information warfare, influencing the narrative surrounding the Israeli-Palestinian war. This investigation delves into how these forces leverage social media to disseminate information and shape public perception. Specific campaigns and instances highlight the instrumental role that social media plays in amplifying the narratives crafted by Zionist forces.

A notable example involves utilizing platforms like X, Instagram, and Facebook to disseminate real-time updates and official statements. Zionist forces strategically utilize these platforms to control the narrative, providing instant updates on insurrectionary operations, illustrating their actions as self-defense, and disseminating information that aligns with their broader strategic objectives. The immediacy and accessibility of social media allow Zionist forces to reach a global audience directly, bypassing traditional media channels and shaping the narrative in real-time.

In addition to official statements, social media is instrumental in disseminating visual content that supports the narrative of Zionist forces. Images and videos shared on platforms like Instagram and YouTube are carefully curated to evoke specific emotions and perceptions. This visual propaganda often highlights instances of alleged violence attributed to Palestinian factions, reinforcing the image of Zionist forces as defenders against external threats. The strategic use of visuals on social media contributes significantly to shaping the emotional response of the global audience. In some cases, pictures of Palestinian suffering are used as if they depict the suffering of Israelis.

Social media campaigns orchestrated on various platforms considerably advance Zionist narratives. Hashtag campaigns, viral videos, and coordinated messaging are deployed to garner support and sway public opinion. These campaigns often employ emotionally charged content, emphasizing the vulnerability of Israeli civilians and portraying Zionist actions as necessary responses to protect the population. The intentional shaping of these campaigns seeks to create a narrative that resonates with a broad audience and garners support for Zionist objectives.

Moreover, social media is a battleground for disinformation and propaganda. Zionist forces exploit the viral nature of content on platforms like Facebook to spread narratives that align with their strategic goals. False or misleading information is disseminated to create confusion, divert attention, or discredit alternative perspectives. The rapid dissemination of such content on social media makes it challenging to counter false narratives effectively, contributing to the manipulation of public perception.

An instance exemplifying the use of social media in shaping the narrative involves the dissemination of images and videos portraying Palestinians as aggressors or using civilians as human shields. These visuals, often shared on platforms like Facebook and X, are strategically framed to elicit outrage and depict Zionist forces as victims forced to take extreme measures. The selective presentation of incidents through social media contributes to a distorted understanding of the confrontation, reinforcing the dominant narrative crafted by Zionist forces.

The role of influencers and online personalities cannot be overlooked in the strategic use of social media. Zionist forces often collaborate with influencers who have a significant following to amplify their narratives. These influencers share content, voice support for Zionist actions, and contribute to the dissemination of curated messages. The reach and impact of influencers on social media platforms further extend the influence of Zionist narratives beyond official channels.

A significant example is the "Protective Edge" operation in 2014, during which Zionist forces heightened their utilization of social media to shape global perceptions. During this campaign, Twitter became a battleground for disseminating real-time updates, visual content, and curated narratives. Hashtags like #ProtectiveEdge were strategically employed to consolidate discussions and amplify the Zionist narrative. Visuals depicting Israeli civilians seeking shelter and the aftermath of rocket attacks were shared widely, evoking sympathy and formulating Zionist forces as defenders against indiscriminate aggression.

The "Protective Edge" campaign also witnessed the proliferation of videos on platforms like YouTube, showcasing the precision of Israeli airstrikes and emphasizing surgical strikes on alleged military targets. These videos were disseminated through official channels and strategically placed on influential social media accounts to maximize reach. The selective presentation of these visuals aimed to convey a narrative of proportionate and targeted responses, reinforcing the self-defense narrative and downplaying collateral damage.

Another case study involves the use of Instagram during the 2018 Gaza border protests. Zionist forces strategically utilized Instagram's visual-centric platform to shape the narrative surrounding these protests. The deployment of carefully curated images depicting Israeli soldiers facing perceived threats contributed to portraying the demonstrations as violent and justifying the use of force. Influencers and official accounts shared these visuals with accompanying captions reinforcing the notion of defending Israeli borders against external threats. The effectiveness of this campaign lies in the emotional impact of visuals on Instagram, where compelling images can influence attitudes with immediacy.

The 2019 social media campaign surrounding the U.S. decision to recognize Jerusalem as Israel's capital is another illustrative case study. Zionist forces orchestrated a coordinated effort across platforms like Facebook and Twitter to shape the narrative surrounding this controversial decision. Memes, infographics, and targeted messaging were disseminated to garner support for the U.S. move, presenting it as a rightful acknowledgment of Israel's sovereignty. The campaign strategically utilized social media's ability to rapidly disseminate information to influence public opinion and garner international backing.

Effectiveness in reinforcing the self-defense narrative is evident in these case studies. The strategic use of hashtags, real-time updates, visual content, and coordinated campaigns allows Zionist forces to dominate the narrative on social media platforms. The emotional impact of visuals, coupled with carefully crafted messaging, contributes to shaping global perceptions of the Israeli-Palestinian war. These campaigns effectively portray Zionist actions as necessary responses to external threats, reinforcing the narrative of self-defense and justifying militant operations.

Apart from Zionist propaganda, individuals from countries with a notable Islamophobic stance, such as India, willingly engage in supporting the Zionist cause without considering the true nature of the decades-long oppression against Palestinians. Various fabricated stories circulate in this context after the Operation Al-Aqsa flood, including false claims like Hamas kidnapping a Jewish baby or beheading a young boy on the back of a truck. Verified Indian users with blue check accounts on X have been identified as leading a disinformation campaign, as revealed by BOOM, a credible fact-checking service in India. These influencers frequently share disinformation, depicting Palestinians in a negative light and or expressing support for Israel. They propagate tropes depicting Palestinians as inherently brutal.

In a specific instance, an account circulated a video claiming to show Palestinian fighters taking dozens of young girls as sex slaves. Despite being false, the video garnered thousands of retweets and accumulated at least 6 million impressions. An analysis revealed that many accounts sharing the video were based in India. Additionally, these accounts frequently post anti-Muslim comments on the platform.

India's challenge with Islamophobia is widely known, particularly intensifying since the rise of Prime Minister Narendra Modi and his RSS-led Bharatiya Janata Party (BJP) government. The majority of Islamophobic tweets were traced back to India in a report. This online manifestation of such sentiments is evident on social media, attracting Islamophobes to the Palestinian cause. The "BJP's IT Cell," actively fueling the flames of animosity, plays a role in fostering this online hatred.

As we reflect on the multifaceted role of social media in shaping the narrative of the Israeli-Palestinian war, it becomes evident that the power to influence public opinion and perceptions is not without its ethical challenges. The digital realm, while a potent tool for communication, demands a discerning audience capable of critically evaluating the narratives presented, ensuring a nuanced understanding of this complex geopolitical brawl.

Demonization of Palestinian Resistance

The media depiction of Palestinian resistance groups by Zionist forces is a critical aspect of understanding the broader theme of media manipulation in the Israeli-Palestinian war. Analyzing the portrayal of these groups in media coverage reveals a deliberate effort to demonize and delegitimize their cause, shaping public perception through strategic language, imagery, and narratives.

In media portrayals, Hamas, a Palestinian defiance group, has been consistently depicted as a notable example. Zionist forces frequently characterize Hamas as a terrorist organization, using charged language that elicits fear and censure. The intentional choice of terms such as "militants" and "extremists" to label Hamas members aims to present them unfavorably, framing their resistance as both illegitimate and inherently violent, as previously discussed. This language not only influences public opinion but also establishes a justification for dissenting actions against these autonomous warriors.

The imagery associated with Palestinian protest groups further contributes to their demonization. Zionist forces strategically highlight instances of alleged violence attributed to these groups, emphasizing destruction and chaos. Images of armed individuals or damaged infrastructure are selectively chosen to reinforce the narrative of a relentless and threatening enemy. This selective representation serves to overshadow the underlying socio-political motivations of Palestinian resistance, reducing them to mere perpetrators of violence in the eyes of the global audience.

Narratives crafted by Zionist forces often overlook the historical context of Palestinian upsurge, outlining it as unprovoked aggression. By omitting the root causes of protest, such as occupation and dispossession, the media narrative perpetuates a distorted comprehension of the conflict. This intentional omission reinforces the portrayal of Palestinian resistance as irrational and driven solely by hostility, undermining the legitimacy of their struggle for self-determination.

Academic studies and independent analyses of media portrayals contribute to the substantiation of these observations. The impact of this interpretation is evident in public discourse, where discussions around Palestinian defiance groups are often framed by the negative narratives perpetuated by media outlets aligned with Zionist forces.

The consequence of such media narrative extends beyond shaping public opinion; it influences policy decisions, diplomatic responses, and international perceptions of the Israeli-Palestinian war. The deliberate demonization of Palestinian resistance groups serves as a tool to justify stringent security measures, militant actions, and political strategies against them. Understanding this aspect of media manipulation is crucial for unraveling the complexities of the razzia and fostering a more nuanced and informed global discourse.

Zionist forces employ a multifaceted approach in portraying Palestinian opposition, emphasizing the perceived threat they pose to Israel's national security. This characterization is not merely descriptive but is intricately woven into the narrative, creating a sense of urgency and fear in the minds of the audience. Terms like "existential threat" and "security risk" become commonplace, contributing to the construction of a narrative that positions Palestinian nonconformity groups as inherently dangerous entities.

In early 2021, Muna el-Kurd, a Palestinian activist, initiated the #save_sheikh_jarrah hashtag on social media, aiming to spotlight the impending forced eviction of her family and others in Jerusalem's Sheikh Jarrah neighborhood. However, Instagram responded by restricting el-Kurd's account, preventing her from livestreaming. This censorship extended to other Palestinian journalists, activists, and influencers, who were barred from publishing posts, stories, and utilizing the livestreaming feature. This occurred precisely when these voices were amplifying news from the field, exposing the Israeli Occupation's assaults on Jerusalem, Al-Aqsa Mosque, and Gaza. Instagram's actions mirrored a broader trend of social media platforms suppressing Palestinian digital content systematically.

Starting in May 2021, social media companies, influenced by the Israeli Justice Ministry's Cyber Unit, began removing Palestinian content without transparent justifications. A report by The Intercept uncovered Facebook's secret blacklist, containing 55 Palestinian organizations and figures, as well as charitable associations, among 4,000 entries. The report revealed Facebook's indiscriminate approach, leading to the deletion of posts documenting Israeli state violence at Al-Aqsa Mosque.

Following the Operation Al-Aqsa flood, X platform made a significant announcement. It declared its collaboration with the Global Internet Forum for Combating Terrorism, emphasizing its commitment to monitor and remove Palestinian accounts from the platform. The reason cited was the recent events in Palestine. According to the platform, it has identified more than 50 million global posts addressing the unfolding events.

The issue extends beyond X platform, as authors, activists, journalists, filmmakers, and regular users globally have voiced their concerns. They report that posts containing hashtags such as "#FreePalestine" and "#IStandWithPalestine," as well as messages expressing support for Palestinians, are being hidden by various platforms. Social media giants like Facebook, Instagram, YouTube, and TikTok have also faced accusations of censoring content that exposes the situations in Palestine or supports the Palestinian cause. In some instances, Instagram has been accused of arbitrarily taking down posts that merely mention Palestine, citing violations of "community guidelines."

The strategic use of threat perception becomes particularly evident in the justification of self-defense measures and militant actions. By framing Palestinian resistance as an imminent threat, Zionist forces create a narrative that positions their actions as necessary and proportionate responses to safeguard national security. This narrative, carefully crafted and disseminated through various media channels, influences both domestic and international perspectives, garnering support for stringent security policies and military interventions.

By analyzing the language employed by political leaders and military officials, one can observe a consistent pattern of emphasizing the perceived threat posed by Palestinian defiance groups. Moreover, examining public discourse and media coverage reveals how these narratives permeate public opinion, reinforcing the idea that robust measures are imperative to protect the nation from imminent danger.

Within Israel, the impact of this is palpable, as the demonization of Palestinian opposition becomes a catalyst for a sense of collective identity and solidarity. The narrative of an ever-present threat reinforces a shared understanding of the necessity for robust security measures. This, in turn, fosters a resilience and unity among the Israeli population, as they perceive themselves as a besieged nation facing constant danger. The impact on public opinion is evident in the support garnered for stringent security policies and pugnacious actions, reflecting a belief that such measures are essential for national survival. The influence on public opinion within Israel can be observed in public discourse, and opinion polls. Public statements consistently echo the notion that a strong response is required to counter the perceived menace posed by Palestinian resistance groups. Opinion polls further substantiate this impact, revealing a correlation between the intensity of threat perception and support for assertive security measures.

On the international stage, the demonization of Palestinian opposition shapes global perspectives on the Israeli-Palestinian war. The narratives crafted by Zionist forces influence how the international community interprets and responds to the actions of both parties. The portrayal of Palestinian defiance as a significant threat prompts empathy for Israel's security concerns, often garnering understanding or support for militant interventions. The impact is evident in diplomatic responses, where nations may align their positions based on the narratives presented through global media outlets.

Victim-Perpetrator Reversal

Examining instances where Zionist forces strategically position themselves as victims despite engaging in quarrelsome actions reveals a nuanced and calculated approach to shaping public perception. This strategy, often referred to as "strategic victimhood," involves crafting narratives and messaging that evoke empathy and garner international support while deflecting attention from their infringement operations.

Operation Protective Edge, and the 2018 Gaza border protests witnessed a continuation of the strategic victimhood narrative, as discussed in detail earlier. In both cases, the language employed by Zionist forces was pivotal in portraying a sense of victimhood, overshadowing their aggressive attacks on Palestinian civilians.

Strategic victimhood is not confined to military conflicts but extends to broader geopolitical developments. The use of victimhood narrative was evident in the aftermath of the International Criminal Court's (ICC) decision to investigate war crimes in the Palestinian territories. Zionist officials framed the ICC's move as an unfair targeting of Israel, portraying the country as a victim of biased international scrutiny. The narrative focused on questioning the legitimacy of the ICC's jurisdiction and presenting Israel as unfairly singled out, despite documented evidence of violations.

The strategic manipulation of blame and responsibility by Zionist forces is a notable aspect of their media tactics, contributing to the broader theme of victim-perpetrator reversal. By skillfully shifting blame onto external actors and portraying themselves as reactive rather than proactive, Zionist forces seek to shape public perception and influence international discourse.

Following the 2014 Gaza skirmish, Zionist forces faced allegations of disproportionate use of force and civilian casualties. Israeli officials responded by asserting that Hamas deliberately used civilian infrastructure for military purposes, placing blame for civilian casualties on the Palestinian group. This narrative aimed to shift criticism by framing the battle as a result of Hamas' actions, portraying Zionist forces as responding to provocations rather than initiating offensive operations. A similar strategy is observed post-Operation Al-Aqsa, with Israeli militant groups intentionally targeting civilian infrastructure and justifying these attacks using a blame-shifting approach similar to the one employed after the 2014 Gaza war.

The impact of such blame-shifting narratives on public perception and international discourse is substantial. By presenting themselves as reacting to external threats, Zionist forces create a narrative that aligns with the broader theme of self-defense. This depiction is designed to garner sympathy and support both domestically and internationally, as it positions Zionist forces as reluctant participants in hostilities forced upon them.

Furthermore, the narrative of shifting blame and responsibility extends beyond individual battles to broader geopolitical developments. For instance, the construction of Israeli settlements in the West Bank, considered illegal under international law, has been justified by Zionist officials as a response to security concerns. By outlining settlement expansion as a defensive measure against potential threats, Zionist forces attempt to legitimize their actions and shift the narrative away from violations of international law.

Understanding the impact of blame-shifting narratives is crucial for critically assessing media representations and recognizing the complexities of the Israeli-Palestinian war. By strategically framing themselves as reacting to external threats, Zionist forces shape narratives that resonate with the broader theme of victimhood. This nuanced manipulation of blame contributes to the construction of a narrative that justifies militant actions, settlement expansion, and other contentious policies.

Counter-Narratives and Fact-Checking

The emergence of counter-narratives in the context of the Israeli-Palestinian tussle represents a crucial aspect of the ongoing media manipulation dynamics. These counter-narratives provide alternative perspectives that challenge the prevailing self-defense account propagated by Zionist forces. Examining the development and contributors to these counter-narratives unveils a complex landscape shaped by various groups, individuals, and movements seeking to present alternative viewpoints.

The international human rights community, represented by organizations such as Amnesty International and Human Rights Watch, serves as a significant reservoir for counter-narratives. These entities outstandingly contribute to scrutinizing and challenging the narratives presented by Zionist forces. Through detailed reports, investigations, and documentation, they present evidence that contradicts the self-defense narrative. For instance, reports documenting civilian casualties, destruction of infrastructure, and war crimes contribute to shaping counter-narratives that question the legitimacy of Israel's actions.

Civil society movements and grassroots organizations also contribute significantly to the emergence of counter-narratives. Activists, both within and outside the affected regions, leverage social media platforms and alternative media outlets to disseminate information that challenges the dominant narrative. For example, the Boycott, Divestment, Sanctions (BDS) movement, advocating for Palestinian rights, utilizes various channels to highlight perspectives that contest the self-defense narrative. Through campaigns, protests, and information-sharing, these movements contribute to shaping a counter-narrative that emphasizes the impact of Israeli actions on Palestinian communities.

Individual journalists are inevitable in offering alternative perspectives to the self-defense narrative. Journalists who prioritize unbiased reporting and independent analysis contribute to the diversification of the media landscape. By investigating on-the-ground realities, conducting interviews, and presenting a more nuanced view of the armed wrangle, these individuals challenge the mainstream narrative perpetuated by larger media entities. The work of journalists like Gideon Levy and Amira Hass, who report from within Israel and the occupied territories, offers a counter-narrative that contrasts with the dominant self-defense narrative.

Social media platforms serve as powerful tools for the dissemination of counter-narratives, allowing individuals and groups to bypass traditional media gatekeepers. Hashtags, campaigns, and viral content contribute to amplifying alternative perspectives. Platforms like X become arena where activists, journalists, and concerned individuals share firsthand accounts, images, and stories that counter the prevailing narrative. The immediacy and accessibility of social media enable counter-narratives to reach a global audience swiftly.

Academic and research institutions also contribute to shaping counter-narratives by providing in-depth analyses and studies that challenge prevailing perspectives. Scholars and experts scrutinize historical contexts, legal frameworks, and the socio-political dynamics of the warfare, offering nuanced perspectives that question the simplistic self-defense narrative. These scholarly contributions enhance our grasp of the Israeli-Palestinian war, fostering a more thorough comprehension.

Simultaneously, fact-checking initiatives, encompassing both independent organizations and media outlets with dedicated fact-checking teams, have a meaningful role in holding media narratives accountable. These initiatives deploy rigorous methodologies, including cross-referencing information, consulting primary sources, and conducting thorough investigations to verify the accuracy of claims made by different parties involved in the confrontation. By providing evidence-based assessments, fact-checkers aim to offer the public a more nuanced understanding of events, thereby challenging the one-sided self-defense narrative.

A noteworthy illustration involves the efforts of entities such as the International Fact-Checking Network (IFCN), which works in collaboration with fact-checkers globally to uphold accuracy in public discourse. Fact-checking outlets such as Snopes, FactCheck.org, and PolitiFact also contribute to the scrutiny of claims related to the Israeli-Palestinian war. These organizations assess statements, images, and narratives circulating in the media, providing readers with clear verdicts on the accuracy of the information.

The impact of fact-checking on public perception is significant, as it influences the credibility attributed to media narratives. When fact-checkers expose misinformation or false claims within the self-defense narrative, it raises awareness among the public about the potential manipulation of information. This, in turn, fosters a more discerning audience that questions the veracity of media portrayals and demands accountability from news sources. The growing prevalence of fact-checking in the media landscape contributes to a shift in public perception from passive consumption to critical engagement.

Fact-checking additionally serves an astonishing function in countering the spread of misinformation on social media platforms. With the rapid dissemination of information online, false narratives can gain traction quickly. Fact-checkers act as a bulwark against the proliferation of misleading content by promptly debunking false claims and providing evidence-based corrections. This proactive approach not only prevents the perpetuation of misinformation but also undermines the credibility of those attempting to manipulate narratives in favor of a self-defense narrative.

Moreover, fact-checking initiatives contribute to fostering transparency and accountability within media organizations. When fact-checkers identify inaccuracies or distortions in reporting, it prompts media outlets to reassess their editorial processes and correct the record. This self-correction reinforces the importance of journalistic integrity and reinforces the credibility of media outlets, especially when facing the scrutiny of fact-checking organizations.

However, it is essential to recognize the challenges and limitations of fact-checking, particularly in a complex and contentious skirmish like the Israeli-Palestinian situation. The subjective nature of some claims, the potential for biases in fact-checking processes, and the constant evolution of narratives pose challenges to achieving absolute objectivity. Fact-checking, therefore, should be seen as one component of a broader strategy to promote media literacy, critical thinking, and diverse sources of information.

Independent journalism, characterized by its commitment to editorial autonomy and impartiality, serves as a bulwark against the potential biases inherent in media narratives influenced by political agendas. Outlets such as The Intercept, ProPublica, and The Bureau of Investigative Journalism exemplify the principles of independent journalism, prioritizing investigative reporting and fact-based storytelling. These organizations actively seek to present a more comprehensive and nuanced understanding of the Israeli-Palestinian war, challenging the one-sided nature of prevailing narratives.

An important facet of the contribution of independent journalism is its emphasis on offering context and historical background, aiding audiences in understanding the intricacies of the warfare. For example, outlets like Al Jazeera English and Middle East Eye delve into historical events, geopolitical intricacies, and the perspectives of various stakeholders involved. By offering a broader narrative canvas, independent journalism aims to foster a more informed public capable of critically engaging with the issues at hand.

These independent entities face formidable challenges in their pursuit of unbiased reporting within the context of the Israeli-Palestinian war. Political pressures, ideological biases, and the risks associated with reporting from battlegrounds can compromise journalistic independence. For instance, journalists reporting on the hostility may encounter obstacles in accessing certain areas or face backlash for presenting narratives that deviate from prevailing discourses, or even be killed, like Shireen Abu Akleh, by the militant forces.

Moreover, the polarization inherent in the Israeli-Palestinian war extends to media coverage, making it challenging for independent organizations to navigate without being accused of taking sides. The mere act of presenting alternative viewpoints or questioning dominant narratives can subject these outlets to criticism and accusations of bias, even when their commitment to journalistic integrity remains unwavering.

Despite these challenges, independent journalism and organizations contribute significantly to the media landscape by amplifying diverse voices and perspectives. By offering a platform to marginalized or underrepresented viewpoints, they provide a more holistic understanding of the conflict. For example, outlets like +972 Magazine and Mondoweiss feature contributions from Palestinian and Israeli writers, offering readers insights often absent from mainstream narratives.

The commitment to transparency and accountability is another hallmark of independent journalism. Many independent outlets openly disclose their funding sources and editorial policies, fostering trust among their audience. This transparency is in stark contrast to the opacity often associated with media outlets aligned with specific political or national interests.

Human Rights
Violations

Extrajudicial Killings and Targeted Assassinations

The documented cases of extrajudicial killings and targeted assassinations by Zionist forces paint a troubling picture of human rights violations in the Israeli-Palestinian war. These incidents, carefully cataloged and analyzed, reveal patterns and trends that underscore the severity and systematic nature of such actions. Targeted individuals frequently include activists, political figures, and those perceived as threats to the Zionist agenda, marking a discernible pattern. These extrajudicial killings extend beyond conventional warfare, reaching into civilian populations and diaspora communities. The documented cases highlight a deliberate strategy of eliminating perceived adversaries, even beyond the immediate combat regions, raising concerns about the scope and ethics of such operations.

Locations of these extrajudicial killings exhibit a disturbing trend, with incidents occurring not only within the occupied territories but also beyond borders. International law delineates the boundaries of military actions, but the documented cases suggest a transgression of these boundaries. The willingness to conduct targeted assassinations in foreign territories raises questions about the ethical and legal considerations guiding such operations.

Methods employed in these cases often involve precision airstrikes, covert operations, or targeted drone strikes. The utilization of advanced military technologies underscores the asymmetry of power in the skirmish. These methods not only violate the principles of proportionality and distinction in international humanitarian law but also pose a significant challenge to accountability, given the covert nature of many of these operations.

The intentional targeting of individuals, irrespective of their status, location, or affiliation, challenges the fundamental principles of human rights and humanitarian law. The systematic nature of these extrajudicial killings calls for a comprehensive examination of the ethical, legal, and geopolitical implications, urging the international community to address these violations and work towards ensuring accountability for those responsible.

The violations of the right to life through extrajudicial killings and targeted assassinations perpetrated by Zionist forces extend beyond the immediate physical harm inflicted on individuals. From a legal and ethical standpoint, these actions starkly contravene international law, particularly the right to life enshrined in various human rights instruments, such as the Universal Declaration of Human Rights and the International Covenant on Civil and Political Rights.

International law unequivocally upholds the right to life as a fundamental and non-derogable human right. Extrajudicial killings, defined as unlawful and deliberate killings carried out by state actors, constitute a barefaced violation of this right. The principle of legality, a cornerstone of international human rights law, dictates that individuals must be afforded due process and legal protection, ensuring that the right to life is not arbitrarily infringed upon. In the context of the documented cases, where individuals are targeted without legal proceedings, these actions stand in direct contradiction to the principles of legality.

The ethical dimensions of these violations are equally profound, as they raise questions about the moral compass guiding state actions. The deliberate disregard for the right to life reflects a departure from the principles of proportionality, necessity, and humanity that underpin just and ethical conduct in armed conflicts. The use of advanced military technologies in targeted assassinations further complicates the ethical landscape, as it underscores the power imbalances and challenges the notion of a fair fight.

While the legal and ethical dimensions provide a framework for condemning these actions, the practical implications demand international attention and intervention. The evidence supporting these violations is often meticulously documented by human rights organizations, investigative journalists, and international bodies. Eyewitness testimonies, forensic analysis, and corroborating reports contribute to a compelling body of evidence that underscores the gravity of the situation.

Addressing these violations requires a concerted effort to hold perpetrators accountable under international law. The legal framework exists, and the evidence is compelling; what remains is the political will to pursue justice. The affected individuals, their families, and the broader community deserve a response that upholds the principles of human rights, ensuring that the right to life is not just an ideal enshrined in legal texts but a tangible reality for all individuals, irrespective of their geopolitical context.

The impact of extrajudicial killings and targeted assassinations on affected communities extends far beyond the immediate loss of life. The social fabric of these communities is intricately woven with threads of shared history, cultural ties, and communal bonds. When these threads are violently severed through unlawful killings, the repercussions are profound, touching every aspect of community life.

Psychologically, the trauma inflicted on individuals within these communities is immeasurable. Witnessing or experiencing extrajudicial killings leaves lasting scars, creating an atmosphere of fear and distrust. The constant threat of violence disrupts the mental well-being of community members, leading to heightened stress, anxiety, and a pervasive sense of insecurity. Children, in particular, bear witness to a distorted reality where the norm becomes a constant state of alertness and fear, shaping their worldview in ways that hinder healthy development.

Socially, the aftermath of targeted assassinations fractures the communal bonds that are essential for the functioning of any society. Fear-driven self-censorship stifles open dialogue and dissent, breeding an environment where silence becomes a survival strategy. The erosion of trust in community members and institutions perpetuates a culture of suspicion, hindering the collective resilience necessary for rebuilding a sense of normalcy.

Economically, the impact is equally profound. Communities that are subjected to extrajudicial killings often face economic downturns as businesses shutter, and investments decline. The pervasive atmosphere of insecurity discourages external investments, perpetuating a cycle of poverty and stagnation. The loss of breadwinners in targeted assassinations further exacerbates economic challenges, leaving families without stable sources of income and amplifying existing socio-economic disparities.

The long-term consequences of these impacts are deeply embedded in the fabric of affected communities. Rebuilding trust, both internally and with external entities, becomes a protracted and arduous process. The psychological shock endured by individuals, especially the younger generation, manifests in various forms, affecting relationships, educational attainment, and career prospects. The economic scars persist, hindering the potential for sustainable development.

Mass Arrests and Administrative Detentions

The occurrence of mass arrests carried out by Zionist forces represents a troubling aspect of the broader issue of human rights violations. These operations, marked by the simultaneous detention of numerous individuals, occur in diverse circumstances, locations, and scales, revealing a worrisome pattern that warrants careful examination. A notable incident highlighting the extent and characteristics of mass arrests took place during the Second Intifada in 2002. IDF launched Operation Defensive Shield, a large-scale militant operation in the West Bank. As part of this operation, Israeli forces conducted mass arrests in several Palestinian cities, including Ramallah, Nablus, and Jenin.

The circumstances surrounding these arrests were marked by the imposition of curfews, house demolitions, and the sealing off of entire neighborhoods. These operations seemingly focused on individuals suspected of engaging in activities against Israel, resulting in the detention of hundreds of Palestinians. The scale of these mass arrests raised concerns among human rights organizations and the international community, questioning the proportionality and legality of such widespread detentions.

In another instance, the mass arrests of Palestinians occurred during the 2014 militant campaign in the West Bank. Israeli forces conducted sweeping operations, arresting over 500 Palestinians. The circumstances of these arrests involved raids on homes, clashes with local residents, and the use of militant checkpoints to control movement.

Specific cases within these mass arrests exemplify the impact on individuals and communities. Take, for instance, the arrest of Palestinian legislator Khalida Jarrar in 2015. Jarrar, a prominent political figure, was detained without formal charges or trial, under administrative detention—a practice that allows for prolonged detention without presenting evidence. Her case highlights the arbitrary nature of mass arrests, where even individuals holding political office are not immune to detention without due process.

The geographical scope of mass arrests extends beyond the West Bank, with similar operations conducted in East Jerusalem. In 2017, during heightened tensions surrounding security measures at the Al-Aqsa Mosque, Israeli forces arrested over 1,000 Palestinians in East Jerusalem. The arrests targeted individuals involved in protests and clashes, illustrating how mass arrests become a tool to suppress dissent and control perceived threats to Israeli interests.

The nature and scope of these mass arrests are further exemplified by the detention of minors. In 2018, the Palestinian Prisoners Club reported that nearly 700 Palestinian minors were arrested by Israeli forces, many subjected to harsh interrogation methods. The circumstances surrounding these arrests often involve night raids on family homes, leading to the traumatization of children and the disruption of family life.

On October 17, 2023, Al Jazeera reported nearly 700 arrests in the West Bank and East Jerusalem since the war began. By October 28, the count reached 1,550, per the Palestinian Prisoners Society. As of October 31, The Globe and Mail stated Israel acknowledged 1,700 prisoners to the Palestinian Authority without disclosing their whereabouts. On November 6, Al Jazeera revealed 1,740 arrests in overnight raids. BBC reported 2,150 arrests on the same day, according to the Palestinian Prisoners Society. The Associated Press cited 2,280 detainees on November 8. On November 10, The Nation reported "at least 2,200". On November 15, Mondoweiss noted ongoing arrests in the West Bank. HaMoked, an Israeli NGO, reported an increase from 1,319 to 2,070 Palestinians held without charge or trial since October 7.

The impact of mass arrests goes beyond the individuals directly detained; it permeates entire communities, fostering an atmosphere of fear and uncertainty. The scale of these operations, coupled with the arbitrary nature of arrests, raises serious questions about the adherence to human rights principles, particularly the right to a fair trial and protection against arbitrary detention.

The legal frameworks—or, more accurately, the lack thereof—surrounding mass arrests and administrative detentions carried out by Zionist forces in the Israeli-Palestinian war are deeply intertwined with the humanitarian implications of these practices. Examining the legal aspects provides a crucial context for understanding the challenges posed by such actions, shedding light on the violations of human rights and the impact on individuals, their families, and the broader community.

In terms of legal frameworks, the Israeli military, through various emergency regulations, asserts its authority to conduct mass arrests and administrative detentions in the occupied territories. The use of administrative detention, in particular, allows Israeli authorities to detain individuals for extended periods without formal charges or trial. This practice is justified under the argument of safeguarding security, a claim that lacks transparency and raises strong concerns about the abuse of power.

The application of administrative detention, a prominent legal aspect, fundamentally violates the principle of due process. Administrative detention allows for the imprisonment of individuals without presenting evidence or allowing them to contest the allegations against them. This practice not only contradicts international human rights standards but also circumvents the basic principles of justice and fairness. The absence of formal charges and the denial of a fair trial undermine the right to a defense, leaving detainees and their families in a state of prolonged uncertainty.

The use of militant orders, often lacking transparency and accountability, further complicates the legal landscape. The wide-ranging powers granted to militant commanders in the occupied territories allow for the issuance of orders leading to mass arrests, house demolitions, and other security measures. This illegal framework, marked by military authority, raises questions about the adherence to the rule of law and the accountability of those involved in decision-making processes.

The legal ramifications extend beyond administrative detention to encompass mass arrests as a whole. The practice of conducting large-scale arrests during armed operations, as witnessed during Operation Defensive Shield in 2002 and subsequent campaigns, raises concerns about the proportionality and necessity of such actions. International law requires that measures taken by occupying powers be proportionate to the security threat and strictly necessary for the maintenance of public order. The extensive use of mass arrests, often targeting broad segments of the population, challenges the adherence to these legal principles.

From a humanitarian perspective, the consequences of prolonged detention without trial are deeply distressing. Families of those detained endure the anguish of not knowing when their loved ones will be released, if at all. The psychic toll on individuals subjected to arbitrary and extended detention is profound, with reports of psychological agony, anxiety, and depression being common among detainees.

Children, unfortunately, are not spared from the humanitarian fallout. The widespread arrests of Palestinian minors, as documented by organizations like Defense for Children International - Palestine, reveal the traumatic impact on the mental and emotional well-being of young individuals. Night raids, arrests, and harsh interrogation methods contribute to a climate of fear among Palestinian children, affecting not only their immediate experiences but also shaping their perceptions of authority and justice.

The broader community also bears the humanitarian brunt of mass arrests. The systematic disruption of daily life, the intimidation imposed by militant operations, and the erosion of trust in legal and judicial systems create a collective sense of insecurity. Communities affected by these practices are left in a perpetual state of vulnerability, with the long-term consequences extending far beyond the immediate impact of arrests.

From an international perspective, mass arrests and administrative detentions conducted by Zionist forces within the land of Palestine have garnered significant attention, drawing critiques and concerns from human rights organizations, legal experts, and diplomatic circles. The global community has expressed unease about the legality and human rights implications of these practices, contributing to a nuanced discourse surrounding the Israeli militant's approach to security measures.

Human rights organizations, such as Amnesty International and Human Rights Watch, have been vocal in their condemnation of mass arrests and administrative detentions. These organizations consistently highlight the violations of international human rights standards, emphasizing the arbitrary nature of arrests, the lack of due process, and the prolonged detention without trial. The reports and investigations conducted by these entities provide a wealth of documented cases, shedding light on the systemic issues within the Israeli militant's approach to security operations.

Amnesty International, for instance, has extensively documented cases where individuals, including minors, have been subjected to arbitrary arrests and prolonged detention without charge. The organization's reports emphasize the detrimental impact on the lives of those affected and call for an end to these practices, urging the Israeli government to adhere to international law and respect the rights of detainees.

Human Rights Watch has similarly criticized the Israeli militant's use of administrative detention, characterizing it as a tool employed to suppress dissent and silence opposition. The organization's detailed analyses of specific cases underscore the need for a comprehensive reevaluation of the legal frameworks governing these practices, stressing the urgency of addressing the human rights violations inherent in mass arrests and administrative detentions.

Legal experts and scholars have also weighed in on the international stage, offering critiques that delve into the legal aspects of these security measures. The lack of transparency in the application of administrative detention and the broad powers granted to military commanders have been subjects of scrutiny. Legal scholars, some of whom are associated with institutions specializing in international law, contend that employing administrative detention without transparent legal justification gives rise to substantial apprehensions regarding the rule of law and the safeguarding of individual rights.

Diplomatic responses from various nations and international bodies further reflect the international community's reservations about mass arrests and administrative detentions. Statements issued by foreign governments, the United Nations, and other international forums often express concerns about the impact of these practices on the broader human rights situation in the region. Diplomatic missions, such as those from European countries and the United States, have ostensibly urged the Israeli government to uphold its commitment to human rights principles and ensure fair treatment for all individuals, including those detained during security operations.

For instance, the European Union has consistently emphasized the importance of respecting human rights and international law in its communications with Israeli authorities. The EU has urged a transparent legal process for individuals detained, emphasizing the need for adherence to due process and the right to a fair trial. Similarly, the United States, while maintaining its strategic alliance with Israel, has conveyed concerns about human rights issues, including the treatment of detainees, through diplomatic channels.

The United Nations, through its various bodies and agencies, has also played a weighty role in addressing the international perspectives on mass arrests and administrative detentions. Reports from the UN Special Rapporteur on the situation of human rights in the Palestinian territories and statements from the UN High Commissioner for Human Rights have superficially underscored the need for accountability and the protection of human rights in the context of security operations.

Torture and Inhumane Treatment

Documented cases of torture perpetrated by Zionist forces in the Israeli-Palestinian war are deeply troubling instances that have raised significant international concern. Human rights organizations, legal experts, and testimonies from individuals affected have shed light on the systematic use of torture and inhumane treatment in various contexts. These cases underscore the urgent need for addressing human rights violations and ensuring accountability for those responsible.

A case that gained global recognition involves the narrative of Samir Arbeed; a Palestinian individual apprehended by Israeli security forces. His case exemplifies the brutal methods employed by Zionist forces during interrogations. According to reports from Amnesty International and other human rights organizations, Arbeed was subjected to severe physical and psychological torture while in custody.

Arbeed was arrested on the accusation of being connected to an attack that resulted in the death of an Israeli settler. During his interrogation, he was reportedly beaten, deprived of sleep, and subjected to stress positions. The extent of the torture was so severe that Arbeed fell into a critical condition and was subsequently hospitalized. The documented details of his case highlight the grim reality of torture tactics employed during interrogations, raising serious concerns about the treatment of detainees in Israeli custody.

Another case that drew international attention is that of Arafat Jaradat, a Palestinian who died in Israeli custody in 2013. According to investigations by human rights organizations, Jaradat was arrested for his alleged involvement in a stone-throwing incident. His death raised suspicions of torture during interrogation. Autopsy reports revealed injuries consistent with physical abuse, including broken ribs and signs of severe beating.

These cases are not isolated incidents, but rather indicative of a broader pattern of torture and inhumane treatment. Palestinians, including minors, have reported similar experiences of torture during interrogations. The methods employed include beatings, solitary confinement, sleep deprivation, urinating on the face and body, and threats against family members. The context in which these acts occur, often within the framework of security operations, underlines the challenges in addressing such violations in a confrontation-driven environment.

Numerous human rights organizations, including Amnesty International and Human Rights Watch, have documented cases of mistreatment and abuse, including sexual violence, in the context of Israeli detention of Palestinian individuals. These reports highlight concerns about the treatment of Palestinian prisoners, both male and female, in Israeli custody.

Female prisoners express grievances regarding degrading body searches, wherein they are compelled to remove all their clothes. Some prison guards have engaged in a degrading and insulting manner of touching their bodies. In instances where a Palestinian female prisoner resists such degrading searches, she is compelled to undress after being handcuffed. There are also reported cases where she may face threats of forced undressing by other guards. The UN Human Rights Committee's General Comment 16 on article 17 of the International Covenant on Civil and Political Rights underscores the significance of conducting body searches in a manner consistent with human dignity, particularly emphasizing examinations by persons of the same sex.

The use of torture is not only limited to interrogations but extends to situations involving protests and clashes. The case of Mohammad Halabi, a Palestinian aid worker, provides insight into how torture can be employed outside the confines of detention facilities. Halabi was arrested in 2015 on charges of diverting funds to Hamas. During his detention, he reported being subjected to torture, including beatings and stress positions. His case sheds light on the broader issue of how torture can be utilized not only as a means of extracting information but also as a tool of intimidation and punishment.

The individuals affected by these documented cases of torture are not only subjected to physical harm but also endure long-lasting psychological disturbance. The use of torture by Zionist forces raises fundamental questions about the adherence to international human rights standards, particularly the absolute prohibition of torture under international law. The systematic nature of these violations suggests the need for comprehensive reforms in the treatment of detainees and the establishment of mechanisms to ensure accountability for those responsible.

The psychological consequences of torture are equally devastating. Detainees subjected to prolonged periods of physical and psychological abuse commonly suffer from post-traumatic stress disorder (PTSD), anxiety, depression, and other mental health disorders. The intentional use of torture as a means of coercion and control leaves lasting emotional scars, disrupting the individual's ability to cope with daily life and exacerbating pre-existing mental health conditions.

The impact of torture extends beyond the immediate victim to affect their families. Families of detainees often endure profound emotional distress, uncertainty, and economic hardships. The psychological ordeal inflicted on the individual reverberates through familial relationships, disrupting the normal functioning of family units. Children, spouses, and parents grapple with the emotional toll of witnessing their loved ones subjected to inhumane treatment, and the long-term ramifications on family dynamics are often profound.

The broader community also bears the weight of the outcomes of torture. When individuals are systematically targeted for torture based on their perceived affiliations or identities, entire communities experience a collective trauma. The fear of arbitrary detention and torture permeates the social fabric, fostering a climate of distrust and anxiety. Communities become fractured as the pervasive threat of torture erodes social cohesion and trust among members.

The long-term implications of torture on detainees, their families, and the broader community demand urgent attention and redress. Rehabilitation and support services for survivors are crucial to addressing the physical and psychological scars inflicted by torture. However, the societal impact requires broader measures, including community-based initiatives aimed at rebuilding trust, fostering resilience, and challenging the culture of impunity that enables such abuses to persist.

The actions taken by Zionist forces stand in stark contrast to recognized legal frameworks, emphasizing blatant non-compliance with fundamental principles of human rights. The Universal Declaration of Human Rights (UDHR), adopted by the United Nations General Assembly in 1948, explicitly states in Article 5 that "No one shall be subjected to torture or to cruel, inhuman or degrading treatment or punishment." The cases of Samir Arbeed and Arafat Jaradat, among others, vividly illustrate the violation of this foundational human right. The severe beatings, stress positions, and psychological torment inflicted during interrogations blatantly contravene the absolute prohibition of torture enshrined in the UDHR.

Furthermore, these documented cases fly in the face of the Convention Against Torture and Other Cruel, Inhuman, or Degrading Treatment or Punishment (CAT), an international treaty that came into force in 1987. Article 1 of the CAT defines torture and explicitly prohibits its use under any circumstances. The acts of physical and psychological torture witnessed in the aforementioned cases squarely fall within the purview of this definition, constituting clear violations of the CAT.

The Geneva Conventions, which outline the humanitarian rules of war, also condemn torture and inhumane treatment. Common Article 3 of the Geneva Conventions prohibits "violence to life and person, in particular, cruel treatment and torture" against persons not taking part in hostilities. In the context of the Israeli-Palestinian war, where civilians often find themselves caught in the crossfire, the cases of Mohammad Halabi and others underscore the breach of these fundamental principles.

The Rome Statute of the International Criminal Court (ICC) designates torture as a crime against humanity. The documented cases of torture by Zionist forces, when viewed through the lens of the Rome Statute, raise serious questions about the accountability of individuals involved. The ICC has jurisdiction over the crime of torture, and these cases provide a basis for the examination of potential prosecutions.

Despite the clear legal frameworks in place, the reality on the ground reveals a disturbing gap between international standards and actual practices. The lack of accountability and the perpetuation of a climate of impunity contribute to the persistence of human rights violations. The challenge lies not only in establishing legal frameworks but in ensuring their effective implementation and enforcement.

The documented cases also highlight the need for an unbiased and transparent investigation mechanism to hold perpetrators accountable. The inherent challenges in conducting impartial investigations within the context of a protracted clash require international scrutiny and involvement. The establishment of an independent commission of inquiry, as proposed by various human rights organizations, could contribute to uncovering the truth, ensuring accountability, and delivering justice to the victims. A comparative analysis of these actions against recognized legal frameworks exposes the disconcerting disparities between international standards and the practices on the ground. The systematic use of torture by Zionist forces underscores the urgency of addressing the root causes of such violations. This involves not only holding individuals accountable but also addressing the broader structural and institutional issues that perpetuate a culture of impunity.

Despite the gravity of these documented cases and the widespread international condemnation, challenges persist in holding individuals accountable for human rights violations. The lack of transparency in Israeli militant operations and security measures complicates efforts to investigate and address instances of torture effectively. Legal frameworks surrounding security operations often provide broad powers to military authorities, contributing to a climate of impunity.

Restrictions on Freedom of Movement

The imposition of physical barriers and checkpoints has become a defining aspect of the restrictions on the freedom of movement faced by Palestinian populations. This systematic approach, characterized by the deployment of walls, checkpoints, and other infrastructure, has profound implications for the daily lives of individuals living in the region. The West Bank stands out as a significant location where the impact of these restrictions is keenly felt, characterized by a network of checkpoints that govern the movement of Palestinians. These checkpoints, often manned by Israeli security forces, serve as critical control points, monitoring and limiting the movement of individuals within the West Bank. The Qalandia checkpoint, situated between Jerusalem and Ramallah, stands as a prominent example. Its strategic location makes it a crucial passage for many Palestinians commuting between these two major urban centers. The meticulous scrutiny and delays at such checkpoints create an atmosphere of frustration and hinder the ability of individuals to carry out daily activities, whether it be work, education, or accessing essential services.

In addition to checkpoints, the construction of physical barriers, such as the West Bank Barrier, commonly known as the separation wall, has had a profound impact on the freedom of movement for Palestinians. The wall, justified by Israeli authorities as a security measure, traverses through the West Bank, separating communities and disrupting the natural flow of life as discussed earlier. The town of Bethlehem, known for its historical and cultural significance, finds itself encircled by this barrier, limiting movement in and out of the town. Residents, once able to freely visit neighboring communities, are now constrained by the physical presence of the wall, altering social and economic dynamics.

The city of Hebron provides a compelling example of the impact of physical barriers. Divided into two sectors, H1 under Palestinian control and H2 under Israeli occupation, Hebron faces a complex reality of restricted movement. Here, Israeli settlements are interconnected by a system of checkpoints and physical barriers, segregating Palestinian residents from Israeli settlers. The daily lives of Palestinians in H2 are marked by stringent security measures, making routine activities a challenge and contributing to an environment of tension and unease.

The implications of these restrictions on freedom of movement extend beyond mere inconvenience. They have far-reaching consequences on the social, economic, and educational aspects of Palestinian life. The limitations imposed by checkpoints and barriers disrupt the normalcy of daily routines. The socio-economic fabric of Palestinian communities is intricately linked to the ability to move freely, and these restrictions pose a significant barrier to development and progress.

In East Jerusalem, home to many Palestinian residents, the construction of barriers and checkpoints contributes to a complex web of restrictions. The neighborhood of Sheikh Jarrah, known for its historical significance, has faced the imposition of physical barriers that disrupt the daily lives of its residents. The intricate network of checkpoints and barriers fragments the community, making it difficult for residents to connect with each other and access elemental services. The impact is not only physical but also psychological, as the constant surveillance and restrictions create an environment of uncertainty and tension.

The systematic limitations placed on the ability to move freely within one's own territory extend far beyond inconvenience, permeating into the very fabric of daily life and contributing to a host of challenges faced by the affected populations. The economic ramifications of restricted movement are acutely felt in Palestinian communities, shaping an environment where access to obligatory services becomes a formidable challenge. The strategic placement of checkpoints and barriers disrupts the flow of goods and services, hindering the efficient functioning of markets and impeding the delivery of crucial resources. Nablus, a vibrant economic hub, serves as a poignant example. The checkpoints surrounding the town create bottlenecks, slowing down the movement of goods and impacting the livelihoods of traders. The economic vitality of Nablus is compromised as restrictions on movement impede the free flow of commerce.

The limitations imposed on access to compulsory services compound the economic challenges faced by Palestinian communities. The town of Ramallah, a political and economic center, encounters difficulties in providing efficient services due to the constraints imposed by checkpoints. Medical services, in particular, are affected as individuals face delays in reaching hospitals and clinics. The physical barriers disrupt the timely delivery of medical care, exacerbating health challenges for the population.

Moreover, the economic impact extends beyond traditional sectors to the ability of individuals to access employment opportunities. The town of Hebron, characterized by a complex system of checkpoints and barriers, exemplifies how restrictions on movement impede the ability of Palestinians to engage in regular economic activities. The division of Hebron posing challenges for Palestinian workers commuting to their places of employment and leading to a loss of income and economic stability for many families.

The social fabric of Palestinian communities is intricately tied to the economic opportunities available to individuals. The restrictions on freedom of movement not only hinder economic prosperity but also contribute to social disparities. In Bethlehem, the impediments to tourism, a significant economic sector, have a cascading effect on the social dynamics of the community. The loss of income and employment opportunities creates a sense of uncertainty, impacting the overall well-being of residents.

The limitations imposed on freedom of movement extend beyond economic and social realms, deeply impacting crucial aspects such as healthcare, education, and overall quality of life. In the realm of healthcare, the town of Jenin stands as a stark example of the challenges posed by restricted movement. The presence of checkpoints and barriers impedes the timely access to medical facilities for residents, causing significant delays in receiving essential healthcare services. Patients requiring urgent medical attention, especially those with chronic illnesses, face hurdles in reaching hospitals and clinics. The restrictions on movement contribute to a humanitarian crisis where individuals are deprived of their right to timely and adequate healthcare.

Furthermore, the town of Tulkarem experiences similar humanitarian challenges in the healthcare sector. The impediments to movement hinder the transportation of medical supplies and equipment, affecting the ability of healthcare facilities to provide comprehensive services. The delivery of indispensable medications and medical equipment becomes a logistical struggle, jeopardizing the health and well-being of the population. The resulting humanitarian consequences underscore the urgent need for unimpeded access to healthcare services, a fundamental right that is compromised by restrictions on freedom of movement.

The impact on education is another facet of the humanitarian crisis wrought by restricted movement. In the town of Jericho, where checkpoints disrupt the regular flow of daily life, students encounter obstacles in pursuing their education. The right to education, a cornerstone of human rights, is compromised as students face challenges commuting to schools and universities. The disruption to the educational process creates a dire humanitarian situation, particularly for the younger generation whose future prospects hinge on uninterrupted access to learning opportunities.

Similarly, the town of Qalqilya, encircled by the separation wall, grapples with the humanitarian implications of restricted movement on education. The isolation imposed by physical barriers disrupts the normal functioning of schools and universities. Students find themselves navigating a complex web of checkpoints and obstacles, impeding their ability to attend classes regularly. The resulting educational challenges contribute to a humanitarian crisis where the right to learn is hindered, compromising the future prospects of the youth in the community.

Beyond healthcare and education, the overall well-being of Palestinian communities is profoundly affected by restrictions on freedom of movement. The town of Salfit, surrounded by checkpoints and barriers, experiences challenges in ensuring the basic needs and rights of its residents. The limitations on movement impede access to innate services, creating a humanitarian crisis where the fundamental rights to a decent standard of living are jeopardized. The ability to move freely within one's own community becomes a vital determinant of overall well-being, and the restrictions imposed undermine the very essence of human dignity.

Destruction of Homes and Property

Throughout the last five decades of Israel's occupation of the Palestinian territory, a prominent aspect of the implemented policies has been the extensive appropriation and destruction of property, encompassing land and natural resources. In recent years, there has been a noticeable rise in the rate of demolitions, seizures, and confiscations of property by the Government of Israel (GoI), particularly across the West Bank.

The documented cases of property destruction by Zionist forces paint a distressing picture of the widespread and systematic violations of Palestinian rights, particularly in the context of the destruction of homes and properties. These instances, supported by concrete evidence and testimonies, provide a factual basis for understanding the enormity of the situation faced by Palestinian communities. Examining specific examples, locations, and circumstances surrounding the destruction reveals the harsh reality endured by individuals and families affected by the actions of Zionist forces.

UNRWA officials have approximated that, within a span of just a few days, the Israeli army wrought destruction upon more than 80 buildings in the Rafah refugee camp. This onslaught followed the purported approval of a demolition plan on May 13, 2004, orchestrated by none other than Former Prime Minister Ariel Sharon, Former Defense Minister Shaul Mofaz, and other high-ranking officials. The profound impact of this orchestrated destruction unfolded rapidly, leaving a stark and distressing imprint on the Rafah refugee camp and its inhabitants. The magnitude of the devastation underscores the coordinated effort and strategic planning behind this unsettling chapter in the region's history.

In the city of Hebron, located in the southern West Bank, the Abu Aisha family home, a residential building sheltering more than 60 Palestinians in Beit Hanina, stands as a poignant example of such destruction. The family endured the devastating loss of their home, demolished by Zionist forces in 2008, leaving them in dire circumstances. The destruction of the Abu Aisha home underscores the systematic nature of property destruction, where families become collateral damage in the broader geopolitical landscape.

Similarly, in the town of Nablus, located in the northern part of the West Bank, numerous cases of property destruction have been extensively documented. One notable example is the destruction of the home of the Al-Masri family in a 2014 Israeli offensive. In this case, Zionist forces carried out a demolition operation, rendering the family homeless and stripping them of their property. The circumstances surrounding the destruction are emblematic of a broader pattern, where homes are targeted without regard for the lives and well-being of the occupants.

Moving to the town of Bethlehem, another documented case sheds light on the pervasive issue of property destruction. The Abu Srour family home became a target of Zionist forces, resulting in its demolition and the displacement of the family. The destruction of the Abu Srour home exemplifies the far-reaching consequences of such actions, as families are uprooted and communities destabilized. The circumstances surrounding this case highlight the severe impact on the lives and livelihoods of those affected.

The village of Bil'in, known for its activism against the Israeli occupation, has also witnessed documented cases of property destruction. The Na'alin family home, situated in this village, fell victim to demolition by Zionist forces. The destruction of the Na'alin home is emblematic of the reprisals faced by individuals and families engaged in resistance against the occupation. The deliberate targeting of homes in Bil'in underscores the broader strategy of suppressing dissent through the destruction of property.

In 2021, the United Nations, through its humanitarian coordinator for the region, Lynn Hastings, provided a sobering estimate of the aftermath of the 11-day war that concluded on May 21. According to the UN's assessment, approximately 1,000 homes bore the brunt of destruction during this battle. Moreover, Hastings noted that the impact extended beyond outright demolitions, with hundreds of additional housing units suffering such severe damage that they are now deemed likely uninhabitable.

The Middle East Monitor (MEMO), a UK-based media organization, reported that Israeli occupation forces demolished 295 Palestinian residential structures in occupied territories in 2021, rendering 895 Palestinians, including 463 minors, homeless. The information was conveyed by the Israeli rights group B'Tselem in a report released on January 4, 2022. B'Tselem highlighted that the number of Palestinian home demolitions carried out by the Israeli occupation in 2021 was the highest recorded since 2016. Additionally, the report disclosed that 548 non-residential structures, encompassing cisterns, warehouses, agricultural facilities, businesses, and public structures, were demolished on Israeli authorities' orders throughout the year – marking the highest number since 2012. Specifically, in East Jerusalem, 160 structures were demolished, with 96 of them being homes, according to B'Tselem.

In 2022, Israeli occupation forces engaged in the demolition of 950 Palestinian homes and the confiscation of over 113 square kilometers of land. The primary objective behind these actions was to facilitate the expansion of illegal Jewish-only settlements in the occupied West Bank and East Jerusalem. The Land Research Centre, which operates in Palestine, released its annual report titled "Israeli Violations Against Palestinian Land and Housing Rights for 2022," highlighting additional measures such as the destruction or damage of 18,900 trees, predominantly olive trees, by Israeli forces. Notably, the report emphasized that 65 of the demolished homes were carried out by their owners under the directives of the Israeli occupation forces.

Within the initial two days of the Israeli offensive attack starting on May 9, 2023, the Government Media Office in Gaza has recorded the total demolition of five buildings, encompassing 19 residential units. Furthermore, 314 residential units underwent partial destruction, with 28 rendered uninhabitable and 286 exhibiting various degrees of damage. According to Al-Haq, an independent Palestinian non-governmental human rights organization based in Ramallah, West Bank, on Wednesday, May 10, 2023, an Israeli warplane launched two missiles targeting the residence of Mohammad Sa'adi Salem Al-Masri, aged 67, situated on Al-Shaimaa Street in the town of Beit Lahiya in the northern Gaza Strip. The singled-out house is part of a two-story residential building, covering an area of 436 square meters, and comprising four housing units. These units are home to four families, totaling 16 individuals, including four women and eight children. The specific house subjected to the attack was entirely demolished, and several nearby residences, along with the Beit Lahiya Development Association headquarters, suffered partial damage.

Jamon Van Den Hoek and Corey Scher, researchers based in the United States, and Al Jazeera's AJ Labs unit, conducted a recent analysis revealing that a minimum of 16 percent of all structures in the Gaza Strip has been demolished. In Gaza City alone, the destruction of buildings has surged to a minimum of 28 percent. Information gathered from the United Nations Office for the Coordination of Humanitarian Affairs (OCHA), the World Health Organization (WHO), and the Palestinian government reveals that within one month of the Al-Aqsa flood, Israeli attacks have caused damage to at least 222,000 residential units. Among these, over 40,000 have been completely razed.

These documented cases represent a mere fraction of the larger pattern of property destruction carried out by Zionist forces. The systematic nature of these actions, spanning across different towns and cities of Palestine, reveals a disturbing trend where homes and properties become targets of deliberate destruction. The circumstances surrounding each case underscore the broader implications for Palestinian communities, as individuals and families grapple with the loss of their homes, belongings, and, ultimately, their sense of security and stability.

The destruction of homes and property, as systematically carried out by Zionist forces, not only leaves physical ruins but has far-reaching consequences on the affected populations. The humanitarian repercussions of such destruction are profound, impacting the lives of displaced individuals and communities in ways that extend beyond the immediate loss of shelter. Examining the effect of property destruction sheds light on the challenges faced by those displaced, encompassing issues related to housing, livelihoods, and social cohesion.

In the wake of the documented cases of property destruction in various towns and cities, the displaced populations are confronted with a dire need for shelter. Families rendered homeless by the destruction of their homes face the daunting task of finding alternative housing in an environment characterized by limited resources and a scarcity of suitable living spaces. The destruction of homes in Bil'in, Hebron, Bethlehem, and other locations has resulted in a growing population of displaced individuals struggling to secure adequate housing, exacerbating an already precarious situation.

The impact on livelihoods further compounds the challenges faced by displaced populations. The destruction of homes often means the loss of not only shelter but also essential belongings and personal possessions. For many, homes serve as the foundation for livelihoods, housing small businesses, workshops, or agricultural spaces. The destruction of these properties disrupts not only the physical space but also the economic activities that sustain families and communities. Displaced individuals are forced to grapple with the loss of their economic foundations, intensifying their vulnerability and dependence on external assistance.

Social cohesion within displaced communities is also profoundly affected by the destruction of homes and property. The communal bonds that are built over generations within neighborhoods and villages are severed when families are forcibly uprooted. Displacement often scatters communities, leading to a fragmentation of social networks and a loss of the collective identity that comes from shared spaces. The destruction of homes in places like Hebron, where communities have deep historical roots, disrupts the social fabric, leaving individuals isolated and communities fractured as discussed.

Specific examples underscore the gravity of these challenges. In Bil'in, families who once shared close-knit communities find themselves dispersed, each struggling to rebuild their lives independently. The destruction of the Abu Aisha family home in Hebron not only left them without shelter but also shattered the economic activities that sustained them, deepening their reliance on external aid. The Abu Srour family in Bethlehem, facing the destruction of their home, experienced not only the loss of physical space but also the erosion of the social ties that had bound them to their community.

The humanitarian consequences of property destruction extend beyond the immediate displacement, influencing the overall well-being of affected populations. Displaced individuals often grapple with trauma, anxiety, and a sense of insecurity resulting from the abrupt loss of their homes. The disruption of daily life, compounded by economic hardships and social dislocation, takes a toll on the mental and emotional health of those affected. The documented cases of property destruction in various locations serve as poignant examples of the multifaceted humanitarian challenges faced by displaced populations.

The destruction of homes and property inflicted by Zionist forces not only displaces individuals but also constitutes a blatant violation of the right to adequate housing, a fundamental human right recognized in international frameworks. This violation, rooted in systematic actions that result in the forced displacement of populations, carries significant legal implications and raises ethical considerations that extend beyond the immediate physical destruction.

Analyzing the destruction of homes and property in the context of the right to adequate housing requires an understanding of the international legal frameworks that safeguard this fundamental right. The Universal Declaration of Human Rights (UDHR) and the International Covenant on Economic, Social and Cultural Rights (ICESCR) explicitly recognize the right to adequate housing as an integral part of the right to an adequate standard of living. According to these instruments, adequate housing encompasses more than just shelter; it includes the right to live in security, peace, and dignity, with access to compulsory services and amenities.

The destruction of homes by Zionist forces, as witnessed in various locations, directly contradicts these principles. Families are forcibly uprooted from their homes, leaving them without shelter and violating their right to a secure and dignified living environment. The documented cases in Hebron, Bethlehem, and other areas highlight the deliberate actions that undermine the very essence of the right to adequate housing.

Legal implications arise from the systematic destruction of homes and property, as these actions violate not only international human rights law but also principles of humanitarian law. The Fourth Geneva Convention prohibits the destruction of property, including homes, unless absolutely necessary for military operations. The destruction carried out by Zionist forces, however, regularly goes beyond military necessity, targeting civilian homes and communities. Such actions contravene the principles of proportionality and distinction outlined in humanitarian law, further underscoring the legal transgressions associated with the destruction of homes.

Ethical considerations surrounding the destruction of homes delve into the profound impact on individuals and communities. Beyond the legal frameworks, there exists a moral responsibility to uphold the dignity and well-being of all individuals, regardless of their background. The deliberate displacement of populations through the destruction of homes raises questions about the ethical standards upheld by those perpetrating such actions. The ethical considerations extend to the international community, urging a collective response to ensure accountability and justice for those affected.

Targeting of Civilian Infrastructure

In the annals of skirmish, a disturbing chapter reveals instances where civilian infrastructure, the bedrock of communities, becomes a deliberate target. In the context of the Israeli-Palestinian war, documented evidence highlights a troubling pattern where schools, hospitals, and other essential structures bear the brunt of intentional attacks by Zionist forces. Human Rights Watch reported a disturbing trend in 2011 when Israeli forces demolished a classroom in Dkaika village in the southern West Bank. By 2017, demolition orders loomed over 111 out of 140 structures in Dkaika. Another incident involved the destruction of the playground of al-Ibrahimiya School and College in East Jerusalem.

In April, Israeli forces razed a school in Khirbet Tana near Nablus, acting on demolition orders issued in March. This wasn't the first time; between 2005 and 2010, the village school had been demolished thrice. The upshot of the demolitions in 2010 led to a drastic reduction in the village's population from 56 to 27 families. Despite residents' resilience in rebuilding the school in 2011, Israeli forces demolished it again in March 2016.

Since 2010, Israeli military authorities have demolished or confiscated Palestinian school buildings or property in the West Bank at least 16 times, with 12 incidents occurring since 2016, often targeting the same schools repeatedly, as found by Human Rights Watch. In Area C, which constitutes 60 percent of the West Bank under exclusive Israeli military occupation per the 1993 Oslo accords, over a third of Palestinian communities lack primary schools. Approximately 10,000 children attend school in tents, shacks, or other structures without heating or air-conditioning, according to the UN.

On February 4, 2018, two primary school classrooms in Abu Nuwar, east of Jerusalem, fell victim to Israeli demolitions – part of the broader assault on 46 Palestinian villages under the "relocation" plan. Israeli authorities maintained a relentless presence in the school, making frequent visits since January, often photographing or interrogating residents. Since 2016, Abu Nuwar endured eight demolitions of donor-funded primary school classrooms and solar panels, along with the destruction of 26 homes. The UN Special Coordinator for the Middle East Peace Process, Nickolay Mladenov, revealed Israel's sustained pressure on Abu Nuwar residents to move, citing the community's location in the strategically planned E1 area for the expansion of Ma'ale Adumim, a significant settlement. The plight of Khan al-Ahmar, also within the E1 area, echoes this challenging reality.

Among the demolished structures were the lone kindergarten serving the Jabal Al Baba Bedouin community, reduced to rubble on August 21, 2017. Another casualty was the primary school in Jubbet Al Dhib, facing Israeli militant offence on August 22. The Israeli authorities didn't stop there; they dismantled and seized the solar panels, the sole power source, from a primary school in Abu Nuwar. This institution had already faced adversity a year before, enduring two attacks that saw parts of it demolished and equipment confiscated.

From January 2018 to June 2020, research conducted by the Norwegian Refugee Council (NRC) unveiled a distressing reality for Palestinian children in the West Bank. The onslaught on education was relentless, averaging 10 attacks per month. Over the 30-month span analyzed by the NRC, a comprehensive examination of a multi-source dataset revealed a staggering 296 attacks on education. These incidents were attributed to Israeli forces, settlers, and private security guards from settlements, occurring in 235 separate instances.

In 2020, Israeli authorities demolished or seized more than 840 structures in the West Bank, displacing at least 518 children and their families from their homes. This troubling trend appears to persist, as Israeli forces have already demolished 707 structures and forcibly transferred 964 Palestinians since the start of 2021. Between June 13 and October 26, 2021, an additional 341 Palestinian structures were destroyed in the West Bank.

In an article dated November 23, 2022, Al-Jazeera reports that Israeli forces have taken down a newly constructed Palestinian primary school in the Masafer Yatta region of the southern occupied West Bank. This area has been grappling with the persistent menace of forced displacement. According to locals and officials who spoke with Al Jazeera, the Israeli force conducted a raid on the Wednesday morning, resulting in the demolition of the school situated in the village of Isfey al-Fauqa.

The school funded by the Consortium in the Jubbet Adh-Dhib community, situated southeast of Bethlehem, underwent demolition by Israeli authorities on May 7, 2023.The UN report uncovered a distressing toll on infrastructure, indicating that within a month from the Al-Aqsa flood, 278 educational facilities, 270 healthcare facilities, and 69 places of worship, including mosques and churches, have suffered damage.

On the 14th of November 2023, Tulkarem city and its refugee camp faced another assault from Israeli forces, marking the second within a week. The aggression unfolded with a show of overwhelming military force, featuring massive vehicles and bulldozers, accompanied by a substantial deployment of soldiers and snipers. To escalate the gravity, Israeli forces introduced suicidal and missile-carrying drones into the scene. Regrettably, the Thabet Governmental Hospital in Tulkarem fell victim to this onslaught, as Israeli forces initiated an attack, bombing its entrance and emergency room with gas canisters. This heedless act resulted in the suffocation of both patients and medical staff within the hospital premises, accompanied by the loss of innocent Palestinian lives and the widespread destruction of the camp's infrastructure, streets, and neighborhoods.

The looming threat of demolition hangs heavily over many West Bank schools, particularly those situated in Area C. Israel's rationale for dismantling these schools and other Palestinian structures in the area isn't rooted in security concerns but rather hinges on the absence of permits from the military. It's worth noting that the military consistently denies the majority of Palestinian building requests, designating a mere 1 percent of Area C for Palestinian construction. Meanwhile, construction in nearby Jewish settlements proceeds with minimal constraints, underscoring a stark contrast in the allocation of building opportunities within the region.

Israeli air raids have resulted in the tragic loss of lives at Al Fakhoura school, operated by the United Nations Relief and Works Agency for Palestinian refugees (UNRWA), located in the Jabalia refugee camp. Another school in Tall az-Zaatar, also in northern Gaza, faced a similar fate. Both schools were shelters for several hundred people seeking refuge from the relentless Israeli attacks. On November 18, 2023, Israeli forces targeted Al Fakhoura school in the Jabalia refugee camp, resulting in the deaths of at least 50 people, including children and women. Additionally, Israeli air raids have claimed numerous lives, including children, across northern, central, and southern Gaza.

Also, the ruthless actions of Zionist forces, as seen in the destruction of The International Eye Care Center, Al-Wafa Rehabilitation Hospital, The Turkish-Palestinian Friendship Hospital, Al-Quds Hospital, and al-Shifa Hospital, underscore a disturbing pattern of targeting vital civilian infrastructure. Beyond these medical facilities, the blockage of water resources and attacks on energy facilities further exemplify the inhumane tactics employed by Israeli forces.

These instances are not isolated; they underscore a disconcerting trend where civilian infrastructure becomes a strategic target rather than a protected space. The intentional destruction of these vital structures amplifies the humanitarian crisis, leaving communities grappling with not only the immediate impact but also the long-term consequences.

Following the intentional targeting of civilian infrastructure, the question of accountability looms large. The impact transcends the physical destruction, extending into the realm of international law and human rights. The deliberate targeting of hospitals, schools, and other essential facilities violates the principles enshrined in various international conventions. A pertinent legal structure that safeguards the rights of civilians during armed ructions is the Fourth Geneva Convention. Under this convention, the intentional targeting of civilian objects, including infrastructure primordial for the well-being of the civilian population, constitutes a grave breach. The deliberate destruction of hospitals and schools goes beyond the acceptable limits of military engagement, demanding scrutiny under the lens of international law.

The systematic nature of these attacks raises ethical considerations as well. The deliberate targeting of civilian infrastructure undermines the fundamental principles of humanity and the distinction between combatants and non-combatants. It challenges the essence of preserving life and protecting the most vulnerable during times of war.

The deliberate targeting of civilian infrastructure, specifically schools, casts a long and ominous shadow over the right to education for affected communities. As the international community grapples with the repercussions of such actions, the broader implications on educational systems, students' access to learning, and the enduring challenges in the pursuit of education come to the forefront.

The disruption of educational systems is a central ramification of targeting schools. The intentional destruction of these institutions disrupts the normal rhythm of academic life, creating a void in the lives of students. The UNRWA Beach Elementary School, once a hub of learning, was reduced to rubble, leaving students without a place to pursue their education. The interruption of the educational process not only robs students of the present but also undermines the foundation for their future.

Furthermore, the profound impact on students' access to learning becomes evident. When schools are deliberately targeted, the once-safe spaces meant to nurture intellectual growth and curiosity transform into zones of danger. Students, who are already grappling with the challenges of clash, find themselves further deprived of a secure haven for learning. This deliberate targeting amid conflict exemplifies how the pursuit of education becomes a casualty in the crossfire, leaving students bereft of the opportunities they rightfully deserve.

The long-term challenges stemming from the targeting of schools are multifaceted. Beyond the immediate physical destruction, there is the enduring misery experienced by students who witness the intentional dismantling of their educational spaces. The emotional cost of living in a community where schools are not sanctuaries but potential battlegrounds leaves lasting scars on the collective psyche of the affected population.

Furthermore, the intentional targeting of schools contributes to a broader erosion of educational infrastructure. The UNRWA Beach Elementary School was not merely a structure; it represented an investment in the future of the community. The purposive destruction of such institutions undermines the very fabric of educational systems, creating gaps that are challenging to bridge. The loss of classrooms, libraries, and other educational resources impedes the continuity of learning for generations to come.

The implications for the right to education extend to the societal level, where the intentional targeting of schools disrupts the social cohesion that education fosters. Schools are not just physical structures; they are the heart of communities, where bonds are forged, and shared values are imparted. The intentional destruction of schools fractures these communal ties, contributing to a sense of disarray and disconnection within the affected population.

Similarly, the deliberate targeting of hospitals, a somber violation of humanitarian principles, carries profound implications for the right to access healthcare for affected populations. As the international community grapples with the consequences of such actions, it becomes evident that the immediate and long-term impact on individuals' ability to receive medical care extends beyond physical health, encompassing profound psychological dimensions.

The immediate impact on individuals' ability to receive medical care is stark when hospitals become intentional targets. Patients, including those with spinal cord injuries and neurological disorders, find themselves stranded without access to specialized medical care. The deliberate destruction of the hospital not only jeopardizes ongoing treatments but also leaves patients without alternative facilities capable of providing the same level of specialized care.

The long-term repercussions of targeting hospitals reverberate through the fabric of affected communities. Beyond the physical injuries resulting from the destruction of medical infrastructure, there is a lasting psychological reverberation on individuals who now grapple with the uncertainty of accessing necessary healthcare. The intentional attack on hospitals not only disrupted ongoing medical treatments but also instilled fear and apprehension among patients who found themselves caught in the crossfire of skirmish.

Moreover, the targeting of hospitals exacerbates existing healthcare disparities, particularly in hostile territories. Vulnerable populations, already facing challenges in accessing adequate healthcare, bear the brunt of intentional attacks on medical facilities. The destruction of hospitals amplifies the existing healthcare inequalities, disproportionately affecting those who are already marginalized and underserved.

The psychological health outcomes of targeting hospitals are equally significant. The intentional destruction of medical facilities creates a sense of vulnerability and despair within affected populations. Patients who once relied on the continuity of medical care now confront a harsh reality where access to primary healthcare becomes uncertain and precarious. The psychological anguish resulting from the intentional targeting of hospitals extends beyond the immediate physical corollaries, leaving a lasting imprint on the mental well-being of affected individuals.

Denial of Access to Natural Resources

Instances of denial of access to natural resources represent a poignant facet of the complex web of human rights violations in the Israeli-Palestinian war. These cases, thoroughly documented, shed light on the severe consequences faced by Palestinian communities, whose access to crucial natural assets has been systematically restricted. Such instances not only underscore the violation of basic human rights but also contribute to the broader narrative of systemic oppression.

The denial is starkly illustrated by the situation in Al-Walaja, a village located in the West Bank. This Palestinian community has faced a protracted struggle for access to its natural resources, particularly land and water. The construction of the Israeli separation barrier, deemed illegal by the International Court of Justice, has not only severed Al-Walaja from its agricultural lands but has also disrupted the natural flow of water sources. The village, surrounded by settlements and the barrier, finds itself in a precarious situation, with limited access to vital resources indispensable for its sustenance. The effects extend beyond mere inconvenience; they undermine the very fabric of community life, creating a precarious existence where every drop of water becomes a contested resource, experiencing a direct assault on its economic foundation. Agriculture, a primary source of livelihood for the residents, becomes increasingly untenable as water scarcity hampers productivity. The economic fallout extends to employment opportunities within the agricultural sector, exacerbating unemployment rates and contributing to financial instability.

Similarly, in the Jordan Valley, Palestinian communities have long confronted the denial of access to their agricultural lands and water reservoirs. The Israeli government's policies, including the establishment of military zones and restrictions on movement, have systematically undermined the Palestinians' ability to cultivate their lands and utilize natural water sources. These policies, ostensibly implemented for security reasons, have disproportionately impacted Palestinian communities, pushing them into a cycle of impoverishment and dependency. The humanitarian implications are stark: farmers struggle to irrigate their crops, families face water shortages for domestic use, and the overall resilience of these communities is compromised. Agricultural activities, deeply intertwined with the economic fabric of the region, also face significant challenges. The economic implications reverberate beyond individual farmers, impacting entire communities dependent on agriculture for their livelihoods. The denial of access to water emerges not only as a logistical challenge but as a direct assault on the basic human right to a dignified and sustainable life.

The village of Susya exemplifies the systematic denial of access to natural resources in the South Hebron Hills. Israeli authorities have exerted relentless pressure on Susya, leading to home demolitions and the confiscation of agricultural lands. Despite the Israeli government's security-driven rationale, it fails to justify the profound impact on the daily lives of Palestinian residents. The denial of access disrupts economic stability and severs the deep-rooted connection to the land, a fundamental aspect of cultural identity. This denial, encompassing natural resources like water, is intricately linked to a broader policy of demolitions and displacement. Through restrictions on well-drilling and water infrastructure development, Israeli authorities intentionally create inhospitable conditions for the village. This imposition of water scarcity is not just an environmental concern but a calculated strategy undermining the foundation of daily life. The corollaries extend to agricultural productivity, livestock health, and the overall well-being of the community.

Moreover, the Bedouin communities in the Negev region have grappled with the denial of access to their ancestral lands. The Prawer Plan, a controversial Israeli government initiative, sought to relocate thousands of Bedouin residents and demolish "unrecognized" villages, further exacerbating the historical injustice faced by these communities. The plan not only denies them access to their lands but also challenges their traditional way of life, eroding the cultural fabric that binds them to their natural surroundings. The implications are catastrophic, and the economic outcomes are profound. Families are forced into precarious situations, struggling to secure alternative sources of income in the absence of their traditional livelihoods. They must navigate the challenges of water scarcity, impacting their ability to maintain traditional livelihoods and sustain a sense of community.

These instances highlight a pattern of systematic target orchestrated through bureaucratic, physical, and so-called legal means. The Israeli government's control over natural resources, often justified by security concerns, perpetuates a cycle of dispossession that disproportionately affects Palestinian communities. This deliberate denial of access not only violates basic human rights but also contributes to the broader narrative of dispossession and displacement.

The denial of access to natural resources, particularly water, inflicts severe humanitarian implications on Palestinian communities, perpetuating a cycle of hardship and undermining the fundamental elements of daily life, agriculture, and overall livelihood. This systematic deprivation has far-reaching implications for the well-being and resilience of the affected populations, deepening their vulnerability in the face of ongoing challenges.

The humanitarian consequences of water denial extend beyond immediate challenges to agriculture and daily life; they permeate the social fabric of communities, affecting health, education, and overall resilience. In the absence of adequate water access, health outcomes suffer as communities struggle to maintain basic hygiene and sanitation standards. Education is also impacted, as students, particularly in rural areas, face disruptions due to water shortages, hindering their ability to pursue learning in a conducive environment.

Furthermore, the denial of access to water amplifies existing vulnerabilities, particularly for marginalized groups. Women, often tasked with securing water for their families, bear the brunt of these restrictions, facing increased burdens and risks. Children, the elderly, and those with pre-existing health conditions are disproportionately affected by the limited access to water, compounding the challenges they already confront in their daily lives.

The violation of the right to livelihood, stemming from the denial of access to natural resources, creates a dire economic landscape in the affected areas. This violation further extends beyond agriculture, encompassing other economic sectors crucial for sustainable development. The intentional targeting of infrastructure, including factories and businesses, further undermines the economic resilience of Palestinian communities. In Gaza, the repeated bombardment of industrial areas has not only led to the destruction of businesses but has also created a climate of uncertainty that deters investment and hampers economic growth. Employment opportunities, particularly in agriculture, are curtailed, leading to heightened unemployment rates and increased dependence on external aid. Sustainable development, a key driver of long-term economic stability, becomes an elusive goal as communities grapple with the challenges posed by restricted access to vital resources.

Violations of Freedom of Expression

The violation of freedom of expression through censorship and media restrictions has been a persistent issue for Palestinian media outlets, journalists, and online platforms. Documented instances reveal a pattern of stifling voices and limiting the flow of information, undermining the fundamental right to express and receive ideas. In the West Bank and East Jerusalem, the Palestinian Broadcasting Corporation (PBC) has faced repeated censorship attempts by Israeli authorities. The closure of PBC's radio station in Hebron in 2019 serves as a poignant example. Israeli forces raided the station, confiscated equipment, and sealed the premises, citing alleged incitement as the justification. This act not only curtailed the station's ability to broadcast but also sent a chilling message to other media outlets about the consequences of critical reporting.

Journalists, the frontline workers in the pursuit of truth, often find themselves targeted by censorship measures. In Gaza, the case of Gideon Levy illustrates the challenges faced by journalists critical of the authorities. Levy, a prominent Israeli journalist, faced backlash and threats for his reporting on the Israeli government's policies, particularly regarding the treatment of Palestinians. The restrictions imposed on him not only impede his journalistic activities but also send a deterrent message to other reporters contemplating critical coverage.

Online platforms, crucial spaces for free expression in the digital age, have not been immune to censorship. The arrest of Ramzi Abbassi, a Palestinian activist and social media influencer, exemplifies this. On the evening of April 2, 2023, Ramzi Abbassi faced a distressing encounter with Israeli police as he returned home to Silwan in occupied East Jerusalem. After visiting his ailing mother at a nearby hospital during Ramadan, he was stopped at an Israeli roadblock, forcibly removed from his car, and subjected to physical mistreatment. He was handcuffed, blindfolded, and taken to the Russian Compound, an Israeli prison. Over the next 90 days, he endured detention, interrogation, and eventually received a one-year prison sentence on charges ostensibly unrelated to his online activities. Despite the official charges, his lawyer contends that his incarceration is primarily linked to his online presence.

This incident reflects a broader pattern of increased charges against Palestinian social media users, especially following the "Unity Intifada" in May 2021. Israeli authorities' surveillance, censorship, and imprisonment of individuals for online expression have been criticized as a form of political persecution, contributing to a systematic curtailment of Palestinian freedom of expression, highlighting the vulnerability of digital spaces to government control. Such cases illustrate the broader trend of limiting online expression and stifling dissent in the virtual realm.

Israeli control over social media content takes another form through the common practice of removing opposing viewpoints, as previously discussed. Reports have emerged of the removal of Palestinian content on platforms such as Instagram, Facebook, and Twitter, including posts that highlight human rights abuses or document instances of violence. This systematic removal not only eliminates narratives but also plays a role in silencing the voices that document the harsh realities on the ground.

Media shutdowns, a drastic form of censorship, have been employed in various instances. The closure of the East Jerusalem offices of Palestine TV in 2019 by Israeli authorities is a notable case. The offices were closed, and equipment confiscated, alleging that the outlet was operating on behalf of the Palestinian Authority in violation of the Oslo Accords. This act not only silenced a prominent media outlet but also restricted the access of Palestinian residents in East Jerusalem to information.

The violation of freedom of expression extends beyond direct censorship, manifesting in deliberate internet disruptions and communication blackouts in Palestinian territories. These instances not only impede the free flow of information but also curtail individuals' ability to express opinions and engage in online discourse, exacerbating the challenges faced by media outlets, journalists, and the general public. In the digital age, access to the internet is fundamental for the dissemination and consumption of information. However, Palestinian territories have experienced deliberate disruptions, hindering the ability of individuals to connect, express themselves, and access information freely. Such disruptions are not only a violation of the right to freedom of expression but also have profound ramifications on various aspects of daily life.

In the West Bank, instances of deliberate internet disruptions have been reported during times of heightened tensions or protests. The Israeli authorities, as part of their security measures, have at times restricted internet access, particularly in areas witnessing civil unrest. This deliberate disruption not only limits the ability of individuals to communicate and organize but also restricts their access to information, hindering their understanding of unfolding events. Gaza, too, has experienced internet disruptions imposed by both Israeli and Palestinian authorities. During periods of war or political tensions, the internet has been intentionally slowed down or cut off entirely. The consequences of such disruptions are far-reaching, affecting not only the ability of journalists to report in real-time but also hindering the general public's access to crucial information.

A significant incident worth noting is the internet blackout enforced by the Palestinian Authority in the West Bank in 2019. In an attempt to suppress dissent and control the narrative, the Palestinian Authority restricted access to various news websites and social media platforms. This blackout not only limited the ability of individuals to express dissenting opinions but also showcased the use of internet restrictions as a tool for controlling the narrative and stifling opposition.

Similarly, this behavior was observed during the war following the Operation Al-Aqsa flood. 15 out of the 19 providers operating in Gaza experienced a complete shutdown of their mobile and broadband services, while the remaining four faced varying levels of significant disruption, impacting millions of people. The complete shutdowns directly affected approximately 411,000 people using these providers in Gaza, along with an additional 34,000 people in the West Bank. Since October 9, connectivity throughout the Gaza Strip has been severely disrupted due to a combination of shutdowns affecting both small and large ISPs. As noted, overall internet traffic across Gaza witnessed a decrease of over 80% in October. Entire governorates were offline between October 27 and 29, affecting networks that had previously been spared from shutdowns, leading to immediate and devastating impacts.

Communication blackouts, often a consequence of broader skirmishes, have also been witnessed in Gaza. During periods of intense fight, such as the 2014 Gaza War, the Israeli military targeted telecommunication infrastructure, leading to widespread disruptions in phone and internet services. The intentional targeting of communication infrastructure not only hampers the ability of individuals to seek and share information but also isolates communities, leaving them vulnerable and disconnected.

The impact of violations on the right to information and freedom of speech for Palestinians extends far beyond individual cases of censorship or internet disruptions. These violations have broader and profound corollaries, shaping the landscape of public discourse, hindering the free flow of information, and impeding the democratic exchange of ideas within Palestinian territories.

The immediate effect of these transgressions is the suppression of public dialogue. When individuals, including journalists and activists, fear reprisals for expressing their opinions or sharing information, a chilling effect ensues. This atmosphere of fear and self-censorship limits the diversity of perspectives and hampers the robust exchange of ideas that is mandatory for a healthy democratic society. However, when certain voices are suppressed or marginalized, the democratic fabric is weakened, and the potential for an informed citizenry to actively participate in the political process is diminished.

The impact on the right to information is equally significant. In a digital age where access to information is crucial for informed decision-making, restrictions on expression limit the public's access to diverse sources of information. Internet disruptions, content removal, and censorship deprive individuals of the ability to seek out alternative perspectives and form their own opinions based on a comprehensive understanding of events.

The cumulative effect of these violations is the erosion of the foundations of a democratic society. When individuals are denied the right to freely express themselves and access diverse information, the democratic process is compromised. Informed decision-making becomes challenging, and the potential for public engagement in shaping the political landscape is undermined.

Struggles and Sacrifices

Displacement and Refugee Experiences

As the golden orb descended below the horizon, casting long shadows across the expansive landscape of collective displacement, a tapestry of personal narratives unfurled. Each story stood as a poignant testament to the profound and enduring impact of forced migration on the lives of Palestinians, weaving a complex mosaic of resilience, struggle, and the unwavering spirit that persists in the face of adversity.

Nestled in the heart of Nazareth's Old City, Ameen Muhammad Ali, known as Abu Arab, presided over a modest shop, a living relic of a bygone era. Amidst traditional sheepskin rugs and faded brass coffee pots, Abu Arab held dear the memories of a lost home, a life disrupted 68 years ago at the tender age of 13. While his village, Saffuriya, lay merely two kilometers away, it remained a distant dream. Despite being an Israeli citizen, Abu Arab was designated a "present absentee," present in Israel but absent from his property. His village had transformed into an exclusively Jewish community, Tzipori, with houses replaced by a pine forest.

Optimistic yet pragmatic, Abu Arab envisioned a return to Saffuriya, acknowledging the challenges. His optimism faded only when recalling the events of July 1948, the bombing of Saffuriya during Ramadan. Despite the tragedies, Abu Arab's spirit persevered. "All the refugees have the right to return – and no one can strip us of that right." In defiance of attempts to silence the Nakba's memory, Abu Arab co-founded ADRID, representing internal refugees. His commitment extended to the Saffuriya Cultural Association, preserving artifacts in a museum, a poignant testament: "The museum is the proof that the Palestinians did exist – and we have a culture and heritage that cannot be erased."

Another victim of Nakba, Umm Omar vividly recalls the day her family was expelled from their hometown of Jusayr in 1948, marking the beginning of a life marked by displacement and loss. Settling in the

Jabaliya refugee camp in the northern Gaza Strip, she reflects on the days when their family lived off the bounties of their farming in Jeseer, a town near al-Fallujah. "Life was good there. We used to grow wheat. I remember going out with my parents in the wheat fields when I was a little girl," she reminisced. Yet, their journey was marred by the violence of Zionist armed groups, reminiscent of the ongoing struggle in Aleppo. "They used to shoot us just like what is happening in Aleppo today," she shared, highlighting the parallels between historical and contemporary struggles.

After her father tragically stepped on a mine planted by Zionist militias, the family's hopes of returning home were shattered. Despite a temporary check on their village that showed it unchanged, the establishment of the Jabaliya camp became a permanent chapter in their lives. Years later, her son, Omar, would take her back to Jusayr, where the remnants of their home were a poignant reminder of what was lost. In the face of successive Israeli military offensives in Gaza and the destruction of their home during the 2014 warfare, Umm Omar and her husband buried their home deeds and keys, a symbolic act of preserving their connection to Jeseer. Expressing a profound desire to return, she asserted, "I still hope that I'll die in my hometown. If they told me I can go back to Jusayr, I'd run all the way." The pain of displacement and the longing for home echo in her last poignant words, "If only God would get rid of this occupation."

Salwa Naser, a refugee twice over, shares a life marked by constant displacement and the enduring hope for a stable home. Forced to leave her family home in Jaffa at the tender age of six due to escalating violence between Jewish and Palestinian militias, she embarked on a journey that would shape her existence. Recalling the beauty of Jaffa and her family's seaside home, Salwa paints a picture of innocence shattered by the eruption of communal tensions. Her family's decision to leave, triggered by an explosion near her school, set in motion a series of migrations from Lebanon to Syria, each stop marked by uncertainty and transience.

The journey, initially perceived as an adventure, soon turned somber as they witnessed their city engulfed in flames from a distance. Settling in various locations in Syria, Salwa's family struggled to establish roots, mirroring the perpetual displacement faced by Palestinians. Marriage at 16 and subsequent relocations within Syria further underscored the theme of continuous movement. As violence escalated in Syria, Salwa and her son sought refuge in Beirut's Shatila refugee camp, only to receive a devastating photo of their home reduced to rubble during the Syrian uprising. Her apprehension in the chaotic camp is palpable, revealing a deep-seated aversion to violence.

Expressing a desire to leave the camp, Salwa dreams of Switzerland or Norway, rejecting the idea of the United States due to perceived difficulties. Her poignant wish encapsulates the essence of her testimony, "I've always hated violence… even arguments make me nervous. Here in the camp, people are always arguing and yelling… It's never, ever quiet, and I'm always nervous. What kind of luck is that … we fled one war only to find another. Where are we supposed to go from here?"

The experience of Palestinian refugees and displacement is not confined solely to the Nakba, nor was the Nakba concluded by 1948. There are hundreds of thousands of testimonials illustrating the profound and ongoing challenges of displacement and refugee life. Trying to encompass all these narratives would demand volumes of books, each page echoing the enduring impact of a history marked by forced migration and the resilience of those who have carried its weight through generations. These personal narratives are not isolated instances but representative of a broader collective experience. The emotional and mental toll of displacement reverberates across Palestinian communities, as families are torn apart, and the fabric of communal life is unraveled. The trauma of leaving one's homeland, with its deep-rooted cultural and historical significance, transcends individual experiences, shaping a shared narrative of resilience and endurance.

Furthermore, interviews with displaced Palestinians reveal the enduring challenges faced in refugee camps and host countries. The struggle for basic necessities, the absence of stable living conditions, and the uncertainty about the future compound the emotional distress of displacement. These firsthand accounts provide irrefutable evidence of the ongoing hardships endured by displaced Palestinians, emphasizing the urgency of addressing the root causes and seeking sustainable solutions.

In documenting these personal narratives, it becomes evident that displacement is not solely a physical journey but a profound emotional and psychological upheaval. The scars left by forced migration run deep, impacting individuals' sense of self, belonging, and community. These stories underscore the importance of acknowledging the human dimension of displacement and fostering empathy and understanding in the broader discourse on Palestinian struggles and sacrifices.

As we confront the complexities of displacement and refugee experiences, it is imperative to amplify these personal narratives, recognizing the resilience of individuals and communities in the face of adversity. By doing so, we contribute to a more nuanced and compassionate understanding of the profound struggles and sacrifices woven into the fabric of Palestinian history and collective memory.

The long-term effects of displacement on Palestinian individuals and communities are profound, permeating various facets of life, from education to mental health and social cohesion. Building upon the personal narratives shared earlier, we delve into the enduring consequences and the resilience exhibited by displaced populations over time. Social cohesion, a cornerstone of community resilience, undergoes a seismic shift in the wake of displacement. Communities, once tightly knit, are dispersed across different regions, disrupting the bonds that sustained them. Despite these challenges, displaced Palestinians exhibit remarkable resilience in maintaining social connections. Cultural preservation becomes a powerful force, transcending physical boundaries. Through festivals, art, and shared traditions, displaced communities actively work to retain their identity, fortifying the collective spirit that binds them together.

Economic Hardships and Poverty

The economic impact of the Israeli-Palestinian war permeates Palestinian communities, unleashing a cascade of direct and indirect corollaries that reverberate through the local economies. This protracted clash has left an indelible mark on various sectors, each contributing stunningly to the economic stability of the region. Agriculture, historically a vital component of the Palestinian economy, has been severely affected by the battle. Land confiscation, restrictions on movement, and the destruction of agricultural infrastructure have impeded the ability of Palestinian farmers to cultivate and harvest their lands. The loss of livelihoods and the disruption of the agricultural sector contribute significantly to the economic hardships faced by Palestinian communities. The inability to access and utilize agricultural land not only hampers individual farmers but also has cascading effects on food security and the broader economy.

Trade, another cornerstone of economic stability, faces formidable challenges due to the tussle. Checkpoints, restrictions on movement, and trade barriers imposed by the Israeli authorities impede the flow of goods and services. Palestinian businesses grapple with delays, increased transportation costs, and uncertainty, undermining their competitiveness in the regional and global markets. This disruption to trade exacerbates economic hardships, hindering the growth and development of local industries.

The industrial sector, though resilient, has not been immune to the economic fallout of the affray. Infrastructure damages, power shortages, and restrictions on the importation of essential materials have stifled industrial growth. The lack of a conducive environment for businesses to thrive results in unemployment, reduced income opportunities, and a weakened industrial base. This, in turn, deepens the economic challenges faced by Palestinian communities, creating a cycle of hardship that is difficult to break.

The economic hardships arising from the Israeli-Palestinian war extend beyond the sectors of agriculture, trade, and industry, impacting individuals' ability to sustain their sources of income. The challenges to livelihoods and employment are profound, shaped by a complex interplay of factors that include limited job opportunities, suppressed wage levels, and constrained access to markets.

Job opportunities, a cornerstone of economic stability, have been significantly curtailed because of the hostility. Palestinians face obstacles in securing employment, exacerbated by the destruction of businesses, restrictions on movement, and the broader economic ramifications of the ongoing hostilities. The dearth of available jobs leaves many individuals, especially the younger generation, grappling with unemployment or underemployment, impeding their ability to provide for themselves and their families.

Wage levels, another critical component of economic well-being, are adversely affected by the skirmish. The scarcity of job opportunities, coupled with the economic disruptions, places downward pressure on wages. Workers often find themselves in precarious employment situations, receiving lower-than-fair compensation for their labor. This wage suppression perpetuates a cycle of poverty, hindering individuals from achieving financial security and contributing to the broader economic challenges faced by Palestinian communities.

Access to markets, indispensable for the success of businesses and entrepreneurs, is hampered by the war. Movement restrictions, checkpoints, and trade barriers imposed by Israeli authorities impede the flow of goods and services. Palestinian businesses struggle to reach broader markets, limiting their growth potential and stifling income opportunities for individuals. This constrained access to markets not only impedes economic development at the individual level but also hampers the overall economic resilience of Palestinian communities.

The challenges faced by Palestinians in securing stable employment have far-reaching implications for household incomes. With limited job opportunities, suppressed wage levels, and constrained access to markets, households experience economic strain. The ability to meet basic needs, access education, and afford healthcare becomes increasingly difficult. This economic fragility contributes to a cycle of poverty, perpetuating the struggles faced by Palestinian families in the wake of the hostility.

In urban settings, where population density is higher and economic opportunities are more diverse, the razzia contributes to elevated poverty rates. The scarcity of stable employment, suppressed wage levels, and limited access to markets disproportionately affect urban dwellers. As a result, individuals in urban areas find themselves grappling with the economic fallout of the tussle, struggling to make ends meet in an environment where the cost of living often outpaces income.

Rural communities, characterized by agrarian economies and reliance on traditional livelihoods, face distinct challenges. The armed ruction disrupts agricultural activities, hampers access to arable land, and impedes the transportation of goods to markets. The result is an exacerbation of poverty rates among rural populations, where livelihoods are intricately tied to the land. The disruption of these traditional ways of life further widens the economic gap between urban and rural areas.

Furthermore, the erosion of infrastructure, including roads, bridges, and utilities, has hindered the efficient functioning of economic activities. The prolonged hostility has impeded the development and maintenance of critical infrastructure, constraining the movement of goods and people. This impediment exacerbates the challenges faced by Palestinian businesses, limiting their capacity to engage in national and international trade.

The socio-economic disparities exacerbated by the brawl extend beyond income differentials to issues of wealth distribution and access to resources. Wealthier individuals, often with connections or resources to navigate the challenges imposed by the hostility, are better positioned to weather economic hardships. Meanwhile, those with fewer resources find themselves disproportionately impacted, facing higher levels of poverty and limited avenues for economic mobility.

Reports from international organizations, economic indicators, and firsthand accounts all converge to paint a comprehensive picture of the socio-economic consequences of the Israeli-Palestinian war. The disparities in poverty rates and access to resources underscore the multi-faceted challenges faced by Palestinian communities, emphasizing the interconnectedness of economic hardships and the broader theme of struggles and sacrifices.

Access to Education and Healthcare

In the poignant narrative of Palestinian struggles, the theme of displacement and refugee experiences stands as a testament to the enduring challenges faced by individuals and families. As the Israeli-Palestinian battle persists, the impact of forced migration on Palestinians reverberates through personal stories and adversities. The echoes of the Nakba, the catastrophic event of 1948, continue to resonate across generations, turning displacement into a multi-generational experience. The first-hand accounts of Palestinians who have experienced displacement offer a humanizing perspective, delving into the emotional and psychological toll of leaving one's home and community. The narratives weave a complex tapestry of resilience and coping mechanisms developed by displaced populations, portraying the profound human cost of the skirmish.

Amidst the persistent Israeli-Palestinian war, the educational landscape in Palestinian communities faces formidable challenges, impeding the access to and quality of education. The fight's impact on educational infrastructure and the learning experiences of students is a poignant reflection of the broader struggles faced by the Palestinian population.

A key obstacle involves the physical harm inflicted upon educational infrastructure. Schools, a requisite foundation for the development of young minds, have become collateral damage in the warfare. The destruction of school buildings, classrooms, and other facilities disrupts the continuity of education. This not only deprives students of a conducive learning environment but also places an additional burden on an already strained educational system.

The geographic dispersion of Palestinian communities exacerbates these challenges. The contention has led to the displacement of families, causing a fragmentation of communities. This dispersion often results in students having to travel longer distances to access educational facilities. The journey to school becomes fraught with uncertainty due to the security situation, impacting students' daily routines and contributing to absenteeism.

Furthermore, the brawl engenders a pervasive atmosphere of insecurity, directly affecting the safety of students and educators. Educational institutions, intended to be sanctuaries of learning, become advertent casualties in the crossfire. The fear of violence or warmongering operations near schools creates an environment of anxiety and fear among students and educators alike. This constant threat not only disrupts the regularity of classes but also instills a sense of trauma and instability in the educational experience.

The restrictions on movement imposed by the tussle pose another significant hurdle. Checkpoints, barriers, and restricted areas hinder the free flow of students and educators, complicating daily commutes to schools and universities. This impediment not only consumes valuable time but also introduces an element of unpredictability into the educational journey. Students, striving for academic pursuits, are confronted with bureaucratic obstacles that hinder their access to educational opportunities.

The disruptions extend beyond the physical realm to the curricular and extracurricular aspects of education. The conflict influences the content of educational materials, often shaping narratives that align with political agendas. This manipulation of educational content can perpetuate biases and contribute to the polarization of perspectives among students. Additionally, extracurricular activities, crucial for holistic development, face limitations due to security concerns, further constraining the overall educational experience.

The perpetual state of hostility also affects the mental health and well-being of students. Living in an environment characterized by violence and uncertainty takes a toll on the psychological resilience of young minds. The constant exposure to traumatic events, be it through personal experiences or media portrayal, creates emotional distress, hindering the cognitive and emotional development of students.

The challenges faced by Palestinian communities extend beyond the realm of education, permeating into the critical domain of healthcare. The Israeli-Palestinian war casts a long shadow over the healthcare delivery system, posing significant obstacles to access and exacerbating public health outcomes. As we delve into the implications for healthcare delivery, the multifaceted impact of restricted movement, damaged infrastructure, and resource limitations becomes starkly apparent.

Restricted movement, a byproduct of the skirmish, stands as a formidable barrier to healthcare access for Palestinians. Checkpoints, road closures, and restricted areas hinder the free movement of individuals seeking medical care. The arduous journey to reach healthcare facilities not only consumes time but also adds layers of stress and vagueness, especially for those facing urgent medical conditions. This restriction on movement is a direct infringement on the right to health, as recognized by international human rights standards, further deepening the humanitarian challenges faced by the Palestinian population.

The war's toll on infrastructure reverberates through the healthcare sector, amplifying the difficulties in delivering essential medical services Hospitals and clinics, frequently situated in hostility-prone areas, constantly face the threat of intentional damage or destruction. This jeopardizes the continuity of healthcare delivery, leaving communities in a precarious state. The damaged infrastructure not only disrupts routine medical services but also compromises the ability to respond effectively to medical emergencies, creating a healthcare landscape fraught with limitations.

Resource limitations compound the challenges, affecting the availability and quality of healthcare services. The tussle diverts resources away from the healthcare sector, redirecting funds and attention to immediate security concerns. This diversion perpetuates a cycle of inadequacy, leaving healthcare facilities ill-equipped to meet the growing demands of a population grappling with both conflict-related injuries and routine medical needs. Insufficient medical supplies, personnel, and infrastructure impede the provision of comprehensive healthcare, contributing to a compromised public health ecosystem.

The consequences of limited healthcare access reverberate through public health outcomes, creating a scenario where preventable illnesses escalate into more severe conditions. The delay in seeking medical attention due to restricted movement, coupled with compromised infrastructure, results in late-stage diagnoses and hindered disease management. Preventative measures, such as immunizations and regular check-ups, become luxuries rather than routine healthcare practices. This, in turn, has a cascading effect on the overall health of the population, contributing to a higher burden of disease and increased mortality rates.

Medical emergencies, a constant reality in battlegrounds, become particularly challenging to address under the constraints imposed by the contention. Emergency response mechanisms, crucial for saving lives, face impediments in reaching affected areas promptly. The damaged infrastructure and restricted movement hamper the swift transport of medical personnel, supplies, and equipment to areas in urgent need. This delay in emergency response exacerbates the severity of injuries and reduces the chances of survival, underscoring the life-threatening costs of limited healthcare access.

In the aftermath of years of battle and disruptions, the implications of limited healthcare access reverberate through public health outcomes and the ability to address medical emergencies. The health infrastructure, already strained by the clash, faces ongoing challenges that impede its ability to provide adequate care. Moreover, the damaged healthcare infrastructure further compounds the challenges. Hospitals and clinics, often caught in the crossfire, experience structural damage, equipment shortages, and interruptions in primordial services. This not only affects the immediate response to emergencies but also undermines the overall quality of healthcare delivery. The long-lasting impact of damaged infrastructure lingers, hindering the recovery and rebuilding process.

The enduring impacts on well-being extend beyond physical health to encompass mental health. Living in a hostile territory induces stress and ordeal, coupled with difficulties in accessing mental health services, contributing to a pervasive mental health crisis. The interaction between physical and mental health challenges creates a complex web of issues that individuals and communities grapple with over the years. As the cycle of war endures, the prospects for improving healthcare access face continuous hurdles. Rebuilding infrastructure, securing adequate resources, and addressing the psychological toll on healthcare providers become integral components of any sustainable solution. The long-term effects on well-being and prospects necessitate comprehensive strategies that go beyond immediate crisis management and focus on rebuilding a resilient and effective healthcare system.

Trauma and Mental Health Struggles

The psychological impact of the Israeli-Palestinian war delves into the intricate layers of trauma, shedding light on the profound and lasting effects that reverberate through individuals and communities. Beyond the immediate and visible consequences of violence and displacement, the nuanced nature of psychological distress requires a deeper exploration to comprehend the complexities at play.

The constant exposure to violence, whether in the form of pugnacious operations, air raids, or clashes, creates an environment where individuals live in perpetual fear. The emotional burden of this sustained threat manifests in heightened stress levels, anxiety disorders, and a pervasive sense of vulnerability. Displacement, a pervasive impact of the skirmish, introduces a unique set of psychological challenges. The forced uprooting from homes, communities, and familiar environments disrupts the continuity of identity and belonging. The psychological distress associated with displacement extends beyond the initial anguish of leaving, encompassing the challenges of resettlement, adapting to new cultural contexts, and the ongoing uncertainty of not having a place to call home. This loss of rootedness contributes significantly to the overarching psychological impact, as individuals grapple with a profound sense of disconnection.

The normalization of adversity, a coping mechanism for survival, adds another layer to the psychological impact. When living conditions characterized by violence, uncertainty, and scarcity become normalized, individuals may struggle to discern what constitutes normalcy. The blurring of boundaries between the expected and the abnormal can lead to desensitization, where individuals develop a tolerance to extreme conditions. This desensitization, while adaptive in the immediate context, contributes to long-term mental health struggles, as the line between coping and distress becomes blurred.

Examining the gendered dimensions of psychological impact reveals additional layers of complexity. Women, often bearing the brunt of societal and familial stressors, face specific challenges, including gender-based violence such as sexual assault and harassment. The intersectionality of gender and skirmish introduces unique traumas that demand targeted interventions. Addressing the gendered aspects of psychological distress is crucial for understanding the diverse experiences within the affected population.

Moreover, the inadequacy of mental health support systems poses a significant barrier to addressing the psychological impact effectively. Stigma surrounding mental health within the cultural context, coupled with limited access to specialized care, leaves many individuals without the necessary resources for healing. Integrating mental health into the broader healthcare framework and challenging societal stigmas are pivotal steps in creating a supportive environment for those grappling with the psychological outcome of the contention.

In the Israeli-Palestinian war, the profound impact on subsequent generations becomes increasingly evident, perpetuating a cycle of psychological distress that is challenging to break. The transmission of gloom from one generation to the next is a deeply embedded aspect of the Palestinian narrative. Parents, themselves scarred by the direct and indirect effects of tussle, inadvertently pass down their experiences, anxieties, and coping mechanisms to their children. This inter-generational transmission manifests in various forms, shaping the worldview, behavior, and mental well-being of the younger generation.

The primary conduit for the transfer of trauma is the family unit. Within the confines of familial relationships, children absorb not only the explicit narratives of displacement, violence, and loss but also the unspoken nuances of emotional distress. The atmosphere of the household, influenced by the unresolved ordeal of the past, becomes a crucible where the psychological struggles of one generation are imprinted onto the psyches of the next.

The displacement experienced by parents during the Nakba, the ongoing cycles of warfare, and the daily challenges of life under occupation create an environment where misery is not only an individual burden but a collective inheritance. The stories of dispossession, the yearning for a homeland, and the persistent threat of violence permeate the family discourse, shaping the identity and consciousness of younger Palestinians.

Children, growing up in this environment, navigate a psychological landscape where the normalization of adversity blurs the distinction between ordinary and distressing experiences. The normalization of anguish becomes a coping mechanism, a way to make sense of a reality marred by clash and uncertainty. As a result, the inter-generational transfer of grief is not always overt; it can manifest subtly in the form of altered stress responses, heightened vigilance, and a distorted perception of safety.

The enduring nature of the armed tangle contributes significantly to the perpetuation of inter-generational wrench. Unlike transient scrimmages that allow for periods of recovery and healing, the protracted Israeli-Palestinian war maintains a constant undercurrent of tension and threat. This chronic exposure to stressors, both acute and chronic, amplifies the psychological impact on subsequent generations.

Moreover, the lack of resolution and the persistent state of limbo regarding the political situation exacerbate the challenges of breaking the cycle of inter-generational trauma. The absence of a clear path to justice, restitution, or repatriation leaves families in a perpetual state of uncertainty, hindering the possibility of closure and healing. The cyclical nature of tussle, marked by recurring bouts of violence and unrest, further entrenches the inter-generational transmission of suffering.

The impact on mental health is not uniform across generations; rather, it evolves and adapts to the changing dynamics of the hostility. Second and third generations, born into an environment shaped by the experiences of their forebears, grapple with a unique set of challenges. The legacy of ordeal intertwines with contemporary stressors, creating a compound interplay of historical and current psychological struggles.

Breaking the cycle of inter-generational tribulation requires a multifaceted approach. Beyond addressing the immediate mental health needs of individuals, interventions must encompass broader societal and systemic changes. Educational initiatives that promote resilience, coping skills, and emotional well-being can have a decisive impact in mitigating the transmission of agony. Creating spaces for open dialogue within families and communities allows for the acknowledgment and expression of collective pain, fostering a sense of shared healing. Furthermore, initiatives that address the root causes of the conflict, advocate for justice, and work towards a sustainable resolution contribute to dismantling the conditions that perpetuate inter-generational throes. Recognizing the interconnectedness of individual and collective healing is essential in developing strategies that break the cycle and pave the way for a future where subsequent generations can thrive free from the weight of inherited anguish.

Family Separations and Social Disruptions

The impact of family separations and divisions within Palestinian communities reverberates beyond the individual level, weaving a complex tapestry of social disruptions that shape the broader social fabric. The wrenching experiences of families torn apart by razzia, forced displacement, and political realities generate profound ripple effects, molding the dynamics of social relationships, community cohesion, and traditional support structures.

At the heart of these social disruptions lies the fracturing of the family unit, a foundational pillar of Palestinian society. The Israeli-Palestinian war, marked by waves of displacement, occupation, and the constriction of movement, has frequently compelled families to navigate the harsh terrain of separation. Whether due to physical barriers, political borders, or the exigencies of survival, many Palestinians find themselves geographically dispersed from their immediate and extended families.

This spatial dislocation not only strains the emotional bonds that traditionally define familial relationships but also catalyzes a reconfiguration of social roles and responsibilities. The absence of key family members disrupts the intergenerational transfer of knowledge, cultural practices, and familial narratives. Grandparents, often repositories of familial history and cultural heritage, may find themselves isolated from younger generations, impeding the transmission of cultural identity and collective memory.

Moreover, the impact extends to the dynamics between parents and children. The burden of maintaining familial ties and economic stability in the face of adversity often falls heavily on parents, who navigate the challenges of raising children within the constraints imposed by contention. The absence of a support network amplifies the strain on parents, affecting their ability to provide emotional guidance and a stable environment for their children.

The disruption of familial networks also reverberates through the community at large. Traditional support structures, built on extended family ties and communal bonds, face erosion when families are fragmented. The organic networks that once provided emotional, financial, and social support during times of crisis are strained, challenging the resilience of communities to withstand the multifaceted impacts of the hostility.

Community cohesion, a cornerstone of Palestinian resilience, faces formidable challenges in the wake of family separations. The collective experience of shared hardship has historically fostered a sense of solidarity and mutual support within Palestinian communities. However, the dispersion of families disrupts the communal drapery, weakening the bonds that traditionally bound individuals together. The shared narratives of struggle and sacrifice lose their immediacy when families are dispersed, impeding the communal solidarity that has been a source of resilience in the face of adversity.

The impact on social relationships extends to the realm of friendships, marriages, and social networks. Palestinians, confronted with the realities of displacement and the uncertainties of the tussle, often find themselves forging new connections in unfamiliar territories. This process of building new social ties is not without challenges, as individuals grapple with the loss of the familiar and the navigation of new cultural landscapes. Friendships formed in the crucible of conflict can be both a source of strength and a reminder of shared traumas, shaping the contours of social relationships in ways that reflect the complexities of Palestinian identity.

Furthermore, marriage patterns undergo shifts as families adapt to the constraints imposed by brawl. The challenges of movement restrictions, economic hardships, and the uncertain political landscape influence decisions regarding marriage and family planning. The quest for stability and security, coupled with the desire to preserve cultural and familial ties, shapes the choices individuals make in the realm of marriage, contributing to the nuanced evolution of social norms within Palestinian communities.

Displaced families contending with the repercussions of forced separations and the far-reaching disruptions caused by the Israeli-Palestinian war encounter a myriad of challenges intricately woven into the web of their daily existence. Negotiating the formidable landscape of displacement unfurls a series of economic, emotional, and practical obstacles that loom over the welfare of individuals and the cohesion of communities.

Economically, the ripple effects of forced separations reverberate through the lives of displaced families. The abrupt uprooting from homes and communities often results in the loss of livelihoods and economic stability. Displaced individuals find themselves grappling with the challenge of sustaining their families in unfamiliar and often hostile environments. The disruption of economic networks, coupled with limited access to employment opportunities, compounds the economic hardships faced by displaced families.

Moreover, the economic challenges extend beyond immediate survival to the broader implications for the well-being of individuals and communities. The erosion of economic stability translates into increased vulnerability to poverty, food insecurity, and inadequate access to basilar services. The economic fallout of forced separations permeates the fabric of daily life, shaping the lived experiences of displaced families and exerting a profound impact on their overall well-being.

Emotionally, the toll of forced separations is immeasurable, casting a long shadow over the mental health and resilience of individuals. The rupture of familial bonds, the loss of homes, and the uncertainties of displacement contribute to a pervasive sense of grief, anxiety, and trauma. Individuals, particularly children, grapple with the emotional scars inflicted by the abrupt disruption of their lives, navigating a complex landscape of loss and uncertainty.

The emotional challenges extend to the functioning of communities, as the collective suffering of forced separations reverberates through the communal montage. The shared experiences of displacement forge a collective emotional landscape, shaping the social dynamics and relationships within displaced communities. The burden of collective tribulation, compounded by the ongoing uncertainties of the contention, contributes to the complex interplay of emotions that define the social fabric of displaced communities.

Practically, the challenges faced by displaced families manifest in their daily struggles to adapt to life in refugee camps or new host communities. The displacement experience often entails a radical shift in living conditions, with families forced to navigate the complexities of life in temporary shelters or unfamiliar urban environments. Access to basic services, including education, healthcare, and sanitation, becomes a pressing concern, with displaced families contending with the disruption of cardinal support structures.

In refugee camps, the challenges are exacerbated by overcrowded conditions, limited resources, and the protracted nature of displacement. Families grapple with the scarcity of resources, inadequate living conditions, and the constant threat of precarious circumstances. The practical challenges of adapting to life in refugee camps further strain the well-being of individuals and communities, shaping the contours of their daily existence.

The economic hardships faced by displaced families intertwine with the practical challenges of adapting to new host communities. The disruption of social and cultural ties resulting from displacement complicates the process of integration into unfamiliar environments. Displaced individuals often find themselves negotiating the complexities of cultural adaptation, grappling with the loss of familiar social networks and the need to forge new connections in order to rebuild their lives.

Amidst the profound challenges of family separations and social disruptions, individuals and communities exhibit remarkable resilience, deploying coping mechanisms and forging community-led initiatives to navigate the intricate ensemble of their disrupted lives. These coping strategies not only enable individuals to weather the storms of displacement but also contribute to the resilience of the broader community, fostering a sense of solidarity and collective strength.

On an individual level, the coping mechanisms employed by those grappling with family separations encompass a spectrum of emotional, psychological, and practical strategies. Emotional resilience emerges as a cornerstone, as individuals harness inner strength to cope with the emotional toll of separation. Drawing upon the bonds of familial and communal ties, individuals often find solace in the shared experiences of displacement, forging connections with others who have weathered similar storms.

Psychologically, individuals often develop adaptive strategies to navigate the uncertainties and traumas of their displacement. Seeking refuge in cultural and religious practices, storytelling, and communal rituals becomes a means of preserving identity and coping with the dislocation of their lives. These psychological coping mechanisms serve as pillars of support, allowing individuals to confront the challenges of displacement with a sense of purpose and agency. Religious institutions also contribute significantly in providing emotional and spiritual support. Mosques, churches, and community centers become spaces where individuals can seek solace, connect with others facing similar challenges, and draw on the teachings of faith to find meaning in the midst of upheaval. The spiritual resilience of individuals and communities becomes a guiding force, offering a source of comfort and fortitude in the face of profound social disruptions.

In practical terms, individuals employ adaptive strategies to surmount the logistical challenges posed by displacement. Demonstrating resourcefulness in securing basic necessities and forging informal support networks within displaced communities, individuals exhibit an inherent resilience confronting adversity. These pragmatic coping mechanisms not only attend to immediate needs but also play a pivotal role in shaping community-led initiatives, laying the foundation for resilience in the midst of social disruptions.

At the community level, the resilience of displaced populations is further exemplified by the emergence of community-led initiatives and support systems. Collective coping mechanisms, ranging from the establishment of mutual support networks to the creation of community-based organizations, become integral components of the response to family separations and social disruptions.

Community-led initiatives often revolve around preserving cultural identity and fostering a sense of belonging. Cultural preservation becomes a potent tool for communities to reclaim agency and counteract the erasure of identity often associated with displacement. Through cultural events, language preservation efforts, and the documentation of collective histories, communities forge a resilient response to the challenges of disrupted social structures.

Moreover, communal support networks have a central function in alleviating the adverse impacts of family separations. Families and individuals find solace in the shared experience of displacement, creating a sense of belonging that transcends the physical separation from their homes. These support networks, often rooted in shared geographical or cultural backgrounds, serve as lifelines for those navigating the complexities of displacement, providing emotional, practical, and social support.

Amid family separations and social disruptions, community-based organizations arise as formidable forces of resilience. Initiated and guided by displaced individuals themselves, these organizations serve as centers of empowerment, providing a spectrum of services encompassing education, healthcare, advocacy, and cultural preservation. Through actively shaping their destinies, these initiatives led by the community epitomize the resilience exhibited by both individuals and communities in the midst of significant adversity.

Towards a Just Resolution

Hypocrisy of UN and Western Countries

In the complex arena of international relations, the inconsistencies in responses to geopolitical conflicts often raise profound questions about fairness and equity. This discussion delves into a particularly sensitive yet crucial dimension of global diplomacy—the contrasting approaches of the United Nations and Western countries towards the Israeli-Palestinian war in comparison to other international situations. The stage is set to scrutinize the nuanced dynamics that underpin these disparities, laying bare the intricate web of political, historical, and strategic considerations.

As the spotlight turns towards the Israeli-Palestinian war, a narrative unfolds that goes beyond the immediate geopolitical landscape. It is a narrative of hypocrisy, where the application of international norms and principles appears to diverge when applied to this enduring conflagration. The world has witnessed the United Nations and Western powers engage with a multitude of global crises, each demanding a unique response. However, the lens through which they view and address the Israeli-Palestinian war reveals a disconcerting discrepancy and speciousness.

Examining instances like the Russia-Ukraine conflict, the Iranian nuclear program, the political crisis in Belarus, and tensions on the Korean Peninsula exposes a notable disparity in how the international community reacts. Swift and impactful sanctions characterize struggles like Russia-Ukraine, standing in stark contrast to the measured and diplomatic approach to the Israeli-Palestinian war.

Despite the protracted history and recurring violence in the Israeli-Palestinian tussle, a comparable level of assertiveness is absent. Diplomatic deliberations, rather than impactful measures, mark the response. This hypocrisy raises questions about the criteria guiding international involvement and the standards used to assess conflict severity.

Entangled in a complex web of historical alliances, Western nations' response to the Israeli-Palestinian brawl is more measured and diplomatic. The UN outwardly engages in addressing the Israeli-Palestinian war through resolutions and actions. Resolution 242, adopted in 1967, emphasizes the inadmissibility of acquiring territory by foray and calls for Israeli withdrawal. However, the ambiguity in its language, particularly regarding the scope of withdrawal, has been a source of ongoing contention. The UN's humanitarian agencies, particularly UNRWA, hold a substantial scope in addressing the socio-economic impacts of the Israeli-Palestinian hostility. This humanitarian focus reflects an acknowledgment of the plight of Palestinian refugees. Nevertheless, the persistent nature of the war raises questions about the adequacy of humanitarian aid in addressing the root causes and achieving a lasting resolution.

A closer examination of UN resolutions reveals patterns in addressing conflicts, with implications for the Israeli-Palestinian situation. The UN's approach leans on diplomatic discourse and peacekeeping efforts. In contrast, conflicts like the Russia-Ukraine struggle see a more assertive stance with sanctions, indicating a willingness to translate discourse into impactful actions. The UN's involvement is inherently multilateral, involving various stakeholders. However, diverse interests hinder cohesive multilateral action. Issues like sanctions against Iran demonstrate a more unified multilateral front.

Unraveling the political and economic interests influencing Western countries' stance on the Israeli-Palestinian war reveals a complex tapestry. Strategic alliances, economic ties, multilateral dynamics, and domestic politics create a landscape where diplomatic decisions are nuanced and contingent on a delicate balance of interests.

Similarly, when closely examining events in and around Palestine and neighboring countries, a noteworthy observation emerges. While some Western nations welcome migrants from Palestine and its neighboring regions, simultaneously, these countries align themselves with Israel and endorse Zionist activities in Palestinian territories. This implies that these nations may, inadvertently or otherwise, contribute to the non-coercive displacement of the indigenous population to make way for Zionist interests.

Amid the inconsistencies in global responses, a chorus of voices emerges—some critical, others supportive. Human rights organizations, such as Amnesty International and Human Rights Watch, criticize double standards, demanding consistency in emphasizing human rights across all conflicts. Scholars highlight disparities in applying international norms, emphasizing the need for a uniform ethical framework. Ireland, within Western countries, witnesses political dissent against selective application of sanctions, questioning the alignment of foreign policies with democratic values.

The expectation of justice and moral responses becomes perplexing when nations take decisive actions against Iran and North Korea, citing potential threats. Instead, Israel enjoys preferential trading relationships with the European Union. Failing to prevent victimization when capacity allows, offering minimal aid in response, is unjust and makes entities complicit in the crime. The inconsistency in approach becomes glaring when contrasting swift actions in other geopolitical scenarios with measured responses to well-documented transgressions in the Israeli-Palestinian war. These entities prioritize personal and political gains over the common good.

Misunderstandings and False Arguments

In the pursuit of a just resolution to the complex tableau of the Israeli-Palestinian war, it becomes imperative to dissect and dispel the misunderstandings and false arguments that have perpetuated discord and hindered meaningful dialogue. Unraveling the intricacies of historical narratives, political rhetoric, and deeply ingrained beliefs is a prerequisite for forging a path toward understanding, empathy, and ultimately, a fair resolution. As we delve into this critical examination, it is essential to sift through the layers of misinformation, unfounded assertions, and misinterpretations that have, over time, become entrenched barriers to progress. Only by untangling these threads of misconception can we pave the way for a more informed, nuanced, and constructive discourse, laying the groundwork for a just and lasting resolution that honors the rights and aspirations of all parties involved.

Zionists often assert that we, as Jews, have an ancestral connection to Palestine, dating back to time immemorial—a homecoming rather than a new arrival. However, as expounded in our preceding chapter, a meticulous examination reveals an incontrovertible truth: Jews cannot lay claim to being the indigenous inhabitants of Palestine. Compelling evidence, as discussed, dispels the notion of an inherent link.

Furthermore, a biblical reference, Genesis 17:8 (New International Version), bolsters this argument: "The whole land of Canaan, where you now reside as a foreigner, I will give as an everlasting possession to you and your descendants after you; and I will be their God." This scriptural passage explicitly denotes Abraham's (PBUH) status as a foreigner in the land. From this scriptural standpoint and our prior analysis, the conclusion becomes unmistakable: Jews do not hold the primordial claim to the territory.

For the sake of contemplation, let us entertain the hypothetical notion that they were indeed among the aboriginal inhabitants of the land. Would such a historical connection serve as unequivocal proof of their present entitlement to the land of Palestine? In response to this assertion, I would succinctly state that, from a standpoint of legitimacy, you cannot sleep with your ex-wife merely because she was once your spouse.

In a parallel vein, as a Tamilian, could I, by mirroring the Jewish assertion, substantiate that my forebears resided in North India? If successful, would the Indian Government, a supporter of Israeli militant actions, acquiesce to granting Tamilians an independent nation akin to Israel, as dictated by the historical claim? Moreover, would the United Nations issue a declaration stipulating that any group substantiating ancestral ties to a particular territory in antiquity is eligible for the establishment of an autonomous nation within that geographical expanse, facilitated by the UN?

Consider the plight of the indigenous populations in America, Australia, Canada, and beyond—historically marginalized and persecuted, their struggles well-documented. In contemplating the perceived entitlement of Zionists to their proclaimed homeland, it raises a pertinent question: why do the governments of the United States, Australia, Canada, and others not formulate comprehensive plans to restore these lands to their native inhabitants? Why not, at the very least, consider declaring portions of these territories as independent nations for the original dwellers?

While advocating for the rights of Zionists, the disparity in treatment becomes apparent. Despite insufficient evidence to substantiate their historical claim, why is there a unique leniency toward the Zionist cause? Is it driven by political motivations or a misplaced sympathy stemming from the Holocaust narrative? The divergence in approach warrants careful consideration and challenges the consistency of principles in addressing historical injustices.

Consider a scenario where a British individual, who had established a business partnership with you, unfortunately meets an untimely demise with no surviving relatives. In such a circumstance, would it be reasonable for any random British claimant, irrespective of their background, to assert ownership and demand partnership? The implausibility of such a proposition is evident. Similarly, even if we were to hypothetically accept that Jews have resided in Palestine, specifically Canaan, since time immemorial, it does not logically follow that any random individual of Jewish descent should be granted ownership of the land. The world's operational mechanisms do not subscribe to such arbitrary allocations based solely on ancestral ties. A nuanced and equitable approach is indispensable in navigating complex historical claims and contemporary realities.

Asserting that Isaac (PBUH) was born in Canaan as a basis for Jewish rights in the region hinges on the presumption that Canaan operated as a "jus soli" nation, granting citizenship by birth. Fortunately, historical evidence validating such a claim is absent, challenging the premise of this   argument.
Even under the assumption that Canaan operated as a Jus Soli nation, it does not necessarily entail that their descendants can claim citizenship today after centuries of absence from the land. Additionally, considerations must extend beyond ancestral claims to address the rights of the actual inhabitants of Canaan.

If the argument is made that Jews have inherent rights to the land, it prompts a crucial question: what about the legitimate rights of the true Canaanites? In the hypothetical scenario of a legal mandate stipulating the return of land to its original inhabitants, the rightful beneficiaries would be the Canaanites and Philistines, not the Zionists. This aligns with the contemporary reality where the modern-day Palestinians, with historical ties to the region, would be the legitimate successors to the lands of Philistia and some parts of Canaan.

The initiation of land ownership documentation traces back to the ancient Mesopotamian periods, yet the widespread implementation of such systems occurred only in recent centuries. During eras preceding this development, people, particularly Israelis, traversed countries and continents driven by the exigencies of their time, devoid of stringent territorial affiliations. Consequently, it appears illogical for their descendants today to assert ownership over lands based on historical movements.

The contemporary insistence on land claims, resembling the assertions made by Zionists, lacks logical coherence. The fluidity of historical migrations and the absence of comprehensive land documentation during those periods underscore the impracticality of contemporary claims rooted solely in ancestral ties. Acknowledging the intricacies of historical context is crucial in evaluating such assertions, promoting a more reasoned and equitable approach to questions of land ownership.

The assertion that Palestinians, hypothetically speaking, sold lands to Zionists does not inherently confer the right to establish an independent country for the latter. This line of thinking oversimplifies the complexities surrounding territorial matters. To illustrate, consider if a group of ten thousand individuals from a particular faction were to purchase land in a designated area within Britain. Would the British government, or any nation supportive of Israel's actions, permit these individuals to declare an independent state by amalgamating these acquired lands? The answer, within the realm of established international norms, is unlikely.

The change in ownership of land within a specific geographical area does not automatically translate into the right to secede and form a new nation. Such lands would typically remain integral to the sovereign nation—Britain, in this instance—regardless of alterations in ownership. Applying this straightforward logic to the rights of Palestinians reveals the complexity and nuances involved, challenging the oversimplified notion that land transactions equate to the establishment of a new, independent state.

If one contends that the land was divinely promised to them, the inquiry necessitates a contemplation of the biblical verses in Genesis 15:18-21 (New International Version): "On that day the Lord made a covenant with Abram and said, 'To your descendants I give this land, from the Wadi of Egypt to the great river, the Euphrates—the land of the Kenites, Kenizzites, Kadmonites, Hittites, Perizzites, Rephaites, Amorites, Canaanites, Girgashites, and Jebusites.'" Additionally, Genesis 13:15 (New International Version) declares: "All the land that you see I will give to you and your offspring forever."

The crux of the matter lies in the interpretation of the term 'forever' in the divine promise, especially when considering the passage of approximately 4000 years since the time of Abraham (PBUH). In stark contrast, the actual period of Jewish control over the land spans only a few centuries. The question thus arises: how do we reconcile the temporal reality with the perpetual nature implied by the word 'forever' in the covenant with God? This contemplation invites a nuanced exploration of the linguistic and temporal dimensions embedded in the divine pledge. Perhaps the term 'forever' carries a symbolic or spiritual connotation, suggesting a perpetual connection rather than continuous geopolitical control. The complexities inherent in interpreting divine promises underscore the challenges of reconciling ancient prophecies with the unfolding course of history.

The biblical promise of a vast expanse, akin to a full large-sized pizza, spanning from the Wadi of Egypt to the great river, the Euphrates, raises perplexing questions. Why, then, did the reality for the Jewish people unfold as a mere slice of this expansive covenant? Did their God find Himself bound by a UN partition plan, or did the Jewish community, perhaps, transgress divine commandments, prompting a retraction of a significant portion of the promised "pizza"?

The paradox deepens when considering the intermittent periods in which the so-called promised land was vacated. The absence of consistent allegiance to this sacred land throughout history invites scrutiny. Why did the Jewish people not ardently contend for their promised land during various epochs, as the current Palestinian inhabitants passionately do today?

Similarly, the ancient Philistines are argued to correspond to modern-day Palestinians, while the Canaanites are seen as Israelis. Logically, the Canaanites predate even the birth of Abraham (PBUH), the patriarch. The term 'Israelite' commonly refers to the descendants of Jacob (PBUH) rather than a specific regional population. The Hebrew Bible itself recounts conflicts between the Israelites and Canaanites, including military campaigns and the Israelite conquest of Canaan. In contrast, the introduction of Christianity and Islam to the region saw locals embracing these religions. This suggests that the present-day inhabitants of Palestine, Lebanon, and parts of Jordan and Syria are the descendants of the original Philistines and Canaanites, with the possibility of some migrants among them.

In parsing these perplexities, one is inclined to ponder whether the divine promise was upheld or if, perhaps, it was a fabrication. The discrepancy between the expansive pledge and the limited reality, coupled with historical vacillations in the Jewish connection to the land, gives rise to poignant questions. Is it a case of a deceitful deity or, rather, a people perpetuating falsehoods and perpetrating violence under the guise of divine mandate? The latter, guided by logical scrutiny, emerges as a compelling conjecture.

A critical observation emerges: if, in the aftermath of the Holocaust, Britain and Western countries harbored a sense of guilt and a desire to provide a homeland for the presumed survivors, the ethical course would have been to allocate land within their own geographical boundaries. Instead, the decision to bestow Palestinian lands upon a group with no logical claims to the region stands as a betrayal of the Palestinian population.

A distinctive feature sets the Zionist movement apart from other nationalist endeavors—the former sought its purported rights within the land of Palestinians rather than within the territory where its adherents resided. Unlike other nationalist movements that typically championed their cause within the confines of their own established communities, the Zionists advocated for their perceived rights in the homeland of the Palestinian people.

While delving into the ancient history of Palestine and the origins of the Jewish people may not be a prerequisite for comprehending the inhumane actions of the Zionists in the region, such historical exploration does illuminate a pertinent truth: the absence of inherent rights for the Zionists in Palestine, even when scrutinized from a historical standpoint.

Examining these historical narratives not only provides context but also reveals a lack of inherent entitlement for the Zionists within the region. The atrocities and inhumane acts committed in the name of their cause become all the more conspicuous when juxtaposed against the historical record.

In the face of compelling historical evidence and logical arguments against the actions of Israel, some pro-Zionists employ the "right to defense" card to justify the killing of innocent people. This stance, however, is flawed in its omission of the broader context, historical ownership of the land, and the protracted nature of the war.

It is irrational to divorce the present circumstances from the intricate tapestry of history and ownership rights to construct arguments solely based on isolated incidents. The ongoing war in the region is not a recent development but rather a protracted struggle endured by Palestinians spanning seven decades. To scrutinize the situation solely through the lens of individual events neglects the root causes and historical injustices that have fueled the enduring strife.

Another argument presented by some pro-Zionists, proposing that if Israel disarms, it would face problems, while a peaceful coexistence could be achieved if Palestinians relinquish their weapons, raises ethical concerns. Skepticism arises when considering historical evidence that challenges the likelihood of Zionists allowing for genuine peace.

To illustrate, let's entertain a hypothetical scenario. A thief intrudes into your home, not only stealing your possessions but also causing intentional harm to you and your loved ones. In an attempt to defend yourself, you manage to grasp something in your hand. The thief then proposes a dubious truce, stating that if he puts down his weapon, you will seek justice and hold him accountable. However, if you disarm, he pledges not to inflict further harm and suggests a semblance of peace, all the while retaining what he has taken from you.

This scenario highlights the inherent injustice in the proposition. It underscores the asymmetry of power dynamics and the impracticality of expecting genuine peace when one party has already suffered profound losses and continues to be denied justice. The analogy mirrors the complexities of the Israel-Palestine tussle, emphasizing the need for a more equitable and just resolution.

Article 23(g) of the Hague Regulations of 1907 states that it is forbidden "to destroy or seize the enemy's property unless such destruction or seizure be imperatively demanded by the necessities of war." Israeli officials have argued that the demolition of property is justified under this provision due to what they perceive as military necessities. The article clearly talks about 'enemy's property,' not about civilians' prosperity. Does their argument mean that Israel considers the entire Palestinian people as their enemies? I know they do, but would they dare to openly accept it?

Some advocate for the forced displacement of Palestinians during times of war, asserting it's for their safety. However, the question arises: if conditions have relatively stabilized, why are these individuals not permitted to return to their homes? The extended denial of repatriation is driven by political, territorial, or demographic factors. In these instances, the emphasis on safety serves as a pretext rather than a sincere concern.

Justification for Israeli attacks on Palestinian civilians and infrastructures often revolves around the claim that Hamas uses civilians as human shields, hiding among them within the same infrastructures. Consequently, Israel is argued to be forced into targeting Palestinian civilians and their infrastructures to combat Hamas fighters. This claim has been proven wrong so many times with strong evidence by numerous entities. But hypothetically, if it's indeed true that Hamas uses Palestinians as human shields, residing in hospitals and schools with the public for this purpose, why not use Israeli hostages in the same way? Why not stay in the same buildings with them so that the losses would be on both sides when Israel conducts airstrikes? On the contrary, Israeli Defense Forces (IDF) used Palestinians as human shields on 1,200 occasions within five years, as revealed by Israeli defense officials in 2005. A UN report in 2013 further highlighted instances where Palestinian children were tortured and used as human shields by the Israeli militant group IDF. There are documented cases of thousands of occasions where Zionists have employed Palestinian civilians, including children, as human shields. In some instances, even activists have been used as human shields by Israel.

The strategic maneuvers of Zionism have led the world to label anyone who doesn't believe in the Holocaust as antisemitic. Those not supporting Israeli activities in Palestine are also branded as antisemitic. Even backing innocent Palestinians is met with accusations of terrorism. Why is the world compelled to support Israel despite their inhumane actions? Logically, why should someone accept the Holocaust when it contradicts reason? Not believing in the moon landing doesn't make one anti-American, so why does Holocaust denial lead to antisemitism?

In candid terms, a genuine adherence to Islam is incompatible with harboring anti-Semitic beliefs. This is because there are many prophets of God from the descendants of Jacob (PBUH). Furthermore, the intention of this work is not to critique the entirety of the Jewish community. Many Jews actively advocate for justice and earnestly pursue peace. The Holy Quran states in Surah Āl-'Imrān, Verse 113-114, "Yet they are not all alike: there are some among the People of the Book who are upright, who recite Allah's revelations throughout the night, prostrating (in prayer). They believe in Allah and the Last Day, encourage good and forbid evil, and race with one another in doing good. They are among the righteous." Additionally, in Surah Al-A'raf, Verse 159, it is mentioned, "Among the people of Moses, there is a group of people who would guide with the Truth and who act justly according to it."

When we delve into mainstream history, we are told that Jews faced expulsion and persecution in various countries: from England in 1290, France in the 14th century, Spain in 1492, Portugal in 1497, Italy in the 16th century, Poland in the 18th century, Russia in the late 19th to early 20th century, and Germany between the 1930s-1940s. From a logical standpoint, the widespread dissemination of the so-called anti-Semitic ideology across geographically distinct countries and varying time periods seems highly improbable, unless it originated from a singular medium. As we delve into the history of Jews, the absence of a singular medium becomes apparent, except for the fact that the majority of Jews themselves bore the reasons for their expulsion and persecution. Their own toxic behaviors acted as the medium that compelled others to act against them. Instead of introspecting and addressing why they faced such treatments wherever they went and whenever they interacted with others, they chose to establish a Zionist state that could support all their personal and political manipulations, atrocities, crimes, and so on.

Based on the historical and logical facts discussed above, we are led to the conclusion that Zionists are capable of committing any evil, pushing the boundaries of immorality and inhumanity for their own benefit. In other words, Zionists are the cancer on humanity that must be eradicated at any cost. They are not deserving of sympathy. IDF is deemed the most dangerous terrorist organization ever because their actions are often shielded by the Holocaust card, and the world is conditioned to overlook and dismiss their crimes and inhumane behaviors when confronted with their crocodile tears.

The intention of this book is not to assert that Palestinians have made no mistakes. On the contrary, Palestinians committed an irreparable and tumultuous mistake in the annals of human history, displaying a unique sympathy towards the historically proven betrayers—the Zionist vampires. They were kind to them and permitted them to reside within the land of Palestine. The predicament of the Palestinians brings to mind an Arabic saying, which means: 'fatten the dog, and it will eventually eat you too.'

Confronted with the historical injustices inflicted upon the Palestinians and the global alignment of numerous countries, including many Arab nations, standing in support of Israel—endorsing its bloodthirsty, inhumane actions either for self-interest or to shield themselves from comparable predicaments from Israel—I am reminded of an Arabic tale. It speaks of a vast meadow where three bulls roamed, their days saturated with grazing, sustenance, and gleeful frolicking. Their hues adorned the canvas of the meadow – one draped in pristine white, another ablaze in fiery red, and the last cloaked in profound black. Little did they know, a shrewd lion harbored ambitions of feasting upon their unsuspecting figures. Yet, confronted with the daunting task of challenging all three simultaneously, the lion concocted a cunning scheme.

Understanding that his triumph rested on isolating one bull at a time, the lion patiently awaited the opportune moment. Fortune smiled upon him when he stumbled upon the black and white bulls strolling alone in the meadow. Seizing the chance, he approached the black bull with hushed advice, slyly highlighting the attention-grabbing essence of the white companion. The lion planted seeds of uncertainty, subtly suggesting that the striking white coat would inevitably lead a hunter to both of them. By eliminating the white bull, he proposed, the meadow's resources could be preserved for the benefit of the black and red bulls, creating a more favorable scenario for the duo.

The words of the lion started to sway the thoughts of the black bull, who wrestled with the notion of eliminating the white companion from the scene. Offering assurance, the lion proclaimed, "Worry not, I will take care of it. Your duty is to distance yourself from here, leaving the rest to me."

Complying with the plan, the black bull stepped away, providing the lion with the opportune moment to strike and claim the life of the unsuspecting white bull. Upon the return of the red bull, the black employed deception, convincing him that the white bull had ventured to graze in the spread-out meadow near its corner and had not yet come back. Over time, the red bull's memory of his companion faded into oblivion.

The lion returned, once again manipulating the black bull by advocating for the advantages of a single ruler of the meadow. With each encounter, he subtly persuaded the black bull that having the meadow to himself was more beneficial than sharing it with the red bull. Eventually, the lion triumphed, devouring the red bull.

When the black bull returned after a few days, the lion's eyes conveyed a knowing look, triggering recognition in the black bull's mind. Understanding that he had been deceived into allowing the lion to consume his companions, he bellowed, " I was eaten on the day the white bull was eaten."

Just resolution

Justice doesn't mean considering the feelings of the parties involved in an incident or to act in favor of all of them. If someone rob you and took all your wealth, it is not just to make a settlement with him on giving him a share of your hard-earned money. However, the entirety of your funds ought to be returned to you, and the perpetrator should face consequences for their crime, even if the punishment inflicts discomfort upon the wrongdoer. Hence, advocating for justice entails supporting the rightful claimant irrespective of any political or personal advantages or drawbacks. To understand who is that right holder in this case, the discussion we have done so far, is good enough to come to a wiser and sound verdict.

Treating the symptoms alone will not cure the disease; the first step is to diagnose the disease and then administer treatment. This is the cardinal process for eliminating the disease and, consequently, eradicating the symptoms entirely. Similarly, establishing refugee camps and providing basic needs for Palestinians is akin to addressing the symptoms without actively engaging with the root cause. The Israel-Palestine war is rooted in the illegal existence of the state of Israel on Palestinians' land, as thoroughly diagnosed throughout this book. The very existence of the state of Israel is a crime. Its flag, to me, embodies betrayal and inhumanity. It's not Nazism that we should fear, but rather Zionism in all its forms. Now, it's time to prescribe the medications for a cure, seeking a just resolution to this longstanding issue.

The Jews who resided in Palestine before the preplanned immigration surge and their descendants have the right to remain there, not as citizens of an independent Israel, but as citizens of Palestine. However, others, including the so-called refugees, should have the right to choose their preferred means of leaving the land of the Palestinians: by land, sea, or air. They also have the right to relocate to the countries where they or their ancestors were before arriving in Palestine, following the strategic plans of the Zionist movement. Additionally, individuals proven to be war criminals or violators of human rights should face appropriate legal consequences, including hard labor sentences or capital punishment, depending on the severity of their crimes.

References

1. Al Jazeera, 2021. Investigative report on Gaza's healthcare crisis.

2. Al Mezan Center for Human Rights, 2018. *Documentation of attacks on medical staff during the Great Return March.*

3. Al Mezan Center for Human Rights, 2021. *Impact of Israeli attacks on Gaza's healthcare system.*

4. Amnesty International, 2014. *Mounting evidence of deliberate attacks by Israeli forces against hospitals in Gaza.*

5. Amnesty International, 2021. *Israel/Palestine: Pattern of attacks on medical facilities and personnel.*

6. Amnesty International, 2023. *Israel/Palestine: New evidence on white phosphorus use.*

7. Aruri, N., 2003. *Dishonest Broker: The U.S. Role in Israel and Palestine.* South End Press.

8. Barghouti, O., 2011. *BDS: Boycott, Divestment, Sanctions.* Haymarket Books.

9. BBC News, 2021. Coverage of the Israel-Palestine conflict.

10. Bishara, M., 2002. *Palestine/Israel: Peace or Apartheid.* Zed Books.

11. B'Tselem, 2014. *Analysis of Israeli military operations in Gaza.*

12. B'Tselem, 2021. *Documenting human rights violations in the West Bank and Gaza.*

13. Carter, J., 2006. *Palestine: Peace Not Apartheid.* Simon & Schuster.

14. Chomsky, N. and Pappé, I., 2010. *Gaza in Crisis: Reflections on Israel's War Against the Palestinians.* Haymarket Books.

15. Cook, J., 2008. *Disappearing Palestine: Israel's Experiments in Human Despair.* Zed Books.

16. Davis, U., 2003. *Apartheid Israel: Possibilities for the Struggle Within.* Zed Books.

17. Efron, S., Fischbach, J. and Giordano, G., 2018. *The public health impacts of Gaza's water crisis.*

18. Electronic Intifada, 2021. Palestinian perspectives on the conflict.

19. Farsakh, L., 2005. *Palestinian Labor Migration to Israel.* Routledge.

20. Finkelstein, N.G., 2003. *Image and Reality of the Israel-Palestine Conflict.* Verso.

21. Foreign Policy, 2021. Analysis of Middle East peace efforts.

22. Ghanem, A., 2001. *The Palestinian-Arab Minority in Israel, 1948-2000.* SUNY Press.

23. Gordon, N., 2008. *Israel's Occupation.* University of California Press.

24. Haaretz, 2021. Israeli perspectives on the conflict.

25. Halper, J., 2008. *An Israeli in Palestine: Resisting Dispossession, Redeeming Israel.* Pluto Press.

26. Human Rights Watch, 2009. *White phosphorus use in Gaza conflict.*

27. Human Rights Watch, 2023. *Israel: Use of white phosphorus during Lebanon confrontations.*

28. Hroub, K., 2010. *Hamas: A Beginner's Guide.* Pluto Press.

29. International Court of Justice, 2004. *Legal consequences of the construction of a wall in the occupied Palestinian territory.*

30. International Criminal Court, 2020. *Preliminary examination of the situation in Palestine.*

31. Khalidi, R., 2020. *The Hundred Years' War on Palestine.* Metropolitan Books.

32. Khalidi, W., 1992. *All That Remains: The Palestinian Villages Occupied and Depopulated by Israel in 1948.* Institute for Palestine Studies.

33. Karmi, G., 2002. *In Search of Fatima: A Palestinian Story.* Verso.

34. Klein, M., 2010. *The Shift: Israel-Palestine from Border Struggle to Ethnic Conflict.* Columbia University Press.

35. Médecins Sans Frontières, 2021. *Providing healthcare in conflict zones: Gaza.*

36. Middle East Eye, 2021. Coverage of the Gaza conflict and human rights issues.

37. Mondoweiss, 2021. Analysis of the Boycott, Divestment, Sanctions movement.

38. Morris, B., 2004. *The Birth of the Palestinian Refugee Problem Revisited.* Cambridge University Press.

39. OCHA, 2021. *Humanitarian needs overview: Occupied Palestinian territory.*

40. Organization for the Prohibition of Chemical Weapons, 2021. *Investigations into chemical weapon use.*

41. Pappé, I., 2006. *The Ethnic Cleansing of Palestine.* Oneworld Publications.

42. Physicians for Human Rights - Israel, 2018. *The health impact of the Gaza blockade.*

43. Qumsiyeh, M.B., 2011. *Popular Resistance in Palestine: A History of Hope and Empowerment.* Pluto Press.

44. Reuters, 2021. Report on the humanitarian impact of the Gaza blockade.

45. Robinson, S., 2013. *Citizen Strangers: Palestinians and the Birth of Israel's Liberal Settler State.* Stanford University Press.

46. Roy, S., 2007. *Failing Peace: Gaza and the Palestinian-Israeli Conflict.* Pluto Press.

47. Said, E.W., 1979. *The Question of Palestine.* Vintage Books.

48. Save the Children, 2021. *Impact of conflict on children in Gaza.*

49. Segev, T., 1999. *One Palestine, Complete: Jews and Arabs under the British Mandate.* Metropolitan Books.

50. Shaban, O., 2015. *The Israeli-Palestinian war: A People's War.* Pluto Press.

51. Shlaim, A., 2000. *The Iron Wall: Israel and the Arab World.* Norton.

52. Tamari, S., 2009. *Mountain Against the Sea: Essays on Palestinian Society and Culture.* University of California Press.

53. The Guardian, 2021. Analysis of recent escalations in Gaza.

54. The Intercept, 2021. Investigative journalism on US involvement in the Middle East.

55. The Lancet, 2018. *Health and healthcare in Gaza: An ongoing crisis.*

56. The New York Times, 2021. *Impact of Israeli airstrikes on Gaza infrastructure.*

57. The Red Cross, 2021. *Challenges in delivering aid in Gaza.*

58. Thrall, N., 2017. *The Only Language They Understand: Forcing Compromise in Israel and Palestine.* Metropolitan Books.

59. Tilley, V., 2005. *The One-State Solution: A Breakthrough for Peace in the Israeli-Palestinian Deadlock.* University of Michigan Press.

60. UNDP, 2021. *Development challenges in Gaza and the West Bank.*

61. UN General Assembly, 1947. *Resolution 181 (Partition Plan).*

62. UN General Assembly, 1974. *Resolution 3236 (Right of the Palestinian People).*

63. UNICEF, 2021. *Children in the State of Palestine: Data and trends.*

64. UNRWA, 2021. *Annual report on the situation in Gaza.*

65. UN Women, 2021. *The impact of conflict on women in Gaza.*

66. United Nations Fact Finding Mission, 2009. *Report on the Gaza conflict.*

67. United Nations Human Rights Council, 2020. *Database of companies involved in Israeli settlements.*

68. United Nations Security Council, 1967. *Resolution 242.*

69. United Nations Security Council, 1973. *Resolution 338.*

70. US Department of State, 2021. *Country Reports on Human Rights Practices: Israel, West Bank, and Gaza.*

71. World Health Organization, 2021. *Health conditions in the occupied Palestinian territory, including east Jerusalem, and in the occupied Syrian Golan.*

72. Ynet News, 2021. Coverage of Israeli military operations.

73. Zionist Congress, 1897. *Proceedings of the First Zionist Congress, Basel.*

74. Zionist Congress, 1917. *Balfour Declaration.*

75. Zionist Congress, 1920. *Protocols of the Zionist Congress.*

76. Zionist Congress, 1921. *Protocols of the Twelfth Zionist Congress, Carlsbad.*

77. Zionist Congress, 1937. *Protocols of the Twentieth Zionist Congress, Zurich.*

78. Zionist Congress, 1946. *Proceedings of the Twenty-Second Zionist Congress, Basel.*

79. Zionist Congress, 1947. *Proceedings of the Twenty-Third Zionist Congress, Basel.*

80. Zionist Congress, 1948. *Proceedings of the Provisional State Council.*

81. Zionist Congress, 1968. *Protocols of the Twenty-Seventh Zionist Congress, Jerusalem.*

82. Zionist Congress, 1978. *Protocols of the Twenty-Eighth Zionist Congress, Jerusalem.*